British Dandies

British Dandies

ENGENDERING SCANDAL AND FASHIONING A NATION

Dominic Janes

BODLEIAN
LIBRARY
PUBLISHING

First published in 2022 by the Bodleian Library
Broad Street, Oxford OX1 3BG
www.bodleianshop.co.uk

ISBN 978 1 85124 559 8

Text © Dominic Janes, 2022
All images, unless specified, © Bodleian Library, University of Oxford, 2022

Dominic Janes has asserted his right to be identified as the author of this Work.

All rights reserved.

No part of this book may be reproduced, stored in a retrieval system, or
transmitted in any form or by any means, electronic, mechanical, photocopying,
recording, or otherwise, without the written permission of the Bodleian Library,
except for the purpose of research or private study, or criticism or review.

Publisher: Samuel Fanous
Managing Editor: Deborah Susman
Editor: Janet Phillips
Picture Editor: Leanda Shrimpton
Production Editor: Susie Foster
Cover design by Dot Little at the Bodleian Library
Designed and typeset by Lucy Morton of illuminati in 11 on 16 Baskerville
Printed and bound by Livonia Print, Latvia,
on 115 gsm Munken Premium Cream paper

British Library Catalogue in Publishing Data
A CIP record of this publication is available from the British Library

Contents

Illustrations

COLOUR PLATES

'Clothes, as despicable as we think them,
are so unspeakably significant.'

THOMAS CARLYLE, *Sartor Resartus*

'There is only one thing in the world worse than
being talked about, and that is not being talked about.'

OSCAR WILDE, *The Picture of Dorian Gray*

ONE

British dandies

The twin cults of glamour and celebrity are often associated with
Hollywood and the rise of the mass media in the twentieth century,
but their origins lie much earlier. Since at least the eighteenth
century, Britain has seen the development of a public audience that
enjoys reading about the lives of the rich and famous. What has been
said about twentieth-century stars such as Marilyn Monroe also could
be said of her predecessors; namely that the perception of glamour
could not 'exist without personal social envy being a common and
widespread emotion'.[1] Dandies – men who enjoy being seen – understand this. They use clothes as one element in a carefully cultivated
performance that may include refined speech, leisured hobbies and an
air of nonchalance. They might be an aristocrat or, due to some other
personal attainment, already be a celebrity, or they might simply be
cultivating the appearance of being one.

   Dandies are men understood as posing as glamorous exceptions
to a norm that establishes women as uniquely passionate about
fashion. Men, such sexist thinking goes, should be distinctive for
their energy, strength or intelligence and not just for their looks.

1 George Bryan 'Beau' Brummell (1778–1840) was the master of understated
magnificence. Line engraving by John Cook, after unknown artist, published by Richard
Bentley, London, 1844.

This rule still operates in the twenty-first century. Column inches in magazines or sections of websites are occupied with figures such as the 'hipster' (one of the contemporary terms for a type of modern dandy). Areas of major global cities such as London are identified as being the haunt of this type that is seen as stylish and yet somehow also slightly ludicrous. The hipster male, it is often thought, takes his personal style a little too far. He is known not just for his beard but for one that is calculatedly too large and ostentatiously overgroomed. Such dandyism is at one and the same time all about, and yet more than just about, appearances. The look must be perfected for it to be remarked upon, but to attempt to be noticed is immediately to make a claim to social status. Hipster excess says: I am special and you should pay attention to me in particular.

It is hardly surprising, therefore, that dressy men as a type of celebrity have played a distinctive role in the cultural – and even in the political – life of Britain over several centuries. But unlike the international phenomenon of the twenty-first century hipster the dandies of the British past provoked distinctively intense degrees of fascination and horror in their homeland. It is a central purpose of this book to explain why this was. The term 'dandy' was not widely used until the end of the eighteenth century. Before then there had been a variety of terms for overtly fashionable males such as 'fops' and 'fribbles'. Their stories illustrate the lives of British dandies *avant la lettre*. These men were typically characterized in stage comedies as being weak and feminine, whereas their roistering rivals the 'rakes' were depicted as recklessly aggressive and sexually overconfident. One particularly intriguing predecessor of the dandies of the Regency was the 'macaroni'. He made a sudden entrance in England in the mid-1760s and, for a decade or so, became an object of popular fascination before vanishing as speedily as he had arrived. His name was derived from his taste for Italian pasta, which at the time was considered by the British to be exotic. He was a man who also, it was rumoured, possessed other supposed Continental tastes including for lace, Catholicism and boys.

In France there had been a variety of terms for dandified men in the eighteenth century such as *petit-mâitre* ('little master'), but widespread discussion of dandyism did not take place until after the French Revolution. The reason for this is that aristocratic ostentation became problematic after 1789 when men were forced to consider how their own personal tastes correlated with their devotion to the new Republic and its exaltation of equality. French dandyism placed reliance on that other revolutionary virtue, liberty. The dandy, it could be argued, did not dress up in order to set himself socially above others but to assert the sanctity of individual self-expression. The Parisian *incroyables* ('unbelievables') of the late 1790s were known at various times either for their reactionary politics or for their real or affected ironic detachment from public affairs.[2]

In Britain the Scottish writer and philosopher Thomas Carlyle denounced the dandy as a mere clothes-wearing man in his satirical novel *Sartor Resartus* ('the tailor re-tailored'), which was initially published in serial form in *Fraser's Magazine* (1833–34). In France, by contrast, the poet and critic Charles Baudelaire was to argue in *The Painter of Modern Life* (1863) that

> contrary to what a lot of thoughtless people seem to believe, dandyism is not even an excessive delight in clothes and material elegance. For the perfect dandy, these things are no more than the symbol of the aristocratic superiority of his mind. Thus, in his eyes, enamoured as he is above all of distinction, perfection in dress consists in absolute simplicity, which is, indeed, the best way of being distinguished. What then can this passion be, which has crystallized into a doctrine, and has formed a number of outstanding devotees, this unwritten code that has moulded so proud a brotherhood? It is, above all, the burning desire to create a personal form of originality, within the external limits of social conventions.[3]

Ellen Moers, in her pioneering study *The Dandy: Brummell to Beerbohm* (1960), argued that 'throughout the nineteenth century the rising majority called for equality, responsibility, energy; the dandy stood for superiority, irresponsibility, inactivity'.[4] Dandies were, in other words, rebellious elitists. This seems particularly clear in relation to the fin-de-siècle art of the 'pose' as cultivated by Oscar Wilde and his admirers.[5]

If it was only on the Continent that high theoretical claims for the value of dandyism were being made these were, nevertheless, based on a specific Briton: George Bryan 'Beau' Brummell (FIG. 1).[6] He had been an undergraduate of Oriel College, Oxford, before becoming an associate of the Prince Regent (the future king George IV). He was a man of independent means, or at least he was once he had come into his inheritance. He was not, however, an aristocrat. His particular ability was to make himself famous by the way he dressed. Brummell's costumes were plain but beautifully fitting. Ostentation appeared in one place only, and that was the necktie, which he wore in a variety of magnificent and complex forms. He eventually fell from social favour, suffered bankruptcy and died in exile in France in 1840.

Brummell's style of understated magnificence was significantly different from the style of the *petit-maître* and other eighteenth-century forms of dandyism since they focused on (alleged over-)elaboration. The switch to plain fashions for men was not something peculiar to the smart set in Britain but was identified, originally by the Anglo-German psychoanalyst J.C. Flügel, as a European-wide phenomenon. Flügel was one of the founders of the Men's Dress Reform Party, whose members advocated rational dress but who were publicly mocked as eccentric dandies.[7] In *The Psychology of Clothes* (1930) he argued that what he called 'the Great Masculine Renunciation' of colour and ornament had taken place as a result of the French Revolution.[8] It was the product of a new imperative towards social inclusivity but was also related to the increasing separation of the social roles and expected performances of men and women. Women became the ornamented sex. This, he alleged, represented a reversal of the natural order in which it was the peacock rather than the peahen that was vibrantly coloured.

Recent critique of these ideas, notably that of John Harvey in *Men in Black* (1995), indicates that it was in Britain rather than in France that the widespread male renunciation of colour first took place and that Flügel's thesis fails to take into account the long-established prestige of dark clothing within Christianity.[9] Black cloth could be expensive and function as a way to show status and wealth.[10] It had been popular at the Roman Catholic Spanish court in the sixteenth century and among English Puritans and Dutch merchants in the seventeenth.[11] Lawyers and the clergy came to be seen as middle-class professionals and their use of black was viewed as a badge of respectability.[12] It had been popular in France at the start of the eighteenth century, although the court of Versailles later favoured brighter and paler colours.[13] It is helpful to think about two distinctions: one, between dark and bright hues, and two, between elaboration and plainness in dress, deportment and speech.[14]

The English Civil War (1642–51) featured a stylistic contrast between the aristocratic flamboyance of the royalists and the Puritan sobriety of many parliamentarians. King Charles II made a significant fashion statement shortly after he returned to power. In October 1666 he appeared in public in a costume that was different from the styles worn at the French court. This ensemble has often been seen as the ancestor of the modern three-piece suit.[15] After some backtracking under King James II the vogue for plainer styles began to take hold again among the elite from the time of the Glorious Revolution of 1688. This was not just about clothing. Continental imports such as silks, pâtés and wine were thenceforward derided by many insular patriots, who preferred to champion home-produced wool, beef and ale. This was not simply xenophobic chauvinism because of the economic dangers inherent in having an elite that spent its money on imported goods and that neglected to patronize local industries. The various British equivalents of the *petit-maître* from the seventeenth century to the eighteenth century included fops, fribbles, beaux and macaronis. If these types had one thing in common it was their passion for luxurious goods, the possession of which they supposedly regarded as more important than sense, virtue and manliness. The belief that interest in French fashions was something inherently feminine – and therefore effeminate when occurring in men – was another distinctively British development.

Brummell's understated style can be understood as an attempt to produce a model for masculine self-display that did not appear quite so frilled, feminine and foreign. Dandyism in its nineteenth-century form was created out of a reaction against its predecessors. Far from being about ostentatious excess, Regency dandyism was known for its pared-back perfection. The precise position of every stitch and button became a matter of social opportunity and peril. It is only from the time of Brummell that the term 'dandy' came into widespread public use, yet there is no evidence that he used it to describe himself and nor was he described as a 'macaroni'. The origin of that last term is uncertain. Its most famous early appearance is in the song *Yankee Doodle*:

> Yankee Doodle came to town,
> Riding on a pony,
> Stuck a feather in his hat
> And called it Macaroni![16]

A later version was to become popular as an American patriotic song, but this verse had originally been written with disparaging reference to provincial soldiery from the New World who fought alongside troops from Britain in the American Wars of Independence. The point of the verse was that to wear a feather in one's hat was not at all the same thing as appearing as a macaroni man of fashion. Just as urban fashionistas were liable to be mocked, so were their backward country cousins.

The macaroni was described as a figure of fun as early as 1711 when the writer and politician Joseph Addison had written in *The Spectator* that the 'common people' give to buffoons the name of the most popular dish of each nation; thus, 'in Italy Maccaronies; and in Great Britain, Jack Puddings'.[17] But it was not until 1764 that the antiquary and politician Horace Walpole reported the existence of a 'Maccaroni [*sic*] Club', which, he explained, 'is composed of all the travelled young men who wear long curls and spying-glasses'.[18] They were called macaronis because of their enthusiasm for Italian pasta and also, perhaps, because of the term 'macaronic', which referred to playful mixtures of vernacular and Latin poetry. The travelling that such men had done was either the Grand Tour down to Italy or a more limited visit to Paris, which was now open to the British after the conclusion of the Seven Years War in 1763. It was widely believed that male preening during the period of the Napoleonic Wars was descended from that of the macaronis and, ultimately, from the fops who had been figures of fun in Restoration comedy.[19] The macaroni look, however, was quite distinct from that of the Regency dandy in that it was inspired by the elaborate styles of the French court, albeit that these were often worn, as they were not in France, at a wide range of unofficial social occasions. Fabrics were bright. Wigs ascended to a peak and descended into a large bag worn against the upper back. Jackets were tight and short. The plain style of the later dandies was an attempt to distinguish themselves from these flamboyant predecessors.

The overall effect can be seen in the 1771 portrait by Thomas Gainsborough of Captain William Wade (PLATE 1).[20] Wade was the master of ceremonies at the new Assembly Rooms, Bath, in which position he oversaw the dress and social arrangements of society as it gathered for the season. This swagger portrait was commissioned to hang on the walls of the card room. It shows Wade in a splendid scarlet suit with a gold-embroidered waistcoat, boutonnière and bag wig. This may be compared with a rare example of an image of a macaroni by himself: a portrait miniature of and by the painter Richard Cosway (*c.* 1770–75; PLATE 2).[21] Cosway came jocularly to be referred to as the macaroni painter.[22] As Peter McNeil explains, 'the height of his powdered wig, the delicate rose brocade of his waistcoat and French needle-lace provide the strongest indication of what a wealthy London macaroni looked like.'[23] The anonymous 'The History of Captain H——, a Macaroni' reported that what had begun as indicating a passion for pasta as served at Almack's (a newly established London club) soon came to be used to refer to men (and occasionally women) who 'exceeded the ordinary bounds of fashion'.[24] A key purpose of this book is to explain why such styles were worn and why their wearers gained an extraordinary degree of both fame and infamy. How was it that – as we shall see – macaronis, dandies and their like were attacked both for swaggering self-assertion and for simpering timidity?

Part of the answer lies in the way in which dandies stirred up a variety of concerns about gender. If fashion-obsessed men were held to be imitating women it raised the possibility that they might share female tastes not merely in fabrics but also in bed partners. Insinuations along these lines can be detected long before the scandalous trials of Oscar Wilde in 1895 highlighted putative links between male dandyism and homosexuality. Wilde, with his adulation of French literature and interest in women's fashion, fitted established stereotypes all too well. But it is also not likely to be pure coincidence that Horace Walpole, who identified the 'Macaroni Club', is now believed by some to have also been a queer man.

Exploring the private life of the dandy requires engagement with the worlds of scandal and gossip. Establishing the truth is often difficult because the most substantial evidence for men spoken of as macaronis or dandies lies in the texts and popular prints that satirized them. Fops and macaronis were originally thought of as being weak men who lacked masculine qualities and who tried to compensate for this through dress. But by the 1770s a series of sodomitical scandals had swept through London society, leaving in their wake an association between the Latin-loving macaronis and tainted forms of love. This process gave a peculiarly sexual charge to British suspicions concerning enthusiasm for the lifestyles of foreign aristocrats and priests of the Roman Catholic Church.

Great Britain should be understood, as Linda Colley has argued, as 'an invented nation that was not founded on the suppression of older loyalties so much as superimposed on them, and that was heavily dependent for its *raison d'être* on a broadly Protestant culture, on the threat and tonic of recurrent war, especially war with France, and on the triumphs, profits, and Otherness represented by a massive overseas empire'.[25] Dandies were a product of British commerce and links with the wider world, but they also highlighted the possession of such connections as a danger to national cohesion. Clothing thus became a focus for patriotism and its discontents. The first sentence of Aileen Ribeiro's *Clothing Art: The Visual Culture of Fashion, 1600–1915* (2017) is: 'This book is about the centrality of clothing in art as in life.'[26] *British Dandies* is about the centrality of clothing to cultural politics in Britain since the eighteenth century.

Because decorative femininity was understood as the appropriate companion to masculine functionality fashion was increasingly associated with women as a frivolous matter that emphasized their exclusion from power. Aristocratic men, meanwhile, donned uniforms and attempted to demonstrate their value as members of a service elite. But the male renunciation that ensued did not so much free men from care about personal appearance as usher in what has been termed the '"tyrannic sway" of inconspicuous consumption'.[27] As the

Georgian period gave way to its Victorian successor 'the black armies of the Nonconformist merchants and ironmasters, and the learned professions and the new professions, and of course the dandies, and Evangelical preachers, converge[d] with new confidence on the same tailors.'[28] The desire for plain style only ended up stoking fears of androgynous effeminacy because a certain butch gravity had itself become a fashion. The homosociality of Britain's ruling elite, seen in the context of the boys' club that was the Westminster Parliament, denied, and yet at the same time cultivated, a self-regard that was potentially homoerotic.

The American War of Independence, the French Revolution and the ensuing Napoleonic Wars all, in their own way, furthered a type of British patriotism that associated manly virtue with disdain for the foreigner. Service in the military became a touchstone of masculine virtue and, perhaps not surprisingly, the tight-fitting jackets that were a vital component of military uniform influenced civilian fashions for men. The more extreme of the resulting looks were parodied as 'monstrosities' in satirical prints created by the brothers George and Robert Cruikshank in the years before and after the defeat of Napoleon in 1815. Whilst the macaroni prints hinted (more or less openly) at the presence of vice in the lives of aristocratic *roués*, images of later Georgian dandies implied that even the fit young male was potentially deviant when overdressed. Exploration of crazes for slumming, boxing and mingling in the quasi-criminal locales of London reveals a variety of ways in which fashionable men came to view attractive male bodies and move in milieus open to the sale of sexual services. This helps to set the scene for an appreciation of the erotic dynamics of Oscar Wilde and his clique as they moved between circles of high culture and working-class contexts in which they sought sexual gratification.

'Mashers' and 'poseurs' were Victorian equivalents of 'rakes' and 'fops'. Understanding these as types of over- and under-masculine behaviour helps us to situate Wilde's poses and performances as copies or reinventions of practices going back to the eighteenth century. The connections between aestheticism and earlier forms of dandyism can be traced via the caricatures of the time. These show some of the ways in which aspects of the scandalous sexual potential of posing and supposing were becoming legible to a wider audience before Wilde's trials of 1895. An example is provided by Max Beerbohm, whose satirical texts and caricatures ranged from the indulgently amusing to the grotesque. He can be seen as representing a characteristic of many of those producing caricature; namely that they were both fascinated and horrified by their subjects and should be seen as not simply criticizing from without but as also actively participating in the development of dandy culture and imagery from within.

The twentieth century was distinctive in that it presented the figure of the well-dressed British gentleman as exemplary, but it also continued to throw up examples of men who took such deportment to improper extremes. There were a series of panics about the antics of what might be termed young style rebels, particularly those with working-class backgrounds. One of the main examples of this was the emergence of youth gangs of 'teddy boys' in the 1950s, whose look was inspired by the classic tailoring of the beginning of the century. This meant that through the twentieth century the figure of the dandy remained a complex one in that he embodied both establish-ment values and a sense of personal autonomy and rebellion. He was sometimes the man whom everyone admired and at other times thought of as not being a proper man at all. The social prominence of the reality and stereotypes of the dandy tells us a very great deal about what the British thought was normal for men. Dandies shaped and fashioned not only themselves but also the nation that observed them with such rapt attention.

TWO

Dressing the sexes in the seventeenth and eighteenth centuries

Fashion has been shaped not only by legal and commercial pressures, but also by changing ideas about embodiment, gender and sexual pleasure. Changes in dress can be seen both as reflecting such wider developments in society and as having contributed to patterns of cultural change. In early modern Europe aristocrats and a proportion of wealthier townspeople and artisans dressed in accordance with changing styles at court. By the end of the eighteenth century, fashion was being embraced by the burgeoning middle ranks of society and was coming to be strongly shaped by their spending power. Social competition spurred on the demand for new modes. Those involved in the production and distribution of clothing and accessories had every incentive to encourage the purchase of new clothes to replace those that were not worn out but were simply out of style.[1] Unwanted items were then sold locally, remade or else handed over to servants, who sometimes expected cloth and clothing as a perquisite. The desirability of the garment in question, as in the case of the erotic allure of a dress, was widely equated with its degree of finery in materials and construction and its adherence to current styles. Many

2 Charles-Geneviève-Louis-Auguste-André-Timothée d'Éon de Beaumont (1728–1810) was widely held to be a woman. *Mademoiselle de Beaumont, or the Chevalier d'Eon*, in *London Magazine* 46, 1777.

female prostitutes, for instance, attempted to dress themselves as much like fine ladies as they could; a practice that appears to have been copied by some of their male, cross-dressing 'molly' counterparts both in European cities and in their transatlantic equivalents such as Philadelphia.[2]

The European centre of fashion was Paris, but status-conscious inhabitants of other countries often relied on local reproductions of French styles. Critique of French patterns of consumption had the effect of promoting the development of plainer styles. This was particularly the case in relation to men's fashion, which sometimes referenced the dress of the country gentry or of the army. In their turn, British sporting styles that were convenient to wear on horseback were adopted and adapted by the French. In addition to these new pan-European fashions many regions of Europe and the wider transatlantic world continued to maintain their own local traditions of dress, in which the mechanisms of fashionable change operated to a greater or lesser extent depending on degrees of prosperity and the extent to which local regimes persisted in maintaining forms of sumptuary legislation.[3]

Fashion during the eighteenth century was increasingly associated with women, but many of those who controlled the fashion industry or commented upon its products were men. The Enlightenment, notoriously, did not produce anything like equality between the sexes. This sometimes resulted in dismissals of the realm of fashion as being something that was essentially frivolous because it was feminine, and feminine because it was frivolous.[4] On the other hand it was often retorted in later eighteenth-century periodicals that it was only natural, and indeed rational, for women to want to please their menfolk.[5] Such debates notwithstanding, fashionable styles for men evolved almost as quickly as did those for women and this generated much of the critical heat that appeared during this period concerning the rationality or morality of styles of dress.

The broad pattern during the eighteenth century was for men's and women's dress to become progressively more distinct. Brightly coloured fabrics and the use of materials such as lace were employed by both sexes in the late seventeenth century, but mostly by women a century later. What underlay this was a momentous shift in the relations between biological sex and the performance of gender. The work of the cultural historian Thomas Laqueur has played a significant role in aiding our comprehension of these changes. In the early modern period men and women were thought of as being different in degree, with the latter being seen as similar, albeit (physically and mentally) lesser, versions of the former.[6] Whilst still retaining theories of female inferiority, scientific opinion changed such that by the middle of the eighteenth century women were seen as distinctly different *in kind* from men.[7] This shift in opinion has been seen by social historians as having originated in a change in the conceptualization of the household from a unit of production in which men and women essentially shared the work, to one in which a female domestic sphere was imagined as distinctively separate from male public life.[8] Men and women were seen as different both mentally and physically, such that the latter were understood as being essentially fragile, vulnerable, emotional, nervous and passionate. A side effect of this process was that it became obvious that some women and men neither matched these evolving stereotypes nor fitted the new fashions that made novel attempts to assert a clear sense of gender distinction.

Randolph Trumbach has argued that it was in this context that we can understand the eclipse of premodern understandings of gender indeterminacy. These were rooted in the classical figure of the hermaphrodite, who was a being who possessed a mix of male and female anatomy. In its place there arose the figure of the effeminate androgyne who was genitally masculine but (supposedly) physically and mentally weak, and the Amazonian woman who was the reverse of this.[9] Fashions which failed to preserve a sufficient difference from those worn by women could threaten to transform the body of the normative male into that of a loathed 'sodomite' (a man who desired perverse sex such as with another man or with an animal). The exaggeration of certain eighteenth-century fashions for women can, therefore, be understood as the result not simply of social competition but also of desires for women to achieve as feminine an outline as possible whilst men strove for the reverse. Status in fashionable society – and this was particularly true of England after the Glorious Revolution of 1688 and of France after the French Revolution of 1789 – was increasingly defined by displays of gendered taste rather than simply of spending power related to rank.

The sexually desirable female form of the period tended to emphasize the hips and the bust through the use of various forms of stays, corseting, panniers and hoops. The aim of the last was to give volume to skirts, and their tendency was to increase in size over time. Thus, in Britain, the hooped petticoat appeared around 1710 and then proceeded to enlarge dramatically to a peak around 1750, at which point fashionable women began to find it difficult to get through the doors of their own dress shops. Such voluminous costumes used up ever greater quantities of material and, as such, acted as an obvious site of conspicuous consumption.[10] The broadening of the woman's profile implied lush fertility and rumours were in circulation that such styles had originated in attempts to conceal pregnancy. Whilst substantial skirts appeared to keep lusting men at arm's length, they also tended to become upset and thus afford sudden glimpses of leg. The danger (or opportunities) in this respect were even greater in Britain than they were in the France of Jean-Honoré Fragonard's *The Happy Accidents of the Swing* (1767), because women of the island race did not wear underwear – since drawers were regarded by the gender-conscious British as being distinctively masculine (PLATE 3).[11]

The use of strips of whalebone with lacing at the front, back or both sides of a separate garment formed an essential element in women's fashions. Medical opinion was frequently hostile to the tight-laced corset, notably in German-speaking areas of Europe. Reports of the dangers of stays spread from the 1740s onwards and even developed legal force in Austria with the intervention of Emperor Joseph II in the 1780s.[12] He was particularly concerned with the health of children, who were typically dressed by the aristocracy in miniature versions of adult styles.[13] That these concerns had specifically sexual connotations is clear from considering the attitudes of the author of *Émile, ou De l'éducation* (1762), which was to have a remarkable impact on fashionable attitudes to child-rearing. Jean-Jacques Rousseau (1712–1778) is one of the founder figures of Romanticism and of the cult of the (supposedly) natural life. In 1751 he had fallen ill and, in a secularized version of Christian renunciation, vowed to lay aside worldly pomp if he were to recover.[14] Not only did he reject elaborate dress in favour of plainness, but he advocated that others should do the same. His enthusiasm for liberating the youthful female body from the bondage of tight constraint was founded on his awareness of the sexual forwardness that this style implied.[15] After all, the fact that mothers and daughters were dressed in the same way meant that there was no clear difference between the dress of sexually experienced women and virgins.[16]

Eighteenth-century fashions for women were meant to be sexually alluring even though women were also required to aspire to virtue as an essential female quality. Flirtation, if not outright seduction, was the order of the day, and its most sophisticated and intense expression was probably to be found in salon society in Paris, where many of the women were far from the empty-headed male fantasies painted by the likes of Fragonard.[17] Masquerades were quite as popular among the London bourgeoisie as they were among the more libidinous elements of *Ancien Régime* France. Under the cover of the masquerade, identities could be swapped and sexual indiscretions committed.[18] By the mid-eighteenth century London had grown to such an extent that fashionable public gardens such as those in Vauxhall on the south bank of the Thames were places where various social ranks could, to a degree, mingle promiscuously. Fashions developed in fancy dress such as the wearing of elements of 'oriental' costume, including loose Turkish trousers by women. These evoked erotic fantasies of the Turkish harem or even forms of gender transgression.[19] Similarly, the taste for chinoiserie in silks, employed both for dress fabrics and for hangings on domestic walls, offered the pleasures of sensual ornament.[20] The parties at which young ladies cross-dressed as soldiers, and footmen as Persian kings, relied for their scandalous effect on the entrenchment of norms of gender and sexual performance.[21] Nevertheless, this evolving society, for all its worries over sex and gender, was on the whole productive of a vast expansion of fashion as an expression of erotic desire. It was in this period that, perhaps for the first time, substantial numbers of people were able to buy clothes the primary purpose of which was to look attractive, rather than to keep their wearers warm and respectable.

CROSSING THE CHANNEL

The fact that ostentation was a key element in the display of power in *Ancien Régime* France does not mean that it was innocent of elements of travesty. Indeed, it can be argued that it was the very strength of the legitimating role of rank in that aristocratic society which allowed play with aspects of gender identity to be seen as a matter of triviality and amusement. That certain aspects of life at the court of Versailles were self-consciously mannered exhibitions of excess is implied by the behaviour of Philippe de France, the brother of Louis XIV, who on occasion dressed in public as a woman and required his attendants on such occasions to do the same.[22] Thus when the king hosted staged ceremonial battles on the 'fields' outside the palace, the attendance of his brother in women's clothing expressed aristocratic entitlement and self-confidence. That notwithstanding, it has been argued that the verb 'to camp' owes it origins to those self-same fields ('champs') of fakery and knowing transgression.

'Monsieur' married twice, fathered several children and advertised that fact in paintings such as *Philippe de France, Duke of Orleans, With the Portrait of His Daughter Marie-Louise*, School of Pierre Mignard (*c*. 1670; PLATE 4).[23] It is possible that he may have been what in later ages would be referred to as a 'bisexual', but it is important to emphasize that his appearance and behaviour need to be judged in relation to the attitudes of his time. By twenty-first-century standards even the male fashions of the French court were colourful and flamboyant, but the message they gave was one of access to wealth and power and not of effeminate weakness. However, the eighteenth century marked a period of transition towards sharp distinctions in the fashions thought appropriate for men and women in terms of colour, cut and materials. The broad pattern was for spending on clothing to rise steadily during this period, with steeper rises for the rich than for the poor and for women rather than men.[24] Nevertheless, society remained strongly patriarchal and the dominant discourses on fashion of the time continued to be shaped primarily by men, even as the role of women as consumers grew steadily in importance. The period was notable for the desire for novelty.[25] Older and cheaper modes were passed down through the social ranks.[26] At the same time, and particularly in Britain, there were tendencies for men's fashions to rise up the social spectrum, notably in relation to sports and country clothing where the aristocracy took up styles previously sported by the gentry.

A key aspect of this latter tendency was that it promoted the wearing by men of simpler and darker clothing, a trend that has sometimes been referred to as the 'great male renunciation', as was mentioned in the first chapter. It is true that the French aristocracy tended to employ lighter shades, and that men in that country took to brighter colours in the course of the eighteenth century. But even in France black was much worn at the beginning of the century.[27] In England, dark clothing was sometimes associated with Puritans but it is, perhaps, better to emphasize that such people advocated 'plain style' in speech and deportment as well as dress.[28] Good-quality black cloth evoked social status simply because it was relatively expensive.[29] Black was a difficult colour to dye successfully and fine gradations were carefully judged. What is revealing, however, is that the tendency for plainness outlasted Cromwell and his Commonwealth. Men of a range of political persuasions duly came to embrace a fashion for a degree of sobriety in dress.

The restoration of the monarchy in 1660 involved more than a modicum of compromise with erstwhile opponents. Charles II, on obtaining his annual financial dispensation from Parliament in 1662, made it clear that the court was not to be a locale of conspicuous consumption. Evidence for the origins of the men's three-piece suit have often been traced to the entry made by Samuel Pepys in his diary on 8 October 1666 in which it was recorded that Charles had declared that he would abandon doublet and hose and appear in a vest (the precursor of the waistcoat, worn with coat and breeches).[30] The king thereby signalled to his courtiers that they should dress similarly. Sartorial splendour was no longer necessary to uphold aristocratic honour, and men at court were expected to adopt the mien of responsible and careful governors.[31] John Evelyn recorded that 18 October was 'the first time of his Majesty's putting himself solemnly into the Eastern fashion of vest, changing doublet, stiff collar, bands and cloak, etc. into a comely vest, after the Persian mode with a girdle or sash, … resolving never to alter it, and to leave the French mode, which had hitherto obtained to our great expense and reproach'.[32] British wool, rather than French silk, was to be preferred in the new sartorial regime. The reference to Persia indicates Mughal court costume, in which trousers and jacket were made of the same fabric. The king may simply have been mainstreaming and popularizing a pre-existing orientalist style. William Fielding, Earl of Denbigh, had Van Dyke paint him in 1633 in red 'paijama', which, for Christopher Breward, was 'surely a foretaste of the two-piece suit'.[33]

The resultant costume was first made fashionable by royal patronage but was subsequently to become widely associated with manly virtue. Its effect was to create a uniform for attendance at court. Something similar took place at the French court in the 1670s, insular protestations of exceptionalism notwithstanding. English modes meanwhile grew more elaborate, before the Glorious Revolution, with its aims of expelling popery, foppery, tyranny and luxury, put a stop to this stylistic drift. In the following century members of all political parties recognized that 'guarding the boundaries of the aristocratic polity meant donning the image of noble simplicity, presenting the landed gentleman as true-born Englishman and the moral backbone of the nation'.[34]

Bourgeois and aristocratic elements mingled in varying proportions in the different parts of Europe. Even after events such as the Glorious Revolution, which pushed the balance of power in Britain towards mercantile as opposed to landed interests, the upper ranks of society continued to be dominated by those who had inherited their wealth and status. Moreover, success among the rich and prominent in society continued to depend heavily upon the management of personal connections. It was, in fact, the persistence of noble forms in the context of weakened aristocratic power that meant that dress and deportment became even more significant as elements of self-promotion. It was the activities of this group of people, sufficiently exclusive that they would come to be referred to as 'Society' (with a capital *S*), who sustained the growth of the 'season' in London. This was when the landed gentry flocked to the capital to meet each other, to shop, and to see and be seen. One of the major differences between the life of the 'beau monde' in London and its equivalent in Paris was that the latter was dominated to a much greater extent by court protocol, although this lessened after 1700 when more and more nobles moved to live in Paris among traders, financiers and their like.

On the British side of the Channel, party politics centred on the opposition between groupings of 'Tories' and 'Whigs' as the power of the House of Lords slowly declined. Many of those in the Commons were, however, the younger sons of peers, and it was not until 1885 that new money was clearly to become dominant in the junior chamber. This did not mean that the upper ranks of society were socially static. The seventeenth century had seen the creation of baronets, a process repeated under Queen Anne. Those who were jockeying for favours from the powerful could employ fashion as a way of calling attention to themselves whilst projecting a self-image of success. Elite clothing, in such circumstances, was not just concerned with personal pleasure because it was of career importance. This applied just as much to a man seeking a sinecure as to a woman seeking a wealthy husband. Those who had a title, power, style and deportment were admired and imitated. This, at least to some degree, descended the social spectrum and, in combination with the importation of new styles from France, egged on by merchants eager for new business, drove an increasingly rapid cycle of consumption. Prosperity led to a steadily rising scale of expenditure on fashion through the course of the eighteenth century, particularly on the part of women. Because the boundaries of the 'beau monde' were ill-defined, it was possible for people to enter it or pretend that they had done so.[35] Whilst those in the upper ranks often knew each other, people of lower station had to judge by appearances. To be able to pass as a lady or a gentleman greatly expanded the potential for obtaining credit from tradespeople.

It has been argued that 'an overriding emphasis on cultural qualifications offered considerable opportunities to certain cohorts within the beau monde, arguably most significantly to women who were able to establish themselves as leaders of fashion in their own right.'[36] Why, then, did many men, when compared to women, apparently take a step back from ostentatious self-fashioning? One answer has been provided by those who regard the Age of Enlightenment as witnessing a radical reorganization of the gendering of men. Thomas King has argued that such changes were pioneered in Britain. He argues that across Europe, and with varying degrees of speed and intensity, an older model of courtly manhood dependent upon the patronage of social superiors was gradually replaced by a new ideal of being the autonomous head of a patriarchal household. In this schema participation in civic life was no longer to be at the whim of a social elite but was, at least in theory, to be determined by personal virtue.[37] Such novel ideas of manliness were reinforced by the denigration of those men who continued to seek the patronage of the elite as being effeminate toadies. In the process sexual normativity became bolted to the performance of duties as father and husband, and practices of vying for favour at court became associated not merely with effeminacy but with associations of aristocratic arrogance and sodomitical favouritism.[38] The new respectability required that men perform sobriety and reject flamboyance and theatricality. This helps to explain why it was that panics over male effeminacy and sodomy were so much more frequent and prominent in Britain than they were in France, where rank more clearly trumped gender as a mark of status before 1789.[39]

One key result of these changes was that an interest in fashion became regarded as being a characteristic preoccupation of women and effeminate men. Sartorial flamboyance was seen as a mark of women's separation from the realm of masculine power, but this does not mean that they escaped censure for supposed exaggerations of style and obsession with Continental modes. It also meant that French men were increasingly viewed in Britain as effeminate. Such notions fed into the development of cultural practices that aimed to secure masculinity as being the peculiar characteristic of individual nations. In Spain the fashion for *majismo* saw the social elites copying forms of lower-class dress and demonizing those emerging from Paris as being those of the *petimetre*.[40] The *petit-maître*, meanwhile, was read in Britain as an effete social upstart who attempted to rise to prominence in society through copying French modes. Under a wide variety of names such as fops, fribbles and beaux, the prominence of such figures in satire is eloquent testimony to the prevalence of concerns about male effeminacy understood in relation not merely to femininity and androgyny, but also to mental and physical weakness, reckless expenditure and unpatriotic enthusiasm for foreign culture and mores.[41] However prevalent they were in real life, such characters were a mainstay of contemporary theatrical comedy, as in Sir Novelty Fashion's appearance in Colley Cibber's *Love's Last Shift* (1696). These stereotypes inverted the older model of the man of mode as the possessor of social power and implied that he was now a trespasser on female prerogatives.

It is important to stress that connections between effeminacy and sodomy were in development during the eighteenth century.[42] Previously, sodomitical desire was associated most often with libertinism and perverse lust as an aspect of masculine excess. It is notable for instance that in John Vanburgh's *The Relapse; or, Virtue in Danger* (1696) it is not foppish Lord Foppington who is a sodomite but another character called Coupler.[43] Tobias Smollett, in his picaresque novel *The Adventures of Roderick Random* (1748), depicted examples of the two forms of male behaviour that fell then under particular suspicion of sodomitical desire, that of the unscrupulous rake (Strutwell) and of the scented effeminate (Whiffle). Whilst Strutwell was wont to take active sexual advantage of men in the pursuit of wealth, it was Whiffle who signalled the presence of innately feminine tastes, implicitly including sexual tastes, through his dress and deportment.

> Whiffle, for that was his name, took possession of the ship,
> surrounded with a crowd of attendants, all of whom, in their

different degrees, seemed to be of their patron's disposition; and
the air was so impregnated with perfumes that one may venture to
affirm the clime of Arabia Foelix was not half so sweet-scented.[44]

Captain Whiffle and his companions are singled out as a certain
type of man who behaves in a feminine way and who associates with
others of similar tastes. The implication is that Strutwells would take
the active part in sex whilst Whiffles would take the passive. It can be
argued that what was being depicted here derived respectively from
an older, libertine model of male behaviour in which evil men might
consort with both whores and boys and a newer model involving dan-
gerously passive effeminate men (sometimes referred to as 'mollies',
who, like women, sought penetration by men, and in search of this
made themselves up to look as young and feminine as possible).[45] The
rakish sodomite, in the process, became complemented as a figure
of social opprobrium by the androgyne.[46] Indeed, it was noticed at
the time that both types might exist together as when it was noted in
John Dunton's 'The He-Strumpets: A Satyr on the Sodomite Club'
(1707, revised 1710), that some 'doat on Men, and some on Boys'.[47]

Sodomy was, nonetheless, simply one of a series of valencies which
informed stereotypes of the ridiculous man of fashion. As Susan
Staves wrote in her article 'A Few Kind Words for the Fop' (1982),
it was often the case that 'the so-called effeminacy of these old fops
was an early if imperfect attempt at the refinement, civility, and
sensitivity most of us would now say are desirable masculine virtues.'[48]
The figure of the fop was meant, above all, to flatter those men in
the audience who felt that they had achieved a polite and cultured
balance between the lurid excesses of the rake, on the one hand,
and the pathetic vapourings of the fop, on the other.[49] This careful
balancing act depended on the cultivation of taste and a discerning
approach to fashionable culture. It required, if anything, ever greater
care in the selection of clothes, so as to avoid mockery for being either
under- or overdressed.[50] Thus, although a fop was not the same thing

as a sodomite, the function of phobic stereotypes was to entrench standards of sexual normality and, arguably, to originate aspects of what would come to be known as the (homosexual) closet.[51]

Whilst sodomy was well known and duly criminalized, there was no such equivalent legal transgression in the case of sexual acts between two women. This was partly because the sexist and phallocentric nature of the law assumed that a penis was required for penetration. Women who were emotional towards one another were, typically, read as sentimental rather than as sexually deviant. The adoption by women of men's clothing was not illegal and was often publicly discussed. Some lesbians in the twentieth century have lived with a same-sex partner in a way that appeared to mimic heterosexual marriage in so far as one partner assumed the dress and mores of a husband and the other of a wife. It is, therefore, tempting to read a household such as that of Mary Hamilton, alias George, who married her partner when disguised as a man, as being a lesbian one. Whilst it is impossible to know exactly what currents of desire were involved, it is revealing to examine male responses to such circumstances as, for instance, displayed in Henry Fielding's *The Female Husband* (1746). What is perhaps most striking is his fascination with the figure of the masculine, 'Amazonian' woman.[52]

Such beings received a significantly better press than did the effeminate male, as can be seen from the case of the Chevalier d'Éon, who was a man who cross-dressed as a woman but was sometimes understood to have been a woman who cross-dressed as a man. As has been seen in the case of Philippe de France, occasional cross-dressing was a feature of court life at Paris. In the service of the king of France, d'Éon had attended masquerade balls at the court of Catherine the Great in 1756–57 where men were required to dress as women and vice versa.[53] However, it was only after he fled into British exile in the following decade that he is recorded as having appeared in women's clothes in daily life. The fact that he was able to do so implies that he did not face immediate hostility for doing so, even though he was noted for his muscular physique and was not able to 'pass' as a woman with ease. He did face some hostility because of his nationality, and mounting panic over sodomy and effeminacy made his position more difficult.[54] Thus his friendship with the politician John Wilkes became something of a liability when the latter began to stir up the anti-sodomitical climate.[55] By 1776–77, d'Éon was being accused of consorting with mollies (sodomites associated with cross-dressing) or even of being a molly himself.

A variety of satirical drawings attempted to engage with this two-gendered figure. One such was *Mademoiselle de Beaumont, or the Chevalier d'Eon*, published in the *London Magazine* in 1777 (FIG. 2), which showed a figure dressed on one side as a man and on the other as a woman.[56] However, d'Éon was never generally shunned by high society, despite the slurs that were flying about in the press. On his return to France he was refused re-entry to the army and was required to remain in women's attire. It seems that he was most widely understood to be a fascinating case of a woman whose masculine nature made her unattractive to men, which was why she remained unmarried. Because masculinity was widely seen (by many women as well as men) as a superior state, it was not considered reprehensible for a woman to aspire to a degree of masculinity. Disputes over d'Éon's status continue today, with opinions that range from those who see them as a trans pioneer to others who argue that this behaviour was rooted in a feminist critique of male norms.[57]

Radical and revisionist stances towards gender reform grew in importance after the outbreak of the French Revolution, but they never attained a position of great influence. Nevertheless, they drew on developing currents of thought that advanced what were presented as more 'natural' styles of behaviour and dress for both men and women. The rise of notions of male politeness and the development of the cult of sensibility were currents that to some degree counteracted the trend sharply to distinguish male and female natures. The degree to which politeness ruled male behaviour in the second half of the eighteenth century is much disputed. Furthermore, male fashions at the end of the eighteenth century were to be inspired by a return to expressions of more overt virility in the context of the militarization of Europe that developed as the French Revolution ended and the Napoleonic Wars began. In 1789 servants' liveries and a variety of other indicators of social distinction were abolished in France.[58] Revolutionary virtue was expressed through short-lived crazes for red, white and blue clothing, or, and perhaps ironically, for an increased enthusiasm for the plainer English modes on the part of leaders such as Marat.[59] Even outside the areas subsequently conquered by Napoleon aristocrats had to work hard to combat the decline of social deference and concomitant accusations of parasitism. Calls for national uniforms generally fell on deaf ears and the fashion industry survived into a new age in which styles were shaped more by the choices of the bourgeoisie rather than by aristocratic attendees at royal courts or the advocates of moral reform.

SEXUAL CONCLUSIONS

The eighteenth century has sometimes been referred to as 'the century of sex'. It was at this time that the concept of fetishism first appeared.[60] The origins of the notion of the fetish lay in European encounters with Africans, who, the former thought, had a tendency to value certain objects disproportionately. In the course of the nineteenth century Karl Marx was to theorize that such mystification was a key element not so much of 'primitive' societies as of the operation of contemporary capital. His concept of 'commodity fetishism' was then joined by that of 'sexual fetishism', which aimed to explain why particular objects, particularly garments, were sometimes regarded as being charged with a degree of eroticism. Sigmund Freud, for example, argued that men tended to identify with objects that they

A MUNGO MACARONI.

3 Racist caricature mocking the idea that a man of fashion might also be a man of colour. *A Mungo Macaroni*, M. Darly, London, 1772.

understood as 'completing' the body of a woman (modelled on that of their mother) viewed as incomplete because it lacked a penis.[61]

Whichever theory of fetishism one may wish to employ, links between sexual desirability and commodity culture had grown stronger in the course of the Age of Enlightenment. Black Africans often appear in paintings of the time as fetishized, exotic possessions or as ciphers for aristocratic luxury and corruption.[62] A 1772 racist print, *A Mungo Macaroni* (FIG. 3), implied that there were also

dandified men of colour.[63] This may be a black-face representation
of the politician Jeremiah Dyson, who had been given the pejorative
nickname 'Mungo' with reference to a slave of that name in a play by
Isaac Bickerstaffe. Or this may be a caricature of Julius Soubise, who
was a former slave freed by the Duchess of Queensberry after she had
named him after a courtier of Louis XV of France.[64]

Fashionable clothing should be seen in relation to the bodies it was
designed to contain and the architectural or landscape contexts those
bodies inhabited. Thus, if sexually fetishized material culture was
often strongly associated with the eroticization by men of women, the
female dressing room became the place of femininity and eroticism
par excellence. Dedicated dressing rooms and closets appear in house
designs from the middle of the seventeenth century.[65] Depending
on the women concerned, such spaces evoked various combinations
of lasciviousness and moral virtue, but in both cases the identity
of the occupant was powerfully constructed through her choice of
garments.[66] In the dressing room 'objects were like extensions of
the body, part of a wardrobe that, correctly worn, could turn the
activities of elite existence into dances of artful persuasion.'[67] The
degree to which clothing accentuated, concealed or displayed the
female body fed the development of an erotic imagination that moved
from the contemplation of classical nudes to the imagined delights of
naked women.[68] In a British satirical print from 1786, *The Bum-Bailiff
outwitted; or the convenience of Fashion*, published by S.W. Fores, a dress
literally stands in for a woman (PLATE 5).[69] With its accentuation of
breast and 'bum', this formidable construction saves a lady from the
attentions of a bum-bailiff (debt collector), between whose legs she is
able to crawl away unnoticed.

In the case of women, social competition could drive the scale of
ostentatious consumption such that items like skirts and wigs had a
tendency to grow in size in order to use up ever greater quantities
of expensive materials. The visible effect of this was to increase the

overall size of a woman's dressed form in a society that also valued the slender waist. The resulting contrast between giant skirt and narrow waist was undoubtedly spectacular but became increasingly impractical, as satirists and caricaturists were quick to highlight. It was to take the revisionist forms of 'citizen chic' disseminated in the course of the French Revolution to bring about a temporary deflation of the fashionable female outline into those more 'natural' forms advocated by founders of Romantic thought such as Rousseau. Competition in masculine dress came, over time, to focus more on precise detailing than on scale of consumption, but such gender distinction as this failed to solve the problem of effeminacy because it simply led to fears that not only sobriety but also masculinity itself had become a fashion to be put on and discarded at whim.[70] The clothes of both men and women were sexually fetishized objects. When the Chevalier d'Éon was shown with men's clothes on one side and with women's on the other the implicit message was that gender fashioning and even the desires attendant upon it were artificial constructions. Fears that sexual tastes might, therefore, be just as well concealed as displayed by fashionable dress were one of the legacies that we have inherited from the eighteenth century.

THREE

A Georgian taste
for macaroni

In March 1773 Parliament passed the General Turnpike Act to regulate the system of road tolls. More fatefully, the following month the Tea Act granted the British East India Company a monopoly in the North American tea trade. In December a group of colonists disguised as Mohawks dumped the cargo of the Company's ships in an action that became known as the Boston Tea Party. Conversation in London, meanwhile, was diverted from such distant discontents by the latest sartorial scandals. The first references to the macaronis date from less than a decade earlier but they had quickly risen to become the talk of the town. They were treated as novelties that were both fascinating and horrifying in equal measure. The frontispiece of *The Macaroni Jester, and Pantheon of Wit; Containing All That Has Lately Transpired in the Regions of Politeness, Whim, and Novelty* (1773) showed a macaroni hatching fully formed from an egg. This type of man was, like his foppish predecessors, seen as a product of commerce rather than morals, arising 'if coxcombs won't be taught / That Manhood is a Thing *unbought*'.[1] He threatened to undermine the superiority of men and usher in an age when women would usurp them, fight

4 Was this a macaroni, or a man mocking a macaroni, or even a macaroni parodying himself? Philip Dawe, *The Macaroni: A Real Character at the Late Masquerade*, John Bowles, London, 3 July 1773.

duels, become priests and prey upon vulnerable males on the public highway.[2]

A play on the subject by Robert Hitchcock was put on at York and London. The reviewer of *The Macaroni* in the *Critical Review* (1773) said that 'extreme self-love, pusillanimity, and *effeminacy*, are the qualities which distinguish his character; these, we must acknowledge, are not unhappily described.'[3] Hitchcock was an actor as well as a playwright. From 1771 he and his wife were members of Tate Wilkinson's travelling company, which was based at York. *The Macaroni* was published not only in York and London but also in Belfast, Dublin and Philadelphia. The connection between comic theatre and forms of dandyism had been almost symbiotic since the Restoration period. Fashionable society went to the theatre in order to view exaggerations of the latest modes of style and behaviour. But there was a new bite to the satirical venom on stage and in print. There was a sense in which this latest form of male performance was especially disturbing. As another contemporary satirist put it, we no longer feared for our peace and the chastity of our daughters since the rakes and libertines had vanished and in their place 'what pigmy monsters teem / What crowds of beaus effeminate are seen'.[4] They are in love with themselves, refuse military service and are despised by women since they only want rich wives whose money will fund their lives of dissipation and vice: 'at first he blushes to commit the deed', but 'at the last his former state's forgot … until grey time, with angry looks, displays / The mirror of his guilt, and wretched days.'[5] Precisely what form this vice took was left to the prurient imagination of the reader.

Men were empowered in all kinds of ways in the early modern period, including sexually. Libertinism, which on occasion strayed beyond heterosexual boundaries, was a pronounced feature of Restoration and Georgian society.[6] Various clubs for men provided venues for group masturbation and entertainment by prostitutes.[7] Masquerade parties facilitated sexual indiscretions and 'molly' cross-dressers

1. Vanity of Age, untoward,
Ever spleeny, ever froward:
Why thofe Bolts, & Miffery Chains,
Squint Suspicion's jealous Pains.

Why, thy toilsom Journey o'er,
Lay'st thou on an ufelefs Store.
Hope along with Time is flown,
Nor canst thou reap of Field thou'st sown.

Haft Thou a Son? In Time be wise,
He views thy Soil with other Eyes:
Needs must thy kind paternal Care,
Look'd in thy Chefts, be buried there.

Whence then shall flow of friendly Eye,
That sweet Converse, homefelt Peace,
Familiar Duty without Dread,
Instruction from Example bred,

That youthful Mind with Freedom mend,
And with y.º Father mix the Friend?

Invented Painted Engraved by W.™ Hogarth, &
Publish'd June y.º 25. 1735. according to Act
of Parliament.   Plate 1.

5 On coming into his fortune the fictional Tom Rakewell has himself measured for new suits of clothes. William Hogarth, *A Rake's Progress*, 1, London, 25 June 1735.

paraded the London streets.[8] As the eighteenth century progressed there were increasing attempts to limit male sexual excesses of all kinds. Men whose behaviour failed to conform to modern expectations of gentility were mocked whether for being overly masculine rakes or allegedly effeminate fops (FIG. 5). Accusations of sodomitical desire provided a convenient way of bringing both forms of gender deviance into line. It was in this climate that an atmosphere of what

might be termed proto-homophobia developed – proto because
there was no such thing as a homosexual or heterosexual person at
this date. Those words, and the identities that derived from them,
originated in the later nineteenth century. Nevertheless, men increasingly had to watch not merely their sexual behaviour but also their
speech and dress lest they be mocked. Sodomitical innuendo on stage
was toned down as actors became targets for whispering campaigns.[9]
It was commented in 1764 that the sodomite Coupler's 'proposals
to young Foppington would be, if that part were acted, sufficient to
congeal the blood in the veins of a modern audience' in Vanbrugh's
The Relapse (1696).[10] The play was either dropped or bowdlerized.
Actors such as David Garrick, who obviously satirized the fops they
embodied on stage, were treated with more respect than those such as
Colley Cibber, who seemed to identify with them.[11]

The theatre was a crucial medium in which gender stereotypes
were displayed and contested. The word 'fop' had been used in
English since the fifteenth century to mean a 'fool'. But under the
Restoration the term became intimately associated, on stage and
off, with clothing, as displayed in the person of Sir Fopling Flutter
in George Etherege's comic play *The Man of Mode* (1676). For the
next century and beyond, the behaviour of such men of fashion
delighted and appalled theatre audiences, who were themselves
largely composed of fashionable individuals of both sexes. These
stock types represented exaggerations whose purpose was not only to
amuse but to distract from the lesser excesses of those in the audience.
The persistence of the allegedly effeminate man in Restoration and
Georgian theatre was sustained by the campaign against male ag-
gression. Men had to tread a fine line between asserting their masculinity and being suitably respectful to women and attendant on their
needs and interests. Fops were usually depicted as men who had failed
at this challenge. They desired female company to the extent that
they almost became like women. It was alleged that women despised

them for this. Effeminacy was associated with a range of qualities including physical weakness, indulgence in luxury, androgyny and feeblemindedness.[12] It was a quality that directly derived from the misogynistic assumption that women and their supposed attributes were inferior to men. This did not mean that effeminacy had no sexual significance since it was a relatively small step from impotence with women to a lack of interest in their bodies. Fashion-conscious fops were, therefore, potentially queer figures, and men who worked in the clothing industry were particularly subject to innuendo.[13]

During the eighteenth century the classical figure of the herm-aphrodite, who possessed the sexual characteristics of both genders,

6 A fribble was, in a variety of senses, meant to be read as something other than a real man. From John Caspar Lavater, *Essays on Physiognomy*, vol. 3, part 1, London, 1789–98, p. 213.

became connected with the medieval category of the sodomite as a sexual transgressor against the laws of God. This produced a kind of third sex in which physical and moral aberrations were linked. This process was complicated by the fact that the strange beings created by this process were on the one hand dangerous sexual predators and on the other effeminate weaklings. The opposition between overly and underly masculine styles made for some of the most compelling scenes in David Garrick's play *Miss in Her Teens* (1747), as in the sparring between the swaggering Captain Flash and the simpering Fribble.[14] Garrick was a physically slight man. He played the latter part by making reference to several of the most prominent contemporary men of fashion in London at the time. That Fribble was, in a variety of senses, meant to be read as something other than a real man was the point of *Contrasted Attitudes of a Man and a Fribble* (1789; FIG. 6), which was copied from *Mr King in the Character of Lord Ogleby in 'The Clandestine Marriage'* (1769).[15] Especially effete fops duly came to be referred to as fribbles. Garrick's exaggerated stage persona was meant as a satirical attack on – rather than affectionate embodiment of – a type. He also took a burlesque approach to cross-dressing on stage, as evidenced, for example, by his performance of the role of Sir John Brute in John Vanbrugh's *The Provoked Wife* (1697). Garrick was depicted by Johann Zoffany with masculine stance ill-concealed by his voluminous frock (PLATE 6).[16] Nevertheless, when the play was reprinted in *Bell's British Theatre* it was accompanied by a print captioned *So! how d'ye like my Shapes now?* which depicted Garrick batting his eyes in a moment of flirtatious camp (1776; PLATE 7).[17]

However absurd his act, Garrick was clearly interested in gender confusion. He returned to the subject in various comedies, including *The Male-Coquette* (1757), which was also notable for featuring the foppish Marchese di Macaroni.[18] He may have got the idea from another play in which he had acted, Benjamin Hoadly's *The Suspicious Husband* (1747), in which there was a discussion of a taste for pasta among young men of fashion.[19] Garrick's new play of 1757 was aimed at the Irish critic Thaddeus Fitzpatrick and his circle, whom Garrick referred to as 'daffodils' and worse than fribbles. Both sides traded various insults in print until the actor published *The Fribbleriad* in 1761. In this poem a band of neutered master-misses is led by Fizgig (Fitzpatrick), who addressed the crowd 'With strech'd out fingers, and a thumb / Stuck to his hips, and jutting bum'.[20] Fashionable coats were being cut short at this point and this posterior performance was specifically meant to ridicule Garrick's opponents as sodomites.[21] This is more or less the same postural innuendo that Marcel Proust was to make about the meeting of two of the queer men in his *In Search of Lost Time* (1913–27): '[Jupien] had – in perfect symmetry with the Baron – thrown back his head, giving a becoming tilt to his body, placed his hand with grotesque effrontery on his hip, stuck out his behind, struck poses with the coquetry that the orchid might have adopted on the providential arrival of the bee.'[22]

There is ample evidence from raids on so-called 'molly houses' (bars with a queer clientele) earlier in the eighteenth century that London had developed a lively sodomitical subculture.[23] Men in search of sex with other men had, of necessity, developed codes of signalling, albeit ones a little more subtle than waving their backsides around. One slightly later source reported that

> these wretches have many ways and means of conveying intelligence, and many signals by which they discover themselves to each other; they have likewise several houses of rendezvous, whither they resort: but their chief place of meeting is the Bird-Cage Walk, in St. James's Park, whither they resort about twilight.
>
> They are easily discovered by their signals, which are pretty nearly as follows: If one of them sits on a bench, he pats the backs of his hands; if you follow them, they put a white handkerchief thro' the skirts of their coat, and wave it to and fro; but if they are met by you, their thumbs are stuck in the arm-pits of their waistcoats, and they play their fingers upon their breasts.[24]

In 1772 Garrick found himself depicted in turn as a sodomite in William Kenrick's poem *Love in the Suds: A Town Eclogue. Being the Lamentation of Roscius for His Nyky*.[25] It was imputed that he had been the lover of the playwright Isaac Bickerstaffe, who had fled to France after a sexual encounter with a soldier had been reported in the newspapers. It is important to be clear that, aside from Bickerstaffe, these accusations may simply have been fabrications. Nevertheless, accusations of dandyism and sodomy represented useful means by which men could challenge their opponents. Nor should it be assumed that such scurrilous publications only provide evidence of prejudice. *Love in the Suds*, for instance, includes reference to various defences for same-sex desire ranging from the mores of the Ancient Greeks to inconsistencies of moral standards in the Old Testament. A man might say one thing during the day and act quite differently when drunk of an evening. 'Love is blind', argued Roscius, leading to 'a common error, frequent in the Park, / Where love is apt to stumble in the dark'.[26]

DESIGNS ON BRITISH MANHOOD

In the eighteenth century, as today, there was no great evidence that less masculine men were inherently likely to be homosexual, any more than there was that sexual indiscretions were more prevalent in some countries than others. The British, however, decided that dandyism and sodomy were both vices that might be caught on the Continent and that sickly young men were the ones most likely to succumb to their allures. An eye for a boy might have bolstered the roistering reputation of a Restoration libertine but by the mid-eighteenth century it had become widely understood as an essentially feminine taste.[27] Men who were of slight build, such as Garrick, who dressed well and might be considered 'pretty', were more likely than others to be the subject of accusations of effeminacy that 'hovered between uses that had nothing to do with sodomy, those that had everything to do with it, and those somewhere in between'.[28] Sometimes the rumour-mongering was well founded, as in the case of Alexander Pope's vicious caricature of the English courtier Lord Hervey as Paris:

> Let *Paris* tremble – 'What? that Thing of silk,
> *Paris*, that mere white Curd of Ass's milk?
> Satire or Shame alas! can *Paris* feel?
> Who breaks a Butterfly upon a Wheel?'
> Yet let me slap this Bug with gilded wings,
> This painted Child of Dirt that stinks and stings.[29]

A few months later Pope revised the piece, changing the name of Paris to Sporus, the eunuch who had been the lover of the emperor Nero, and added the following:

> His wit all see-saw between *that and this*,
> Now high, now low, now master up, now miss,
> And he himself one vile Antithesis.
> Amphibious thing! that acting either part,
> The trifling head, or the corrupted heart,
> Fop at the toilet, flatt'rer at the board,
> Now trips a Lady, and now struts a Lord.[30]

The artist William Hogarth was apt to put the occasional sodomitical allusion into his satirical works, including *Lord Hervey and His Friends* (1738). This has been interpreted as the depiction of an 'all male pseudo-family' in which both Hervey and his lover Stephen Fox obliquely catch the eye of the viewer.[31] Hervey fathered several children and appears to have been bisexual, but his stylish, petite figure made him an easy target for satire.

But were men attracted to the same sex likely to advertise that fact by overdressing? A possible answer is provided by John Chute, who appears in the *Oxford Dictionary of National Biography* as an 'architect and connoisseur of the arts and literature … of unimpressive appearance, frail and near-sighted' and who, in the judgement of historian

Timothy Mowl, was a 'defiantly affected old queen'.[32] A portrait of 1758 preserved at his house, The Vyne, shows him displaying a splendid embroidered waistcoat under a plain jacket (PLATE 8).[33] Two suits that were probably owned by Chute dating from 1765 have also been preserved.[34] They are not especially ostentatious but are carefully constructed, notably in their interior tailoring. The queer man of fashion was perhaps in reality, if not in caricature, elegantly understated.[35]

It was a custom of the upper ranks to send their sons to Italy on the Grand Tour, often, but not always, in the charge of a tutor.[36] This was meant to crown their education with judicious appreciation of the classical past and disdainful reflection on the Roman Catholic present, but was often an excuse for drinking and whoring at lower cost and with less chance of public scandal than at home.[37] Catholic priests, being unmarried, were widely suspected of sodomy in a scurrilous line of thinking that derived directly from Henry VIII's promulgation of the Buggery Act in 1533 in the context of the suppression of the English monasteries. As one anti-Catholic text put it, noting that men and women mingled in the afterlife: 'Heaven is not shut like the Pope's court, / To all but priests, eunuchs and boys.'[38] Italians were reputed to be highly sexed, impoverished and prone to pimping their daughters and even, on occasion, their sons.[39] There was, in effect, a strong element of sex tourism in the reality as opposed to the ideals of the Grand Tour. Some men – including Chute, who went in later life – made their home in Italy for extended periods of time. It was there in the 1740s that he met Horace Walpole.

The centre of queer British life in Italy at this time was Florence, where the British diplomat Horace (Horatio) Mann held court. William, second Earl Fitzwilliam, wrote that

> Sir Horace is the most finical man in the world: if you speak a little loud, he can't bear it, it hurts his nerves, he dies – and he v–m–ts if you eat your petite patee before your soup; take him as he is,

without the least notice, he is a perfect character for the stage. He has been so long out of England, that he has lost the manliness of an Englishman, and has borrowed the effeminacy of Italy. But with all his little airs, he is a good kind man, and is very civil.[40]

Walpole's correspondence would have been spruced up for publication, but cheerful references to buggery are still preserved in his irony-filled letters.[41]

The same weaknesses, the same passions that in England plunge men into elections, drinking, whoring, exist here and show themselves in the shapes of Jesuits, cicisbeos and *Corydon ardebat in Alexin*'s [a same-sex passion in Virgil's *Eclogues*]. In England, tempers vary so excessively, that almost every one's faults are peculiar to himself. I take this diversity to proceed partly from our climate, partly from our government: the first is changeable and makes us queer; the latter permits our queernesses to operate as they please.[42]

Johan Zoffany was in Florence thirty years later and painted Horace Mann, the caricaturist Thomas Patch and other members of their coterie of fellow connoisseurs rapt in the contemplation of classical statuary in the foreground of his painting *The Tribuna of the Uffizi* (1772–77; PLATE 9).[43] They are apparently admiring Titian's *Venus of Urbino*, but the eye of the viewer drifts to a nearby sculpture of two nude wrestlers in an intimate clinch. Some years later the artist William Beechey reported that George III had said that the Queen would not allow it to be hung in her apartments – 'Zoffany having done so improper a thing as to introduce portraits of Sir Thomas Man[n], [Thomas] Patch, & Others who were considered as men addicted to improper practices'.[44]

We cannot be sure that these bachelors were, in modern terms, queer men. Queer theorist Eve Kosofsky Sedgwick spoke of Walpole as being 'iffily' homosexual.[45] Nevertheless, some historians have taken a stronger stance. George Rousseau has denounced later homophobia for widespread misinterpretation of the eighteenth-century evidence and argued that 'the activities of English homo-sexuals abroad – Walpole, [Thomas] Gray, and their circle – have caused confusion and falsification in the standard biographies and cultural histories in which these figures appear.'[46] Timothy Mowl, in his biography of Walpole, likewise argues that we can tell from the set of letters from Horace to Lord Lincoln written between 1739 and 1744 that the two were lovers. They did, notably, share a taste in clothes, since both appear wearing similarly gorgeous garments in portraits by Rosalba Carriera.[47] George Haggerty has found Mowl's interpreta-tion to be an anachronistic reading of modern sensibilities into the past:

> what the letters reveal is a bitchy, playful, arrogant, self-satisfied, intriguing, acquisitive, loving and devoted friend who loved deeply and long and devotes himself to his house and his collections with the same kind of energy he puts into friends and (sometimes) politics. This is the person who emerges so vividly and richly in the letters that he himself preserved for posterity: isn't it enough?[48]

Walpole, whatever his sexuality, is important to the story of the British dandy because it was he who first recorded the appearance of 'the Maccaroni Club' in 1764 comprising well-travelled youths with curls and 'spying-glasses'.[49] Italy may have been the expected destina-tion of those on the Grand Tour, but the journey usually took them through France with a lengthy stop for shopping and socializing in Paris. The fact that the United Kingdom was frequently in a state of hostilities with its neighbour meant that there were periods when such journeys were no longer possible. Furthermore, even in times of peace the purchase of certain French goods was subject to legal controls. In 1745 the Anti-Gallican Society was set up with the aim of discourag-ing the importation of French goods and culture into Britain. Four years later an Act of Parliament banned the import of embroidery, brocade and precious-metal thread, and from 1765 there was a ban on the shipping of silks.[50] The aim was to redirect spending to British products and prevent gold coin from leaving the country. Travelled young men, particularly if they dressed the part, could therefore be attacked as unpatriotic. The restriction on imports, however, meant that those who had finery were able to stand out even more at social occasions.

The ostentatious use by young men of eyeglasses composed of a lens with a handle was an exercise in fashionable affectation. Such items would normally be required by older persons whose sight was no longer what it had once been. To flaunt the use of an eyeglass that one probably did not need was to advertise the exhibitionistic character of their deployment. The statement they made was: See me looking![51] Groups of young men toting eyeglasses as a fashion accessory may have been pretending to peer at young ladies while they were really admiring each other. This playful quality is perhaps one reason why later writers sometimes connected these men with 'macaronic' light verse in Latin such as might have been written by bored pupils after a hard day spent translating Virgil.[52] To give one example, a newspaper article on the 'Origins of Macaronism' from 1827 suggested that the name derived from Theophilus Folengio of Mantua, who wrote trifling verses that were known as macaroni after the 'little Italian cakes' (in the eighteenth century pasta was often eaten using the hand and without sauces).[53] This is indeed what contemporary writers recorded; that the macaroni style began with a club for those who, having been on the Grand Tour, wished to reassemble with friends to eat the Italian food that they remembered. The term 'macaroni' then became a variation on the themes of fop and fribble.

At this time there was a wide range of London clubs focused around dining, some formally constituted with premises and others simply being the occasional and informal gatherings of friends. William Hogarth was one of the original members of the Sublime Society of Beefsteaks. This was founded around 1736 in order that men might gather, eat beef and sing 'The Roast Beef of Old England', which was a patriotic refrain from Henry Fielding's *The Grub-Street Opera* (1731). Beef ranked alongside ale and wool as prime British products. Around this time *rosbifs* came into use in Paris to refer to English tradesmen, and by the 1770s it had come to mean anyone English (in much the same way that the French are sometimes referred to as 'frogs'). In France the aristocracy distinguished itself from the lower orders in the variety, expense and subtlety of its cuisine. This was copied by many members of the British elite, including Robert Walpole, who employed a French chef.[54] Whilst the problem for the poor in Britain was getting enough to eat, there was also a fashion among the middling ranks to make a virtue of necessity and laud the values of good, plain food. Elaborate French sauces, it was alleged, were deployed to conceal inferior meat. Great stock was set by the value of British beef and its relative affordability was associated with the tradition of political liberty that was supposedly absent on the Continent. It was alleged by anti-Catholic propagandists that across the Channel only despots and priests grew fat while the people starved. Subsisting on vegetables was seen as enfeebling. In Britain, by contrast, young men grew strong as a result of their diet.

These themes were explored by William Hogarth in his painting *O the Roast Beef of Old England*, or *The Gate of Calais* (1748), in which a cook staggers under the weight of a huge joint of beef that he is carrying through the streets of Calais to the British inn in the town.[55] He is watched by spindly French soldiers and manhandled by a leering and rotund friar. The painting provided inspiration for Tobias Smollett's novel *The Adventures of Peregrine Pickle* (1751), in which the character of Pallet, an artist, appears to have been modelled on Hogarth.[56] Pallet at one point remarks that 'I am none of your tit-bits, one would think, and yet there's a freshness to the English complexion, a *ginseekeye*, I think you call it, so inviting to a hungry Frenchman, that I have caught several in the very act of viewing me with an eye of extreme appetite as I passed.'[57] The implication is of equivalence between visceral and sexual hunger on the part of the French, and for beef in both bovine and human forms.[58] Admirers of British beef looked askance at pasta as unpatriotic and unmanly. It was supposedly only fit for foreigners and those like babies, invalids and feeble women who did not have the powerful jaw and strong teeth needed to chew meat. This helps to explain why a taste for pasta was promptly held up to mockery.

Whether there was a formally constituted 'Maccaroni Club' in 1764 is not known, but the term came into general circulation soon after. In May 1765 the 'Macaroni Sweepstakes' were anounced at Newmarket racecourse. Forty-four men subscribed 5 guineas each, including the Duke of Ancaster, Lord Rockingham and Lord Grosvenor.[59] Perhaps the earliest image of a macaroni was drawn around this date by Henry Bunbury when he was a schoolboy at Westminster. It survives bound into an album of material collected by his friend Horace Walpole and is captioned 'THIS CLUB was instituted and kept at ALMACKS and called the MACARONNI society' (PLATE 10).[60] Almack's Club opened in 1765 and was to play an important role in the operations of fashionable society. Entry was controlled by lady patronesses and it was to some degree modelled on French salon culture, in which conversation and matchmaking between the sexes was encouraged.[61] It might therefore seem a less likely venue for queer homosociality than hearty men-only clubs, but to individuals such as Hogarth frequent intermingling with society women was liable to be an effeminating activity in and of itself.

Just as was the case with the fops and fribbles before them, much of the evidence for the macaronis is in the form of satire against them. This sometimes took the form of stage performances such as Hitchcock's aforementioned play *The Macaroni* (1773), but surviving visual representations are mostly in the form of prints. Britain at this time was noted for its lively print culture, which initially took as its subjects the public and private lives of the members of the upper ranks. Compared with paintings, the cost of prints, especially small ones, was low and so an expanding market developed composed of those in the middling section of society. Prints were not only bought by private collectors but pinned up in bars and coffee houses where their subjects duly became, quite literally, the talk of the town. Macaronis were sometimes depicted in groups but many of the prints show a particular individual. These were often drawn by friends or opponents and handed in to a print shop for duplication. They were typically anonymous but were provided with hints as to their real subjects. Walpole annotated his collection of macaroni prints with the names of the individuals he thought they were. It seems that although the term 'macaroni' started off referring to a small and exclusive group, it was soon deployed to mock anyone with social pretentions. However, bearing in mind Oscar Wilde's quip from *The Picture of Dorian Gray* (1890) that there is 'only one thing in the world worse than being talked about, and that is not being talked about', to be derided as a macaroni implied that at least one had the status that invited mockery.[62] Some of the prints equated individuals with stereo-types of the man of fashion but others focused more on individual particularities and eccentricities.[63] These could even, in some cases, be aligned with British liberties, including the possibility of being a trifle peculiar.[64]

Walpole himself drew Clotworthy Skeffington, second Earl of Massareene, around 1765 in a style that was typical of many of the macaroni prints. His slight figure is shown prancing on its toes, his wig juts upwards perkily and he wears a huge boutonnière (FIG. 7).[65] He was in real life an extravagant and (until 1789) unmarried man of fashion. Walpole records meeting similar Englishmen in Paris in the winter of 1765–66 who were wearing 'coloured frocks, satin waistcoats and breeches, and huge nosegays with bunches of ribbands', all this being most improper at a time of mourning for the Dauphin (the

7 Clotworthy Skeffington, 2nd Earl of Massareene (1742–1805), presents a slight, prancing figure, complete with pert wig and vast *boutonnière*. Horace Walpole, *Clotworthy Skeffington*, c.1765.

heir to the French throne).[66] A very similar effect appears in one of the prints in Walpole's collection *Lord —— [Grandison] or the Nosegay Macaroni*, which was published in *The Macaroni and Theatrical Magazine* in 1773.[67] If one compares the figures contrasted in another print, *Macaroni Dresses for 1740 and 1776* (*c.* 1776) – there were, of course, no macaronis in 1740 – one sees that the (overly) fashionable male image

8 The overall impression is of someone who is not an impressive figure of a man trying and failing to use clothes to achieve that effect. *Macaroni Dresses for 1740 and 1776*, in *New Lottery Magazine*, c. 1776.

for men had become thinner and was positioned more upright, with, it was alleged, the strategic employment of tiptoe so as to accentuate the height (FIG. 8).[68] The clothing has become closer fitting and the jacket shorter. The overall impression is of someone who is not an impressive figure of a man trying and failing to use clothes to achieve that effect.

The firm that was most associated with the macaroni prints was that run by a married couple, Matthias and Mary Darly, between 1766 and 1781.[69] Their establishment was the subject of Edward Topham's print *The Macaroni Print Shop* (1772).[70] This shows a wide range of other identifiable Darly prints in the windows of the shop and various men (mostly thin but one corpulent) in conversation on the pavement.[71] Most but not all of the prints in the window are also of men. This emphasizes the heavily homosocial nature of the macaroni prints and also the importance not only of fashion but of the male bodies beneath the clothes.[72] There were some female macaronis who were interested in such prints, as shown in the window displays featured in *Miss Macaroni and Her Gallant at a Print-Shop* (1773).[73] Although we can establish that the mass market for prints was expanding rapidly at this time, we do not know how many were typically produced or how widely they were circulated. We can, however, be sure that far more people in London bought such prints than ever ate macaroni.[74]

The rich person of fashion could, of course, commission a flattering self-portrait in oils. Richard Cosway had a particular reputation for this sort of work. It is thought that he may be the subject of Robert Dighton's *The Macaroni Painter, or Billy Dimple Sitting for His Picture* (1772).[75] Unsubtle references to buggery featured in a story concerning Billy Dimple and his valet in a magazine article published the following year.[76] Cosway was a social climber of small stature and was widely mocked for wearing an outsized wig and sword.[77] He was not to marry his wife Maria until 1781. She had also been attacked in *The Paintress of Maccaroni's* [*sic*] (1772) and it was suggested that the marriage was a sham.[78] But Cosway's letters show him, in the words of one historian, as having been 'rampantly heterosexual'.[79] The image, as opposed to the reality, of the macaronis did become more powerfully associated with sodomy than had those of the earlier types of fop. The term become a byword for the supposedly effeminate extravagances of men who exceeded the normal bounds of fashion such that 'the Macaronis' painted, patched, amazingly coiffed heads and slender, delicate, beribboned bodies filled the print-shop windows'.[80] Peter McNeil, a historian of fashion and design and an expert on the macaronis, argues that 'by the 1760s when the macaroni emerged, such attention to fashion was read as evidence of a *lack of interest* in women, or as potentially unattractive to women.'[81]

Such macaroni men had, it was thought, 'taken on women's aims and objectified themselves'.[82]

It was in this climate that the London publisher and art dealer Carington Bowles brought out *How D'Ye Like Me?* in November 1772 (PLATE 12).[83] This shows a simpering man in the stance that might be expected of a sexually desirable young woman. The classical discourse of the hermaphrodite was referenced by depicting this figure with but a vestigial sword and with a prominent vulva-like crease where his penis ought to be.[84] The British Museum's two differently hand-tinted copies of the print show him either as a youth, albeit one who was heavily made up, or as an aged roué: the one implies someone wanting to sell their favours, the latter someone seeking to pay for them.[85] He is wearing the towering style of wig, the back of which was tied up by an enormous bow, that was characteristic of the macaronis at this date. Complex wigs were expensive to buy and maintain, and were a convenient marker of high social status.[86] However, they became objects of ridicule when they appeared to be worn not as reflections of high rank but of social insecurity. Such excessive wigs 'came to proclaim one's dependence upon things rather than independence from them'.[87] Furthermore, the tall wig was the fashion for women in France and its use by macaronis would have been seen not only as effeminate but also as un-British. In Paris, by contrast, this fashion for men was known as the English style.[88]

Another print that hinted at perverse sexuality was Philip Dawe's *The Macaroni: A Real Character at the Late Masquerade* (1773; FIG. 4).[89] He is shown having attended to his complex toilette at a woman's dressing table. Such a boudoir was a room associated with seduction.[90] The objects with which women were made up were regarded with an almost fetishistic degree of attention by admirers.[91] Much the same could be said of household furnishings: 'social seduction in eighteenth-century France was impossible without furniture. Objects were like extensions of the body, part of a wardrobe that, correctly worn, could turn the activities of elite existence into dances of artful persuasion.'[92] On the chair back behind the macaroni is the face of a cat. This alludes both to brothels, which could be referred to as cat houses, and to catamites.[93]

There is, however, even more than first meets the eye taking place in this representation. Innovations in fashion, particularly those that referenced the more elaborate elite styles of the past, were supposedly a feature of macaroni practice. Horace Walpole wrote to William Hamilton, who was the British Ambassador to the Kingdom of Naples, in 1774, saying that 'if you were to come over you would find us a general masquerade. The maccaronis, not content with producing new fashions every day, and who are great reformers, are going to restore the Vandyck dress' (i.e. the style of the court of Charles I as depicted by Anthony Van Dyck).[94] Masquerade parties were a popular form of both public and private entertainment. The masks themselves drew attention to the wearer as much as they disguised them.[95] At venues such as the newly opened Pantheon the social ranks and sexes mingled with opportunistic glee.[96] Costumed events often had a theme, but famous people might come 'as them-selves'.[97] The 'real character' in this print may, therefore, have been a macaroni unaware of the ridiculous figure that he was cutting, or else a macaroni who was deliberately courting attention by pushing fashion to its extremes, or even an ordinary member of the public who had dressed up to impersonate an outrageous macaroni.

The rapid rise in queer innuendo in the macaroni prints was partly the result of the sensational trial of Captain Robert Jones, who was convicted at the Old Bailey in July 1772 for sodomizing a 13-year-old boy and sentenced to death. He was subsequently given a royal pardon if he left the country. Jones was well known in London's fash-ionable world and was noted for his work in popularizing skating and fireworks. The military had a reputation for sodomy partly because the common soldiery was badly paid and sometimes made themselves sexually available for hire. The civilian militia were depicted as effete dilettantes who were just playing at being soldiers.[98] These suspicions were referenced in *The Relief* (1781) by Walpole's friend Henry Bunbury. This showed the tailcoats of three pretty young soldiers on parade blown back so as to reveal their shapely thighs and buttocks (PLATE 11).[99] It was suggested that a *corps de beaux* was to be formed: 'all genteel, nice, neat, pretty, elegant, beautiful, smooth-faced, red-cheeked, white toothed, long fingered, narrow shouldered, unbellied young men of fashion' were supposedly to join up. There shall be no unpleasant use of gunpowder, but rather 'the cartouch box is to be filled with scented hair powder, wash balls, pomatum, and paints, particularly the latter, as it is in orders, that every man's cheeks be painted on parade, and in the field.'[100] This takes well-established tropes of effeminacy and re-presents them in the context of a social world in which men were ceasing to employ cosmetics and would soon abandon wigs as well. But this was not the only mode in which the military could be queered in the later eighteenth century. The even more transgressive idea that a macaroni might be so perverted as to sexually admire a masculine tough – as opposed to an andro-gynous youth – was mocked in Richard St George Mansergh's *Refin'd Taste* (1773; FIG. 9).[101]

A letter to the *Public Ledger* on 5 August 1772 attacked Captain Jones. It claimed that this 'MILITARY MACCARONI' was 'too much engaged in every scene of idle Dissipation and wanton Extravagance … therefore, ye Beaux, ye sweet-scented, simpering He-she things, deign to learn wisdom from the death of a Brother'.[102] Three days later another newspaper reported that an 'effeminate prigg of a Macaroni' had said he was glad that Jones had been 'respited' and was set on by the mob.[103] A crowd gathered in Islington on the northern edge of London and 'proposed hanging a Sodomite in effigy'. They were only prevented when a magistrate read the Riot Act.[104] It was reported that Jones was going into exile in Florence, and that he had letters of credit and recommendations 'to many people of fashion there'.[105] By November it was reported that it had become 'common practice with the vulgar, whenever a well-dressed person passes, to call out Macaroni, whether young or old, male or female, 'tis just the same'. The writer continued, 'if I consult the prints, 'tis a figure with something uncommon in its dress or appearance; if the ladies [think of it, they see] an effeminate fop; but if the 'prentice-boys [do so they see] a queer fellow with a *great large* tail. 'Tis remark-able, that the ladies never thought effeminacy was its characteristic, 'til the affair of Capt. Jones.'[106] This brings out the fact that the tail

9 A macaroni might prefer a masculine tough to an androgynous youth. Richard St George Mansergh, *Refin'd Taste*, M. Darly, London, *c.* May 1773.

Refin'd Taste.

or back of the macaroni wig was now being vulgarly associated with the penis and that effeminacy could be used as code for sodomy.

The topic of sodomy was also in the news because of the aforementioned scandal in theatrical circles over the conduct of Isaac Bickerstaffe, and because of the case of Samuel Drybutter. Drybutter was a jeweller and bookseller who had been arrested for attempted sodomy on 23 January 1770 and put in the pillory. Sodomy was a hanging offence, but a guilty verdict was hard to secure because it required proof not only of anal penetration but also of emission of semen. Lesser offences, which involved masturbation or oral sex, were treated as attempts to commit anal sex and were punished by a period in the stocks. This had the effect of exposing the convicted felon to public ridicule and liable to private acts of retribution either at the time – since objects were often thrown at the chained-up prisoner – or at a later date.[107] Drybutter was subsequently re-arrested, suffered various assaults upon his person and died after a mob attacked his house in 1777. Several Darly prints have been identified as showing him even though he was not a pretty man of fashion. In fact, his physical unattractiveness, complete with hunched back and squat legs, was made into part of the joke in a print that showed him in the character of Ganymede, the boy-lover of the Greek god Zeus. 'Dammee Sammy', says the executioner, 'you'r a sweet pretty creature and I long to have you at the end of my string' (i.e. my penis/my rope).[108] A squib by 'Punch' in the *Morning Chronicle* published on 7 August 1772 claimed that 'Mr. Dr—b—tt—r's club are desired to meet at the Gomorrah, to-morrow evening, to consider of a proper address of thanks to the throne for the respite of brother Jones. The Macaroni, Dilettanti, and other Italian clubs will bring up the *rear* of the cavalcade.'[109]

It is easy to understand how the increasingly public association of sodomy and macaroni style would have led to the rapid decline in its ability to function even as an ironic amusement in fashionable society. But this should not obscure the fact that most of those men who embraced the bold macaroni styles are likely to have been sexually attracted to women. They were acting in accordance with a long tradition of the use of power-dressing to intimidate rivals and lure partners. Nevertheless, those who disdained such impudence could use the stereotype of effeminate foppery to confound their opponents. Picture a scene on 30 July 1773 in Vauxhall Gardens on the south bank of the Thames. It would become briefly famous through the publication of *The Vauxhall Affray; or, the Macaronies Defeated* (1773).[110] This described the confrontation of a group of men by Henry Bate, editor of the *Morning Post*. He was a priest and assertive journalist whose conduct on this occasion was to earn him the nicknames the 'Fighting Parson' and the 'Reverend Bruiser'.

These commercially run pleasure gardens were frequented both by persons of fashion and, partly because entrance was free, by prostitutes. Respectable ladies would be escorted there, and on this occasion Bate was discharging just such as duty. He and his female companion were bothered by the attentions of some men who stared in a most impudent manner at the lady. The leader of the group, Fitzgerald, was a dangerous man who was known as a gambler and a duellist. Nevertheless, Bate drove them off by resorting to ridicule of what he termed this 'little effeminate being... The dress, hat and feather, – miniature picture [of himself], pendant at his snow-white bosom, and a variety of other appendages to this *man of fashion*, were naturally seized upon by me.' Bate won the day as the crowd joined in on his side.[111] The *more is more* style of the macaronis was being laughed into extinction. It was time for the man of mode to rethink his sartorial plan of attack.

On 5 September 1772 it was reported in *The Craftsman; or Say's Weekly Journal* that

> It is said that a measure has been hit upon, which will certainly put an end to every species of *Maccaronism* for the future, by laughing it entirely out of countenance. Several persons of fortune (Ladies as well as Gentlemen) are subscribing a sum, to purchase a number of dresses in the highest Maccaroni taste. These are to be given to chairmen, porters, carmen, watermen, and other low people, who are to be handsomely paid for wearing them, not only in their several occupations, but in traversing the Park, and other public places, arm in arm, in groups. Some of the clubs for the Irish chairmen's hair [i.e. 'tails' at the back of the wigs] are made as thick as the wearers legs; and all their other habiliments equally *outre*.[112]

It was in this spirit that the Darlys produced a stream of prints purporting to show macaroni farmers, tradesmen and builders.[113] The macaroni style of sartorial overstatement fell out of fashion for a number of reasons, including fear of sodomitical innuendo, but what was also critical was that it lost its social cachet as it was copied down the social spectrum.

It is notable that we do not find people calling themselves macaronis, although the statesman Charles James Fox, who was associated with this group earlier in his life on his return from the Grand Tour, did use the term *petit-maître* to describe himself.[114] As we have seen, this was a French equivalent of the fop and Fox's use of the term was partly ironic. His aim was to depict himself as a cut above the middling order of the town, on the one hand, and the country gentry, on the other, through stressing his international connections.[115] This also involved displaying a calculated lack of respect for the homely court of George III.[116] Fox and his grand friends in the Whig party had a penchant for adopting items of elaborate Continental dress, such as red-heeled shoes, but they wore them without reference to the elaborate codes of propriety expected at the French court. Such showing off was intended to display their wealth and self-confidence, but the cultural tide was starting to turn against such displays. As the eighteenth century progressed, a social model in which men courted men and women of higher rank in search of preferment fell into some disrepute. It was replaced by the valorization of the autonomous participant in politics who maintains his own patriarchal household.[117] As the upper ranks of society became gradually less exclusive the performances of social climbers were watched by established members of the elite. After all, accusations of sodomy could be deployed to undermine aristocratic authority since it was associated with effete men who had no need to work and who appeared to favour Catholic regimes on the Continent.[118] Penalties for sodomy in eighteenth-century France were less severe than in Britain and, except in the case of sexual assaults involving boys, generally involved retirement from public life rather than the death penalty.[119]

The growth in the ideal of polite relations between men and women, which had given rise to parody of overly demure fops, also had the effect of reducing the acceptability of libertine behaviour and public displays of eroticism. As one historian has commented of this process, 'the polite gentleman never has sex'.[120] However, society was still far from entertaining Victorian levels of hypocritical secrecy over sexual indiscretions, and politeness was far from the rule in political life. Indeed undue meekness might be seized upon by opponents as evidence of effeminate unfitness for a public career.[121] Nevertheless, it is striking that during the 1780s Fox transformed his image from that of a flamboyant aristocrat into that of a dishevelled man of the people.[122]

So what choice was left for the dandy who did not wish to be denounced? One option, although not of much use to a politician, was to assume a pose of profound interiority. This had the advantage that it aligned the individual in question with progressive intellectual opinion. Jean-Jacques Rousseau had famously advanced the ideal of the natural man as opposed to the courtier.[123] His thought was central to the development of Romanticism and the embrace of the emotions as opposed to the intellect. Where the macaronis had seemed to be without authentic feeling the new fashionable type was composed of little else. At the time that the macaronis were being mocked into extinction, therefore, a new enthusiasm arose for 'the man of feeling'. This development was directly connected with the publication in 1771 of Henry Mackenzie's novel of this title.[124] Its hero, Harley, was in some ways a quintessential fop in that, amidst his tears, he fails miserably in his attempt to win the woman he loves.[125] Such sentimentality in men has been seen as a kind of cross-dressing in that it imitated the traditional sensitivity of women.[126] Sighing men might equally divulge their souls to one another such that, in the opinion of one queer historian, same-sex desire was also the 'open secret of sensibility'.[127]

Joseph Wright painted one such devotee of fashionable introspection, Sir Brooke Boothby, lying, somewhat camply, in a woodland glade in 1781 (PLATE 13).[128] There is, incidentally, a miniature portrait of Boothby, attributed to Cosway, that presents its subject as distinctly dimpled.[129] Boothby had got to know Rousseau in the 1760s during the latter's stay in Derbyshire, and when in Paris in 1776 was entrusted with the manuscript of the first part of the writer's *Dialogues*. Boothby published the text in 1780 and reminded the public of this fact by having himself shown holding it. The painting duly attracted a good deal of attention when it was put on display at the Royal Academy's exhibition in London.[130] Richard Etlin has commented that 'if you had not learned that the broad-brimmed black hat, the reclining pose with the head on the hand, and the unbuttoned sleeves were all signs of "melancholy" well established in Western art, you certainly would miss that aspect of the "meaning" of Joseph Wright of Derby's portrait of Sir Brooke Boothby.'[131] The man does not look like he is reclining broodingly in the countryside far from thoughts of worldly splendour because he has been captured by the artist precisely as he was: posing in Wright's studio when dressed in the height of understated fashion. The bright colours and spectacular appendages of the macaroni costume have gone but not the ostentatious tightness, which meant that the sleeves must have needed to be unbuttoned in order that the sitter might bend his arms at all.[132] Wright was capable of painting dishevelment, as he did in his portrait of Thomas Day (1770).[133] Boothby, in comparison, appears to be impersonating sensibility while wearing a hat set at a jaunty angle, dog-skin gloves and formal shoes with Artois buckles.

The expression that Boothby bears in this portrait is one of shrewd detachment and reminds one of that shown in Joshua Reynolds's painting of Horace Walpole (PLATE 14).[134] His self-presentation as an object of the gaze evokes comparison with a visual in-joke that was played in Walpole's circle of depicting an individual from front, side and back, as if he were a figurine.[135] Just as the macaronis represented a ironic reaction to the improving ideals of the Grand Tour, so the fashion for the man of feeling can be seen as equally rooted in forms of dandified performance. Boothby, unlike Walpole, did marry and father children, although there are grounds for exploring a queer reading of his painting as a representation of male passivity.[136] Walpole, by contrast, had been accused, albeit implicitly, of being a sodomite as a result of having defended his cousin, the general and statesman Henry Seymour Conway, from a series of political attacks. This happened, interestingly enough, in 1764, the same year that Walpole reported the appearance of a macaroni club. He found himself mocked as 'by nature maleish, by disposition female'. The writer William Guthrie continued by saying of Walpole that 'it would very much puzzle a common observer to assign him to his true sex'.[137] The object of these hermaphroditic insinuations seems to have thought that this was about more than simply his sex for he wrote to

Conway that 'they have nothing better to say, than that I am in love with you, have been so these twenty years, and am no giant'.[138]

Accusations of sodomy alongside those of effeminacy were bandied about in eighteenth-century male discourse as one of a range of strategies aimed at undermining one's opponents. The idea that eighteenth-century dandies were essentially neither male nor female but neuter was a particularly comforting illusion since it drained these men of sexual threat. The intensity with which the satire was pursued displayed the depth of men's own insecurities about how distinct gender differences really were. Dandyism as a term had yet to come into use but similarly contested practices of male self-fashioning were a major preoccupation in earlier Georgian Britain. The associated stereotypes of the fop and his various successor types flattered 'those men able to solve the conundrum of being both polite *and* manly', and of being able to dress well without indulging in excess.[139] It has even been claimed that 'violence toward the fop [and I would add the macaroni] *produced heterosexuality as we know it*, as a companionate relationship between the sexes'.[140] Such violence was fought out in the world of parody and satire and resisted by fashionistas on a daily basis as they stalked the streets and the salons.[141] And yet, despite all the controversy, or perhaps because of it, the man of fashion remained a central figure – alternately admired, envied and despised – in debates over British values. Perhaps part of the reason for this was that, even as the whiffles and macaronis were increasingly demonized in terms not only of gender but also of sexual tastes, there remained a yearning for 'loving, mutually vulnerable connection among men', as well as for the sheer fun that comes from dressing up.[142]

FOUR

Fine and dandy in the Regency

> In the Year 1772 one Captain Jones was convicted of Crimes
> against Nature, and sentenced to die: He was a Gentleman famous
> for his Invention in the Art of making Fireworks, and adapting
> Subjects fit to be represented in that Genre… If he is pardoned …
> He may shew off the Destruction of Sodom and Gomorrah; it will
> have an admirable Effect.[1]

So wrote Hester Lynch Thrale, later Mrs Piozzi, when looking back
at the macaroni scandals in 1778. By that time fashion had moved
on and Britain was in the midst of fighting the rebellious American
colonies. She was an independent-minded woman, an author and
friend of Samuel Johnson. Her first husband was a rich brewer and
her second an Italian musician and composer. In 1776 she began
to keep a record of her reminiscences. She was notable for spotting
connections between personal style and what she at one point termed
'the unnatural Vice among the Men (now so modish)'.[2] In 1794 she
recorded that she and a woman friend 'call those Fellows Finger-
twirlers; – meaning a decent word for Sodomites: old Sir Horace
Mann and Mr [George] James the Painter had such an odd way of
twirling their Fingers in Discourse; – and I see Suetonius tells the
same thing of one of the Roman Emperors.'[3]

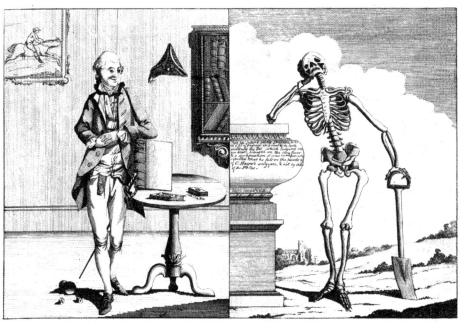

MACARONIES DRAWN AFTER THE LIFE

10 A life that combined foppish styling with rakish sex and gambling might be a short one. *Macaronies Drawn After the Life*, M. Darly, London, 1 December 1773.

The case of Robert Jones, to say nothing of his classical predecessors, gave the lie to the notion that supposedly effeminate vices were incompatible with masculine service to the nation. This revelation was important at that time because it came in the context of a wider 'gender panic' in Britain. The British failure to prevent American independence would soon lead to renewed fears for the state of the nation and the potency of its manhood.[4] These concerns were to be reinforced during the long period of the Napoleonic Wars. Some of those hanged for sodomy by the military courts can be understood as having been scapegoated by a nation beset by fears of military and political catastrophe.[5]

Eighteenth-century moralists had seen the shadow of death lurking behind the beribboned silhouettes of beaux. Marrying elderly ladies for their money implied the end of family lines and, thereby, a kind of social death. Lives of vice might lead to an early grave or even to the noose. One of the collected volumes of macaroni prints published by the Darlys presented the anti-sodomy print *Refin'd Taste* (see FIG. 9) below *Macaronies Drawn After the Life* (FIG. 10), which implied that a life of sex and gambling would be a short one.[6] On the table in the left-hand panel there is a pack of cards and a copy of John Cleland's pornographic novel *Fanny Hill, or the Memoirs of a Woman of Pleasure* (1748–49). There is a picture of a racehorse on the wall and a dice box and two dice on the floor. In the right-hand panel a skeleton leans on a funerary monument inscribed: 'Here lies Interr'd Dicky Daffodil, who in a fit of Despair on a run of ill luck swallowed the Die which lodging on his heart, brought on the bone fever and a Mortification, it was maliciously reported that he fell on the points of C. Hayes's scizzars.' A similar comparison was made a few decades later in *Fashionable Ties or Modern Neckcloths* (1810; PLATE 15).[7] Again there are two panels, with 'The Dandy' on the left and 'The Dangle' on the right. The figure on the left is saying 'I declare these Large Neck-cloths are monstrously Handy, They [serve] for a shirt too and make one a Dandy.' On the right the same figure dangles on a noose with a cloth over his head. The comment by this reads: 'When a man comes to this there's little to hope, His neat Dandy Neckcloth is changed for a Rope.' Life extinguished, the corpse is nothing more than a sack covered in its clothes.

The implications of overindulgence with women in this particular macaroni print are missing in the dandy equivalent. As we shall see, the early-nineteenth-century dandy was often associated with a lack of interest in women and a queer obsession with self-appearance. Sodomy was one of a range of capital offences in Georgian Britain, but it had a peculiar power to inspire horror.[8] Violence and perverse desire hang about the dandy prints in a way that was not quite the case with their macaroni predecessors. Part of the reason for this lies in the bloodthirstiness of the years around the turn of the eighteenth and nineteenth centuries. Masculine probity was one of the grounds on which anti-revolutionary Britons relied to prevent the spread of radical ideas from France in the wake of the momentous events of 1789. The French had long been alleged to be both rapacious and effeminate. For instance, the habit of polite kissing between men had fallen out of favour in Britain since the seventeenth century but had not done so in France.[9] Louis XVI's participation in a celebration of the storming of the Bastille was satirized by Isaac Cruikshank as a *A New French Bussing Match* in which men jumped into each other's arms or lasciviously embraced phallic pillars.[10]

Macaroni style had been based on dressing to excess. The reaction against it ushered in a period in which men's fashion was dominated by an aesthetic of plainness, and ostentation in terms of colour and decoration was mainly restricted to military uniforms. Aristocrats rushed to rebrand themselves as men in service – particularly in the army – to avoid being accused of social parasitism. Military uniforms had played an increasing role in fashion during the eighteenth century on both sides of the Channel, but the early nineteenth century was a time when 'fops, nay, cowards, are in gorgets clad, and all the world is military mad'.[11] A satirical poem published just after the end of the Napoleonic Wars presented what purported to be the 'Journal of Sir Valentine Sleek, a Colonel in the —— [regiment], and Finished Dandy'.

> ... PIERRE drew on my patent boots
> With six-inch heels; – look'd very tall – ...
> My pigeon breasts, and padded sleeves,
> Made my whole front *en militaire*;...
> By their aid a youth receives
> The approbation of the fair.
> Look'd very noble PIERRE confessed.[12]

There was, furthermore, no guarantee that men who dressed in such a fashion had ever seen military service even if they managed to look the part.[13]

The use of wigs was progressively abandoned by the end of the eighteenth century and trend-setters began to aim for more than a touch of machismo. These successive innovations were recorded in great detail in the satirical prints of the time, which found a new market in the expanding middle classes. These works continued to show a fascination with various types of dressy male from the 1770s to the 1820s when the sales of prints went into a rapid decline as innovations in printing technology allowed the cost-effective production of illustrated books and magazines.[14] Developments in Britain need to be seen in association with events in France. Clothing was highly politicized during the French Revolution. The abandonment of the styles of the French court and traditional forms of livery led to widespread innovation in dress. Conservative groups attempted to bring back more ostentatious costume, but they did so in the face of concerted opposition from those who thought that this was a betrayal of the values of 1789. The British government had, of course, set its face firmly against revolutionary agitation, but it also relied on forms of patriotism that rejected the ways of the ousted French monarchy. The result was that men's dress became plainer and darker on both sides of the Channel.

A characteristic dandy type of the time was the 'crop'. This was a person who had embraced the rising cult of the natural man by abandoning the wig and cutting the hair short. In place of the macaroni's beribboned sword, the crop carried a knobby and cudgel-like cane. This thuggish appearance notwithstanding, satirists of the time such as Cruikshank insinuated that this was all done for show. Two men exchange a manly British handshake rather than an effeminate Continental kiss in *The Knowing Crops* (c. 1791, reprinted 1794; FIG. 11).[15] However, the delicate pointed foot and spying glass of the

HA! JACK IS IT YOU___HOW ARE YOU DAM-ME.

11 It takes one to know one, or, trying (too) hard to be butch. Isaac Cruikshank, *The Knowing Crops*, Laurie & Whittle, London, 12 May *c*. 1794.

man on the left implies that he is of the macaroni persuasion. Men who attempted to fake masculinity in this way might find themselves condemned as 'monstrosities'. Purchases from collectors of prints were facilitated by a rapid development of sartorial styles that provided distinctive monsters of fashion for each passing year. The man on the right of James Gillray's *'Monstrosities' of 1799* (1799) appears, at first glance, to be a fine figure of a man (PLATE 16).[16] Yet his shoulders are puffed up in a quite unnatural fashion, which may allude to the contemporary practice of inserting pads so as to fake an impressive musculature. The drooping tassels on his boots imply a failure of potency. This print also makes clear that male monstrosities were sometimes considered in relation to their female equivalents. Gillray emphasized extremes of fashions in both sexes but, unlike some of his compatriots, did not tend to draw men and women of fashion as if they were becoming like one another.[17]

Insinuations of effeminacy and queerness did not vanish during these years, as can be seen from *Modern Bloods, or, Acoat-ation* (1803) in which the crack of a pretty young man's buttocks is visible to his companions because of the extreme shortness of his fashionable jacket.[18] This print is unsigned but was published in a series consisting of the work of either Richard Newton or Isaac Cruikshank. As has already been seen, the latter had form in the field of sodomitical innuendo. It may just be coincidence that he had a tendency to depict the beaux of the time – variously now called bucks, bloods or dandies among other things – going about arm in arm.[19] But it should also be pointed out that what might appear to be a gaze indicative of heterosexual lust may in truth have been motivated by the need for a convenient marriage to a rich woman, as in *Money Hunting Deigned* [sic] *by an Amature* (1823) by Isaac's son George.[20] Appearances certainly could be deceiving.

THE BEAU

It is interesting that the man who has been acclaimed the foremost of the dandies, and indeed the creator of dandyism as a stance of principled individualism, was neither married nor associated with sexual scandal at a time when rakish behaviour in young men was generally expected if not always admired.[21] The origins of the word 'dandy' are obscure. Derivation from Scots dialect or from the French word 'dandin' have been suggested, but either way it seems to have referred originally to fools or vulgar and awkward upstarts.[22] George Bryan 'Beau' Brummell was a social upstart but one whose fame rested on his ability *not* to appear vulgar. Born in London in 1778, George was the son of William Brummell, private secretary to Lord North, and Jane, née Richardson, who was the daughter of the Keeper of the Lottery Office. At Eton College and then Oxford University the beau was noted for setting new standards in the wearing of the cravat. In June 1794 he joined the Tenth Royal Hussars, the personal regiment of the Prince of Wales (later the Prince Regent and King George IV). Brummell's inheritance from his father was substantial but so were the expenses of an army officer, which included elaborate uniforms and frequent banquets. He resigned his commission in 1797 when the regiment was posted from London to Manchester, but he continued to play a prominent role in society in the capital thanks largely to his friendship with the prince.

Brummell's downfall began in 1811 when he lost royal favour and accumulated the debt from which he was to flee into exile in France in 1816.[23] His final years were ones of poverty and increasing decrepitude caused, it has been alleged, by syphilis.[24] In his glory years, however, Brummell was thought remarkable for his cleanliness. He insisted on the whiteness of his linen and, to widespread astonishment, took immense care over brushing his teeth, cleaning his skin, shaving and depilating. His day look centred on a dark blue coat, buff waistcoat and tight trousers, rather than knee breeches, worn with black boots. The one item of elaboration was his cravat, which was tied with such great care and deliberation that he was all but forced to hold his nose in the air.

When not at court, many men of taste and distinction spent time at their clubs. In 1811 a bow window was installed at the centre of the facade of White's Club.[25] This venerable institution – it had been founded in 1693 – functioned as an unofficial headquarters of the Tory Party. To see and be seen in such a place was not simply a matter of personal vanity but of importance in establishing and maintaining a public career. Brummell's genius lay not only in negotiating the snobberies of these social circles but in becoming an arbiter of 'correct style' for men from both old and new money. The effect was to disguise the ramshackle nature of aristocracy, on the one hand, and the crude reality of social climbing, on the other. His was a deeply conservative social performance, but it contained within itself a radical possibility – that all social positioning was performative.[26]

There is no evidence that Brummell called himself a dandy since this was, after all, at the time, a term of satirical abuse indicating a new type of fop.[27] William Jesse, who published a biography of the beau four years after his death in 1840, also denied that he had been a dandy on the grounds that his aim had been correct rather than flamboyant dress.[28] What Jesse appears to have had in mind here was a revived tradition of ostentatious dandyism as had been exemplified in the London of his own time by Count Alfred D'Orsay. The Count's sartorial expenses were supported, in a somewhat unusual arrangement, by Lord and Lady Blessington, both of whom appear to have found him attractive.[29] He was also the kind of man that Thomas Carlyle attacked in his extraordinary novel *Sartor Resartus: The Life and Opinions of Herr Teufelsdröckh* (1834).[30] It was the opinion of Carlyle's fictional German professor that 'clothes, as despicable as we think them, are so unspeakably significant'.[31] This text, like the myriad satirical prints over the previous decades, had a huge impact in reinforcing the idea that dandyism was not simply a matter of personal eccentricity but reflected, if in reverse like a photographic negative, the core values of British society. Carlyle's attack was not specifically aimed at elaborateness of costume but at inauthenticity. Somewhere, between the aristocratic, or pseudo-aristocratic, performances of the dandy and the soul-destroying labours of the working-class drudge, there lay a realm of meaningful and useful middle-class labour such as he himself exemplified.[32]

Carlyle's wife Jane was engaged in rereading her husband's finished thoughts on dandyism when D'Orsay was ushered in.

I had not seen him for four or five years. Last time he was as gay in his colours as a humming bird – blue satin cravat, blue velvet waistcoat, cream-coloured coat, lined with velvet of the same hue, trousers of a bright colour, I forget what … and length enough of gold watch-guard to have hanged himself in. To-day, in compliment to his five more years, he was all in black and brown … and only one fold of gold chain round his neck tucked together right on the centre of his spacious breast with one magnificent turquoise. Well! that man understood his trade; if it be but that of dandy, nobody can deny that he is a perfect master of it, that he dresses himself with consummate skill![33]

Nineteenth-century dandyism, therefore, when consummately practised, was an art that combined renunciation and flamboyance.

Ironically enough, George, Prince of Wales, who was the man at the centre of the dandified social scene during the Napoleonic Wars, was a poor pupil of George Brummell. The Regent's style aligned itself much more closely to the 'more is more' aesthetic of the macaronis than it did to the pared-down discipline of his slim friend. It was this collision between ideals and reality that was irresistible to satirists both literary and artistic.

George acted formally as Prince Regent from 1811 to 1820 when his father was both mentally and physically incapacitated. The antics of the playboy prince were widely seen as a national embarrass- ment in the context of the threat posed by the armies of Napoleon Bonaparte. Victory in 1815 was not enough to stave off a bout of renewed economic and political instability and continued attacks on the monarchy. Meanwhile, grandeur came to London's West End shopping district courtesy of the construction of Regent Street. The widened pavements were thronged with strutting soldiers dressed in a wide range of ostentatious national uniforms. Their presence reflected the complex nature of the military alliance against the French. Such men were duly satirized in prints such as George Cruikshank's *Ancient Military Dandies of 1450: Sketch'd by permission from the Originals in the*

Grand Armory at the Gothic Hall Pall-Mall; Modern Military Dandies of 1819:
Sketch'd without permission from the Life (1819; PLATE 17).[34]

It was in this period, which Christopher Hibbert has characterized as one of 'repasts and riots', that expenditure on the Regent's
Indo-Islamic pleasure palace, the Brighton Pavilion, was mounting
steadily.[35] Court life by the seaside was mocked in a range of prints,
including George Cruikshank's *The Court at Brighton à la Chinese!!*
(1816). The prince appears twice: first as a bloated figure in faux
Chinese costume sitting on a divan, and second in corseted profile as
'the British Adonis'.[36] This statue shows him walking like a dancing
master with his posterior projecting in a grotesque manner so as to
match 'Regency Taste' opposite. This second statue is a representation of Sara Baartman, a South African woman, who was referred
to as the 'Hottentot Venus' and exhibited as a freak-show attraction
because of her large buttocks.[37] A further connection between the
monarchies of England and China, although it was not explored
in this print, was the use of feathers. High-ranking mandarins
sometimes wore caps adorned with peacock feathers.[38] Since the
peacock was associated in Europe with narcissism it was no great
surprise to find the ostrich plumes from the Prince of Wales's coat of
arms transformed into peacocks' tails in other illustrations by George
Cruikshank.[39]

Isaac Cruikshank and his two sons, Isaac Robert and George,
collaborated on so many prints that it is not always possible to
disentangle their work.[40] Isaac died in 1811 but his sons continued
a vast production of prints, many of them of dandies, throughout
the Regency. Some of them were directly scurrilous, but many
dandified men, including the Prince of Wales, bought large numbers
of the prints. This indicates a similar situation to that during the
macaroni craze: that the worst thing was not to be laughed at but
to be ignored.[41] And, just as had been the case forty years earlier,
print designers were immersed in the practices that they mocked.

Isaac Robert spent time in the merchant fleet of the East India Company after his parents deflected him from serving in the military. On marrying in 1816 he moved his household from Holborn to fashionable St James's Place. He possessed, according to a leading Cruikshank scholar, 'an oddly divided sensibility, Robert sought after fashionable society one day and savaged it the next'.[42] His brother George signed up with the volunteer militia but never saw service.[43] This might have made him sensitive to the phenomenon of military imposters. He was, nevertheless, more of a rake than a fop and 'his extravagant conduct, exceeding that of his father, gave his family and friends much concern. All-night drinking bouts, raids on unsuspecting watchmen, riotous excursions with boon companions to theatres and pleasure gardens, trips to races and cock pits and visits to brothels consumed his leisure hours, his energy, and his money.'[44] He only married in 1827, a few years after he had turned away from prints towards the new market for book illustrations.[45]

An argument has been made that George used aspects of his own appearance, such as long legs, in his depictions of dandies.[46] It is notable, however, that when he was himself drawn in 1833 his askance look and crossed legs imply someone who did not entirely relish being the centre of attention (PLATE 20).[47] This is significant bearing in mind that his profession required him to spend much of his time looking at other men. It could be argued that those who mock the masculinity of their fellows may be insecure in their own. On the wall behind him in the sketch is the picture of a boxer. During the last decades of the eighteenth century boxing moved from a barbaric, lower-class activity related to criminal violence to a fashionable spectator sport.[48] It became understood as representing the sublimation of manly urges to the extent of even being a patriotic duty. As one early Victorian writer argued, 'foreigners, in general, know nothing of it; they handle their arms like the flapping of a duck … and they dare not await the assault of the British battering-ram.'[49]

George publicly identified himself with the contemporary enthusiasm for boxing as evidence not of vulgar barbarity but of un-
varnished manhood. *The Boxers Arms* (1819) is based on an aristocrat's
coat of arms, but in the place of traditional heraldry we find a paean
to the 'fancy' (PLATE 18).[50] The shield is divided into four sections
containing, respectively, a pair of boxing gloves, a man uncorking a
bottle, and two different moments during a fight. Two bottle holders
stand in support on each side and above there is a clenched hand
surrounded by victory laurels. Compare this with Cruikshank's *The
Dandies Coat of Arms* (1819; PLATE 19).[51] In this case the shield is an
ornamented tailcoat supported on each side by monkeys dressed as
dandies, who hold phials of eau de cologne. The comparison between
dandies and monkeys represented a racialized slur and implied that
they were both exotic pieces of goods.[52] The dandy at the centre is all
but disembodied. The effect is similar to that of the stinging attack
launched by the novelist William Makepeace Thackeray on George
IV: 'I try and take him to pieces, and find silk stockings, padding,
stays, a coat with frogs and a fur collar, a star and blue ribbon, a
pocket handkerchief prodigiously scented, one of Truefitt's best
nutty-brown wigs reeking with oil, a set of teeth, and a huge black
stock, underwaistcoats, more underwaistcoats, and then nothing.'[53]
Thackeray, like the Cruikshanks, was a social satirist who affected to
detest dressy theatricality but was clearly also fascinated by it.[54]

At the centre of the dandies' coat of arms is a figure dressed half
as a woman and half as a man. This is described below as 'the sexes
impaled improper between two butterflies'.[55] A similar attack on
alleged androgyny occurs in many prints by the brothers, including
in Isaac Robert Cruikshank's *A Dandy Fainting, or, An Exquisite in Fits:
Scene a Private Box Opera* (1818).[56] The singing of the Italian castrato
Signor Nonballenas has caused one of the young dandies to faint.
The print has a variety of phallic innuendo – candle melting against
its neighbour, phial of perfume in the young man's face – that hint

at what other things might have been taking place in this curtained private box.[57] The bodies of these dandies are drawn such that they appear to lack musculature and to have breasts. The notion that dandies were, in effect, women, was also the conceit of a composition by Alfred Henry Forrester, *Beauties of Brighton*, which was engraved as a print by George Cruikshank (PLATE 21).[58] This showed a dandy standing directly in front of a woman so that the viewer – who also observes the man's buttocks – imagines him wearing her clothes. Yet it should be noticed that Forrester also depicted himself as a prancing buck to the far left, arm in arm with his brothers. The conceit of the dandy as a figure of gender confusion was, therefore, for him at least, more of an in-joke than it was a phobic attack.

It is notable that the rejection of elaboration in men's clothing – those complex cravats notwithstanding – did not render Regency dandies immune from accusations of effeminacy similar to those with which the macaronis had had to contend. Early-eighteenth-century parody, both literary and visual, rejoiced in depicting bodily functions such as vomiting or shitting.[59] Critique developed, in line with evolving expectations of decency, more towards a focus on the body shapes of the men concerned and not just on their attire or what they were doing physically. A further comparison between the macaronis and the dandies relates to social class. Just as many of the macaroni prints parodied social upstarts, so did more than a few of those produced during the Regency. An example is provided by the illustrations to *The Dandies' Ball; or, High Life in the City* (1819) by Isaac Robert Cruikshank. A fashionable couple give a ball which is largely attended by impoverished single men in search of wealthy wives. One such man, Mr Mopstaff – a splendidly emasculate name – is shown darning his own socks in a shabby room with a feeble fire and a bare floor.[60] Akin to the female macaroni was the phenomenon of the female dandy or 'dandyzette'. But because a fascination with fashion was an expected attribute in young women it was only those individuals who took things to an extreme, or who associated with highly dandified men, that were singled out for attention. In Paris an assertive and allegedly masculine woman might also be discussed in these terms.[61]

Satirists were intent on queering the world of the dandy, but most of those advancing a dandified lifestyle, even if they did not use that term about themselves, depicted it as a milieu of heterosexual high enjoyment. This is the world of Pierce Egan's best-selling novel *Life in London; or, the Day and Night Scenes of Jerry Hawthorne, Esq., and His Elegant Friend Corinthian Tom, Accompanied by Bob Logic, the Oxonian, in Their Rambles and Sprees Through the Metropolis* (1821). Pierce Egan was a successful journalist and sportswriter noted for, among other writings, *Boxiana; or, Sketches of Antient [sic] and Modern Pugilism* (1812).[62] He dedicated his novel to the new king, George IV. It was subsequently dubbed by Thackeray the 'schoolboy's delight', even though he went on to add that all London had read it.[63] Boys and men of slender means could borrow a copy from the circulating libraries or else they could save up as they did for the latest satirical prints. 'Did we not forgo tarts, in order to buy "…monstrosities?"' (i.e. prints of dandies), was Thackeray's further comment about his own earlier years.[64]

According to William Blanchard Jerrold, as recounted in his nineteenth-century biography of George Cruikshank, the designs for the illustrations to *Life in London* came from Isaac Robert, who based his depictions of Tom and Jerry on himself and his brother.[65] The city of Corinth in Greece had been associated with luxury in the ancient world. But for George's modern biographer this does not imply a critique of 'Corinthian Tom', who, although not a dandy, 'is nevertheless a fellow of fashion, and expert boxer and whip, well versed in the subjects of the day, accomplished in polite society, a man of honor'.[66] In one of the illustrations in the novel, *Jerry in Training for a 'Swell'*, the tailor, Mr Primefit, watched by Tom, measures up Jerry in a room lined with pictures of racehorses, fighting cocks, boxers and other sporting scenes (PLATE 22).[67] Primefit is singled out as a dandy by his distinctively puny body and stance. Meanwhile, we read in the novel that 'the CORINTHIAN smiled to himself at the lusty, unsubdued *back* of his merry rustic Coz [i.e. cousin], at the same time making comparisons, in his own mind, at the vast difference of the hinder parts of his *dandy*-like friends at the west-end of town, when put into the scale of the country breed of JERRY.'[68] Jerry in his turn is allowed to 'admire' Tom when he was taking part in sport, such as fencing, as can be seen from the plate entitled *Jerry's Admiration of Tom in an 'Assault' with Mr. O'Shaunessy, at the Rooms in St. James' St.*[69] Unselfconscious homosociality (which might, of course, have contained within it elements of same-sex desire) was facilitated by muscularity. A manly physique, and concomitant interests in sport, supposedly insulated an individual from both dandyism and queerness. Any further cause for sexual concern was allayed by the appearance of two good-time girls in *Gay Moments of Logic, Jerry, Tom and Corinthian Kate*.[70] The fact that Logic is left on his own at the piano, rather than dancing or canoodling on a sofa, may be attributed to the short-sighted ugliness of the stereotypical scholar.

Tom's behaviour is in line with Brummellian standards of exactness in dress, but part of the purpose of his scrupulous attention to sartorial detail was to avoid accusations of dandified excess: 'It was considered a good idea of the CORINTHIAN, to have every article that was NEW first placed in the *Chaffing Crib*, to undergo the ordeal of the visitors.'[71] In other words, any new clothes were put on display, and only when they had passed the test of not being mocked ('chaffed') by friends would they be worn in public. Tom and Jerry, therefore, perhaps like Isaac Robert and George in real life, were men who enacted sartorial dandyism whilst avoiding being labelled as dandies because they put enough energy into establishing their masculinity.

A WHIFFLE OF SCANDAL

There was a form of dandyism that actively flirted with the possibility of sexual scandal. Andrew Elfenbein has argued in an article, 'Byronism and the Work of Homosexual Performance in Early Victorian England' (1993), that a variety of men copied the mixture of dandyism and dangerous sexual indeterminacy associated with the poet Lord Byron in order to achieve social prominence: 'for young men aspiring to enter the fashionable world, performing Byronesque effeminacy was a dangerous but certain way to attract attention. It operated as a form of symbolic capital that might compensate for the lack of more conventional forms of social capital, such as family connections.'[72] Widespread recognition of this pattern in the later nineteenth century helps to explain why the young Wilde was generally assumed to be merely posing as a scandal rather than embodying one. As one writer commented in 1829, five years after Byron's death, 'open shirt-collars, and melancholy features; and a certain *dash* of remorse, were… indispensable for young men, and are so still.'[73] Byron himself commented that 'I like the Dandies – they were always very civil to *me* – though in general they disliked literary people.'[74] It is important to note, however, that although he did not think of himself as a dandy he did admire exotic costume such as that of Albanians, in which he had himself painted (PLATE 23).[75]

What has been termed the 'vexed issue of Byron's sexuality' has attracted a considerable amount of discussion. Louis Crompton's *Byron and Greek Love: Homophobia in Nineteenth-Century England* (1985) has index entries for heterosexuality, homosexuality and bisexuality. At one point homosexuality is listed as 'co-extant with his heterosexuality'.[76] This indicates that Byron did not easily fit into twentieth-century labels based on sexual identity.[77] Thomas Moore's *Letters and Journals of Lord Byron* (1830) openly discussed the scandal of Byron's seduction of women but explained male friendships only in terms of homosociality. Nevertheless, the orientalist author William Beckford, who had had to temporarily leave the country after a sodomitical scandal in 1784, annotated his copy of the book with comments such as 'attachments à la *Greque*' that showed that Byron's sodomitical interests were obvious to him.[78] When he was a student at Cambridge in 1807 Byron had, for his part, declared Beckford's novel *Vathek, an Arabian Tale* (1786) to be his 'gospel'.[79]

The poet's interests in women and boys fitted a paradigm of rakish masculinity. This was found scandalously intriguing in contradistinction to effeminate styles, which were subject to more overt ridicule because they violated expectations of male potency. It is notable than when Byron was attacked it was sometimes through accusations of effete dandyism. This was the mode employed in *Lord Byron and Some of His Contemporaries* (1828) by Leigh Hunt, who knew the poet through his friendship with Shelley.[80] Hunt described Byron as handsome but 'tending to fat and effeminacy' and lacking facial hair.[81] He would appear dressed in 'brown and silver, buff-coloured boots, a green cloak, and a star! And this was his "usual travelling dress"; … in order to avoid being stared at, which could have been his only object in wearing it.'[82] Hunt continued by alleging that Byron 'had a delicate white hand, of which he was proud; and he drew attention to it by rings. He thought a hand of this description almost the only mark remaining now-a-days of a gentleman; of which it certainly is not. … He often appeared holding a handkerchief, upon which his jewelled fingers lay imbedded, as in a picture.'[83] Elfenbein suggests that the reason Byron was depicted in this way was not that he was in reality an androgyne but that he inspired a kind of 'gender panic' in other men.[84] This came about because Byron did not feel impelled to identify himself with developing sexual norms for men, which mandated exclusive cross-sex attraction. As a man of Romantic genius, he was simply free to express himself.[85] It is striking, therefore, that the one quality that is absent from images of the stereotypical

12 So young, so well-groomed and so ambitious. Attributed to Alfred Henry Forrester/ Daniel Maclise, *Benjamin Disraeli*, early 1830s, pen and ink.

dandy is individuality. They were depicted as identically dressed and equally vacuous.

One of the reasons for the sensitivity of elite men to charges of dandyism was that these were often associated with the behaviour of social parasites. The deliberate cultivation of a dandified image implied a high degree of self-confidence. Byronism – that is to say posing as Byron – has been attributed to several Victorian literary figures, including Oscar Wilde and, before him, the prime minister

13 Monstrosities of the eighteenth and nineteenth centuries astonish each other in the park. George Cruikshank, *Monstrosities of 1788 and 1823*, 1 January 1823, George Humphrey, London.

Benjamin Disraeli. Both Wilde and Disraeli were social climbers in their youth who presented themselves to a sometimes-sceptical public as promising writers. They were both parodied for allegedly undue attention to their own appearance.[86] This is how Disraeli appeared in a representation by or after Alfred Henry Forrester and Daniel Maclise in '[James] Fraser's Gallery of Illustrious Literary Characters' which featured in *Fraser's Magazine* in the 1830s (FIG. 12).[87] This, it should be remembered, was the same periodical that had published Carlyle's attack on dandyism.

Fashions changed from year to year, but out-of-date modes reappeared at masquerade balls and, occasionally, from the pens of satirists. In 1823 George Cruikshank produced a comparison between the 'monstrosities' of his own day and of half a century earlier

(FIG. 13).[88] The park was a fashionable place to parade and in it he has imagined two generations of fashionistas scrutinizing each other in bemusement. The left-hand section of the print sees a prancing macaroni staring at a woman of the 1780s – a time when puffed derrières, huge hats and muffs were all the rage. They are watched by a modern dandy, arm-in-arm with an officer in the regiment of Lifeguards. The macaronis were, originally, rich youths back from the Grand Tour and with the tastes and wardrobes to prove it. Their successors looked increasingly to sartorial restraint and to patriotic models of British masculinity.[89] However, the apparent renunciation of colour and elaboration in dress that this entailed created rather than prevented the appearance of the Regency dandy. This was a figure whose distinction in dress was established through careful attention to detail. The self-regard that this entailed was called out by caricaturists through depicting dandies as having effeminate bodies even if not effeminate clothes.

The figure of the man of fashion remained a central preoccupation not just for Britain's elite but also for many others well down the social spectrum who could not buy the clothes but could afford the satirical prints. Formal dress remained a crucial mark of social distinction in an age when all such costumes were relatively expensive, whatever cloth they were made from, because they had to be sewn by hand. As a rising mercantile and imperial nation, Britain was proud of its wealth but also wary of social instability. The dandy was of importance because he was poised between social self-assurance, class transgression and criminal imposture. He mirrored the situation of the country as a whole: an upstart nation built on aristocratic foundations. Satirists were often implicated in dandyism if only because they seemed to be fixated by it. Priggish moralists, after all, would have kept well away from the vulgar and rambunctious world of Georgian visual satire.[90] Dandies themselves were admired and feared since, as was said at the time, 'it is the very soul of their occupation to ridicule others'.[91] To dress in high style was, in effect, a rebuke to anyone who was less well attired.[92] The cutting looks and remarks of an occasional dandy, such as Brummell, could amuse high society – although even he eventually fell from favour. What was unconscionable was that large numbers of men of the lower orders should attempt to self-fashion their way to social prominence. The accusation of effeminacy was a highly effective way to frighten parvenus away from such behaviour, although this raised the social visibility of those who insisted on persisting.

The styles adopted by dandies continued to vary and evolve through the nineteenth century. The dominant theme was elegant plainness but there were colourful exceptions to this rule.[93] A clear divide between men of muscle and men of fashion staved off the fear that modern man was becoming gender-indeterminate. One early Victorian writer remarked with astonishment that 'I remember seeing a pretty, effeminate little dandy at a picture exhibition, whom I heard make some sensible remarks on the paintings. He turned out to be an eminent prize-fighter.'[94] The behaviour of a bizarre minority who failed to conform could be seen as underlining the probity of the mainstream. Exaggerated behaviour could be viewed as a source of 'camp' amusement, using that term in the sense in which it appeared in Ware's *Passing English of the Victorian Era* (1909): 'actions and gestures of exaggerated emphasis. Probably from the French. Used by persons of exceptional want of character.'[95] Connections between such exaggeration and sodomy had been discussed during the macaroni craze and were to be again in relation to the later Victorian aesthetes of whom Oscar Wilde was perhaps the most (in)famous.[96] Camp, of course, can be a highly self-aware practice, the purpose of which is to undermine normative expectations of manhood. There is nothing inherently homosexual about camp but there are good reasons why queer men have often been interested in it.

It was in the early Victorian period that dandies came to be understood as more than the latest type of the foolish man of fashion and that dandyism began to be taken seriously as an aesthetic stance. The pioneer in this line of thinking was the French novelist Jules-Amédée Barbey d'Aurevilly, who published *On Dandyism and George Brummell* (*Du dandysme et de George Brummell*) (1845) in the wake of the appearance of William Jesse's biography.[97] It is only fair to point out that his preoccupation with the quasi-aristocratic Englishman was initially regarded as eccentric and, by those of a left-wing persuasion, politically suspect. For Barbey d'Aurevilly, however, the dandy was a radical figure in his austere focus on individual self-fashioning. This perfectionism, he thought, could only have emerged in a country with a history of puritanism. He also hinted at the gender-indeterminacy of the dandies by referring to them as 'hermaphrodites of history'.[98]

Such lines of thought led to an expectation that the essence of dandyism lay less in dressing and undressing than in an intellectual construction of the self. Fear of such radical autonomy may have led to the vehemence and frequency with which satirists insisted that dandies had no real intelligence and were mere slaves of their possessions. Perhaps it was only behind the armour of their clothes that such men were fully able to foster their own sense of self, by appearing not to have one.[99] The Regency dandy was a creation of the closet in more ways than one.

1 PREVIOUS PAGE Captain William Wade (1734–1809) dressed in a splendid scarlet suit with a gold-embroidered waistcoat, nosegay and bag wig. Portrait by Thomas Gainsborough, 1771, oil on canvas.

2 Richard Cosway (1742–1821) came jocularly to be referred to as the macaroni painter. *Self-Portrait*, c.1770–75, paint on ivory.

3 Voluminous skirts were no guarantee against sexual impropriety. Jean-Honoré Fragonard, *Les Hasards heureux de l'escarpolette* (*The Happy Accidents of the Swing*), 1767, oil on canvas.

4 Philippe I, Duke of Orléans (1640–1701) combined fatherhood with a taste for cross-dressing. School of Pierre Mignard, *Philippe de France, duc d'Orléans, prés du portrait de sa fille aînée, Marie-Louise d'Orléans* (*Philippe de France, Duke of Orleans, With the Portrait of His Daughter Marie-Louise*), c. 1670, oil on canvas.

The Bum-Bailiff outwitted; or the convenience of Fashion.

Suky like the Syrinx changes shape,
Her vain pursuer to escape:

Ye Snapps of Piers hard fate beware,
Who thought his arms embraced the fair
But found an emty Bum-case there

Published May 6th 1786 by S.W. Fores at the Caracature Ware house Piccadilly

5 A formidable costume, complete with jutting breast and 'bum', saves a lady from the attentions of a bum-bailiff (debt collector). *The Bum-Bailiff outwitted; or the convenience of Fashion*, S.W. Fores, London, 6 May 1786.

6 The actor David Garrick's (1717–1779) masculine stance was ill-concealed by his voluminous frock. Johan Zoffany, *David Garrick as John Brute in the 'Provok'd Wife' by Vanbrugh*, Drury Lane, c.1763, oil on canvas.

7 But Garrick could also be depicted batting his eyes in a moment of flirtatious camp. James Roberts, *Mr Garrick in the Character of Sir John Brute*, Bell, London, 1 June 1776.

8 John Chute (1701–1776) wearing a splendid embroidered waistcoat under a plain jacket. Gabriel Mathias, *John Chute*, 1758, oil on canvas.

9 Men of diverse sexual interests admired the art and antiquities of Florence. Johan Joseph Zoffany, *The Tribuna of the Uffizi*, 1772–77, oil on canvas

10 *The Macaronni Society*, by Henry Bunbury (1750–1811) explained that 'THIS CLUB was instituted and kept at ALMACKS and called the MACARONNI society'. Pen-and-ink drawing, c. 1765, from an album collected by Horace Walpole.

11 The tailcoats of three comely young soldiers blow back to reveal their shapely thighs and buttocks. *The Relief*, after Henry Bunbury, William Dickinson, London, 1781.

12 A man simpers in the stance that might be expected of a sexually desirable young woman. *How D'Ye Like Me*, Carington Bowles, London, 18 November 1772.

13 A 'man of feeling' lies, somewhat camply, in a woodland glade. Joseph Wright, *Sir Brooke Boothby*, 1781, oil on canvas.

14 The shrewd gaze of Horace Walpole (1717–1797), who first recorded the appearance of 'the Maccaroni Club' in 1764. Joshua Reynolds, *Horace Walpole*, 1756–57, oil on canvas.

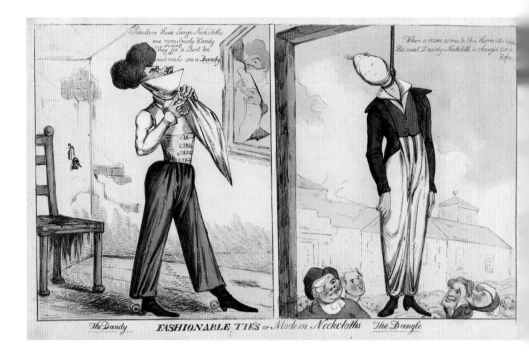

15 A necktie and a noose might not be so different. *Fashionable Ties or Modern Neckcloths*, 1810.

16 The rapid development of sartorial styles provided new monsters of fashion for each passing year. James Gillray, *'Monstrosities' of 1799: Scene, Kensington Gardens,* Hannah Humphrey, London, 25 June 1799.

17 Did military uniforms become more ostentatious with every passing year? George Cruikshank, *Ancient Military Dandies of 1450... Modern Military Dandies of 1819*, G. Humphrey, London, 8 February 1819.

"MONSTROSITIES" of 1799 — Scene, Kensington Gardens.

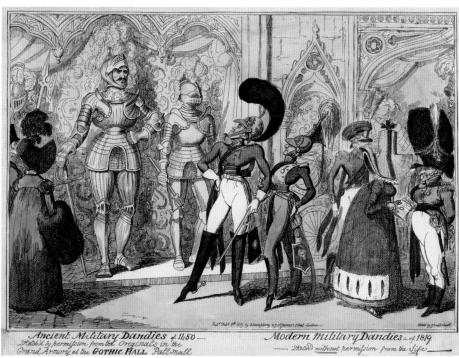

Ancient Military Dandies of 1450
Etch'd by permission from the Originals in the
Grand Armory at the GOTHIC HALL Pall-Mall

Modern Military Dandies of 1819
Sketch'd without permission from the Life

18 Boxing was celebrated as a way of building and displaying a manly body. George Cruikshank, *The Boxers Arms*, c.1819, watercolour with pencil, pen and ink.

19 Dandyism was disdained as an attempt to conceal a want of brain and muscle. George Cruikshank, *The Dandies Coat of Arms*, c. 1819, watercolour with pencil, pen and ink.

20 The artist George Cruikshank (1792–1878) at work. Attributed to Alfred Henry Forrester/Daniel Maclise, *George Cruikshank*, 1833, pencil.

21 A dandy stands directly in front of a woman so that the viewer imagines him wearing her clothes. Alfred Henry Forrester, *Beauties of Brighton*. 1825, pen, ink and wash.

22 Clothes made the man, even when clothiers were less than men. Isaac Robert and George Cruikshank, *Jerry in Training for a 'Swell'*, London, Sherwood, Neely & Jones, 31 August 1820.

Beauties of BRIGHTON

23 Lord Byron's (1788–1824) exotic tastes were matters of considerable interest. Thomas Phillips, *George Gordon, Lord Byron in Albanian Dress*, c. 1835, based on a work of 1813, oil on canvas.

24 Oscar Wilde (1854–1900) looked suitably respectable in the portrait given to him as a wedding present. R.G. Harper Pennington, *Oscar Wilde*, 1884, oil on canvas.

25 The aesthetic challenge of living up to one's teapot. James Hadley, *Aesthetic Teapot*, 1882.

26 The aesthetic pose was to become identified with stereotypes of gay men in the twentieth century. *Guy-ing Him* by 'Shirl', in *Funny Folks*, 10 March 1883.

GUY-ING HIM.

["Oscar Wilde has revived the costume of Beau Brummel."—*World*.]

'*Arriet.*—LOR, 'ARRY, WHO'S THAT CHAP?
'*Arry.*—WHO IS IT? WHY, ONE O' THEM GEERHARDS, AS WE SEE AT THE MUSIC
'ALL—A-GOING TO GIVE THE SWELLS A SHOW AFTER DINNER, OF COURSE!

27 Noël Coward (1899–1973) made an art out of not quite revealing his homosexuality. Dorothy Wilding, *Noël Coward*, 1951, chlorobromide print.

28 OVERLEAF Male dandyism crossed over into lesbian celebrity. Karl August Büchel, *Radclyffe Hall*, 1918, oil on canvas.

Victorians and
the aesthetic pose

In 1883 the *Illustrated London News* published a cartoon entitled *Athletics v. Aesthetics* by Henry Stephen Ludlow (FIG. 14).[1] This showed a recreational scene of young persons by the river. To the right are two fashionably attired ladies in conversation with a pair of well-built athletes in rowing-club jackets. To the left and in the background two scruffy-looking figures scuttle past eyed only by a small dog. The joke is that these ugly specimens are the aesthetes. The clue is that one of them is wearing a sunflower, which, like the lily, was associated with dandified aestheticism at this time. The same joke was applied to aesthetic women in *The New Aesthete-Athlete Era* (1881). This depicted a group of unattractive women rowing past with sunflowers on their frocks.[2] Manly men were assumed to be the natural athletes, but they were supposedly free of excessive concern for their own attractions. These attempts to disavow dandyism as the preoccupation of a lunatic fringe were important because being well turned out had never been so easy. Britain at its imperial zenith was, for its times, an immensely wealthy society in which men of relatively modest means were encouraged to spend money on looking good. As a historian of male consumption has explained, 'the commercial cultivation of male display helped bring about the public re-emergence of the male body as aesthetically pleasing and sexually desirable.'[3]

14 The fashionable ugliness of the modern aesthete. Henry Stephen Ludlow, *Athletics v. Aesthetics*, in *Illustrated London News*, 17 March 1883.

The legacy of Regency dandyism was that elite men aimed to show their status through self-control and discernment in their sartorial choices and had a tendency to disdain what was then termed 'vulgar ostentation'.[4] Openly asserting one's own aesthetic superiority fell into this category of behaviour, as did assuming the airs and graces of one's social betters. Working-class dandies were often referred to as 'mashers' who aped the heavy drinking and sexually adventurous behaviour of upper-class 'swells'.[5] Dandyism as a disciplined art – and its public disavowal as perverse or declassé – continued to be central to maintaining male status. Aesthetes such as the academic critic Walter Pater threatened this closeting of male narcissism because of their 'canny recognition of the erotics of such sublimation'.[6] Perhaps the most famous aesthete was Oscar Wilde. He drew his inspiration from French ideas that dandyism, while invented by the British, now involved the cultivation of decadence as an act of intellectual dissent.[7] Even ugliness could thus be embraced as an aesthetic choice. Texts that were to become important to the decadents of the *fin de siècle*, such as Charles Baudelaire's 1863 essay *Le Peintre de la vie moderne* (*The Painter of Modern Life*), were overtly anti-utilitarian and can be understood as part of a reaction against the growing power of commodity culture in the first age of mass consumerism.[8]

The dandyism of Wilde and his circle, however, focused on an ironic engagement with contemporary popular culture. It also drew energy from distancing itself from earlier Victorian disdain for the Georgian era as unpleasant and corrupt.[9] The orientalist tastes of the aesthetes for items such as blue china directly recalled the consuming passions of eighteenth-century 'Chinamania'. This partly had its origins in the collection brought over by Catherine of Braganza when she married Charles II in 1662.[10] The modern man of sensibility in George Du Maurier's *Intellectual Epicures* (1876) was depicted surrounded by blue china, Japanese fans, medieval snuff boxes and 'his favourite periodicals of the eighteenth-century'.[11] It is also pertinent that the so-called 'Orient' was racialized as effete. When a group of 'Japanese ambassadors' arrived at North Seaton Colliery in Northumberland in 1862 it was commented 'how striking [was] the contrast between the English bone and muscle, the clean-cut Teutonic face of the miner, and the almond-shaped-eyed, effeminate-looking Mongolian by his side ... the most casual spectator could see at a glance the difference in mental calibre.'[12] But where the fop had been the dupe of his material tastes his late nineteenth-century equivalents, such as Wilde, delighted to proclaim that they were finding it ever harder to live up to their own porcelain.[13] It was perhaps only fitting that James Hadley fashioned a satire of the aesthetes in the form of a teapot for Royal Worcester with the figure of an effete man on one side mirroring that of an affected woman on the other (PLATE 25).[14]

The background to late Victorian aestheticism lay in the activities of groups such as the Syncretics and the Pre-Raphaelites. These proclaimed the value of art for its own sake and were duly mocked in line with mainstream expectations that moral advancement or accurate representation should be its purposes. Fault was also found with representations of empowered women and enervated men that challenged popular assumptions concerning gender roles.[15] A squib in *Punch* magazine mocked George Stephens's poem *The Hungarian Daughter* (1841) by showing an ugly-looking poet in modern dress staring into a pool and seeing Shakespeare reflected therein.[16] Forty years later George Du Maurier drew a Wildean figure narcissistically reclining by a pond in *A Love Agony. Design by Maudle* (1880). The young man's androgynous body and rubbery shoulders are in a direct line of satirical representation from those of the Cruikshank dandies of the Regency (FIG. 16).[17] Du Maurier knew a good deal about the objects of his satire. He had lived for a time in Paris with another dandified artist, the American James Abbott McNeill Whistler, and was to use those experiences as the basis for the popular and sensational novel *Trilby* (1894).[18] Du Maurier had already hinted at the homosexual aspects of male aestheticism in his cartoon 'Nincom-poopiana' in which he drew a group of aesthetic men drooping together beneath a bust labelled 'Antinous', who was famous for

being the youthful male lover of the emperor Hadrian (FIG. 15).[19]
The cartoonist was to push things as far as the libel laws would allow
in *Maudle on the Choice of a Profession*, in which a figure resembling
Wilde exclaims 'how *consummately* lovely your son is, Mrs Brown'.[20]
What is striking about this innuendo is that Wilde had only just
arrived in London and had not, so far as we are aware, yet had any
homosexual affairs. He was best known as an aspiring poet and as
an Irishman who had assumed airs of superiority that seemed unsuit-
able in one so young. When the 'The Man about Town' column in
Country Gentleman commented a couple of years later that 'Byron was
a notoriety on similar grounds' it was making a moral rather than a

NINCOMPOOPIANA.

(*Surfeited with excess of "cultchah," Prigsby and his Friends are now going in for extreme simplicity.*)

Prigsby. "I CONSIDAH THE WORDS OF '*LITTLE BOPEEP*' FRESHAH, LOVELIAH, AND MORE SUBTILE THAN ANYTHING SHELLEY EVAH WROTE!"
[*Recites them.*

Muffington. "QUITE SO. AND SCHUBERT NEVAH COMPOSED ANYTHING QUITE SO PRECIOUS AS THE *TUNE!*" [*Tries to hum it.*

Chorus. "HOW SUPREME!"

15 A group of aesthetic men droop together in the presence of classical male beauty.
George Du Maurier, *Nincompoopiana*, in *Punch*, 20 December 1879.

literary comparison.[21] As mentioned in the previous chapter, a series of dandified writers from Disraeli to Wilde appeared to perform 'Byronism'; that is to say that they cultivated a personal style in which genius and scandal were apparently combined.[22]

In 1881 aestheticism was the subject of parody in London from the major theatres of the West End to the music halls of the East End. 'It is a sign of the times', commented one newspaper, 'when Whitechapel becomes *intense*.'[23] The epicentre of this satirical storm was the hugely successful production of Gilbert and Sullivan's *Patience, or Bunthorne's Bride* (1881). This show opened at the Opera Comique in April before moving to the Savoy Theatre, where it became the first theatre production in the world to be lit entirely by electric light. The run lasted for 578 performances. The original concept for the operetta had been the rivalry between two priests who excelled in camp displays of mildness. Unmarried clergy were becoming associated with suspicions of affectation and queerness, so it was not too much of a leap to transpose the characters into a pair of aesthetes.[24] The key joke focused on the notion of nonentities posing as men of talent: '"If this young man expresses himself in terms too deep for me, / Why what a very singularly deep young man this deep young man must be!"'[25] The production was overseen by the theatre impresario Richard D'Oyly Carte, and it was he who sponsored Wilde's lecture tour of the United States the following year. The aim was to raise awareness of aestheticism across the Atlantic and ensure a successful New York run of the play.

The aesthetic pose was derived from the characteristic stance struck by male aristocrats in their portraits in past centuries. It involved standing contrapposto with the weight on one leg, one arm on the hip and the other arm extended with the wrist bent. This camp stance has in the twentieth century become identified with stereotypes of gay men. It was how Cruikshank had drawn an 'ancient military' dandy in 1819 and it was the way in which Wilde was often to be caricatured (see PLATES 17 & 26).[26] The nobility were increasingly in danger of being associated with effeteness because work, which they did not have to do by virtue of their inheritances, was seen as toughening and masculinizing. Parody of Wilde as a faux aristocrat came thick and fast during his months in the United States, and it was to accompany him throughout his career. This display of what might at first sight appear to have been unremitting hostility was not however without its benefits, since it generated immense publicity. It may also have contributed to the copying of aesthetic styles down the social spectrum. As Charles Ross, journalist and (un-successful) theatrical impresario, wrote in 1881, the world would soon see 'the adoption by the million of the very tastes and eccentricities now laughed at'.[27] Meanwhile, another columnist opined that 'Mr. Du Maurier laughed Mr. Oscar Wilde into a lucrative notoriety.'[28] One thing this satire had in common was an insistence that whatever skill Wilde possessed it was not originality. There was even discussion of who was responsible for inventing him. Whistler was suggested as one candidate, and Napoleon Sarony was another.[29] The latter was a New York-based celebrity photographer who had achieved a commercial triumph by posing Wilde in items of supposedly aesthetic dress such as quasi-Georgian knee breeches.

The suits that Wilde had made when he went up to Oxford as a student were loud unaesthetic checks, and many of his early opponents assumed that his subsequent performances in the United States were aimed at turning the heads of women. The Wilde who featured in the anonymous pamphlet *Ye Soul Agonies in ye Life of Oscar Wilde* (1882) was sent up as a hearty type who is a pal of the Prince of Wales.[30] Yet, even if Wilde was not always associated with queer desire, nor were other aesthetic types always thought of as merely effete. For example, in 1883 *Punch* published a skit on proceedings in Parliament featuring Edward White Benson, the Archbishop of Canterbury:

'Looks as if it was washing-day, and they had got the clothes out early', Randolph [Churchill] says, gazing upon the scene from the Gallery. New Archbishop present. Looks Aesthetic. Got his speech ready. Intended when he came down to deliver it, but so nervous couldn't get it off.

'Pity your Grace should have had all this trouble', I say (always like to be polite to an Archbishop); 'sure great loss to the world so much eloquence, argument, and common sense'.

'Don't think it will be lost', said his Grace sweetly. 'Preaching shortly on the destruction of Sodom and Gomorrah; shall be able to use up a good many of the passages'. His Grace ought to carry a lily or a sunflower.[31]

Wilde took pains sartorially to distance himself from the 'aesthetic costume' with which he had become associated courtesy of Sarony during the lecture tour around the United States. He loved his wedding gift of a portrait from the American artist R.G. Harper Pennington which showed a sombrely dressed man who was aged 27 in 1884 (PLATE 24).[32] Photographs of Wilde tend to show an unflamboyant but well-dressed individual who presented himself as a gentleman. This is how even the by then embittered Lord Alfred Douglas was to describe his former lover in the memoir that he published in 1914.[33] All this was also in accordance with what the *Boy's Herald* had proclaimed a few years earlier:

In dress and manners the Puritan triumph has been complete …
we, if we met such a ruffed and ruffled worthy as used to swagger
by hundreds up and down St Paul's walk, not knowing how to
get a dinner, much less to pay his tailor, we should look at him
as, firstly, a fool, and secondly a swindler; while, if we could meet
an old Puritan we should consider him a man gracefully and
picturesquely dressed, but withal in the most perfect sobriety of
good taste.[34]

This is only unexpected in the case of Wilde because we tend to be more familiar with the decadent images of him that were drawn by Aubrey Beardsley, Max Beerbohm and others in the early 1890s.[35]

A period of intense public scrutiny and mockery had brought about the eclipse of the macaroni style, and something similar can be said about aestheticism. As was commented at the end of the decade, 'aestheticism "went out" [of fashion] long before Oscar Wilde cut his hair and got married'.[36] This is not to say that there were no more aesthetes, nor any more love for art for art's sake, but aestheticized dandyism had to be carried out with circumspection if it were not to face ridicule. That is why Wilde's performance of a dandified aesthete during his American tour has been spoken of as a caricature of a caricature.[37]

DANDYISM ON TRIAL

Two years into his marriage Wilde took Robert Ross as his first male lover. This was not public knowledge. The reasons that Wilde was sometimes identified in the early 1880s as queer was not because of his private life but because this had already become established as a potential attribute of dandyism. An obsession with effeminacy was endemic in Britain because masculine probity was built into concepts of national identity. Effeminophobia flared up periodically, often due to sensational trials such as that of Robert Jones in 1772. A century later the media fixed on the lives and costumes of Frederick William Park and Thomas Ernest Boulton (known familiarly as Fanny and Stella), who had been arrested on the basis that their public cross-dressing was evidence of soliciting for queer sex. The beadle of the Burlington Arcade in London's West End attested that he regularly saw the men powdered and rouged, sometimes in drag and sometimes not. He testified that they 'caused much commotion' and that 'everybody was looking at them'.[38] The court, however, found them not guilty. Digby Seymour, in his summing up, argued that the blatant behaviour of the defendants implied that they were simply dressed up as a lark since in the case of sexual perversion one would 'expect a secret hiding from the sights of men and women ...

[and that] they would shrink and hide away and draw over themselves and their horrible deeds a pall of darkness'.[39]

It seems likely that Boulton and Park were guilty as charged and
the judge was attempting to sweep scandal under the carpet. A
cover-up was deemed necessary because the defendants were middle-
class men from apparently respectable homes.[40] One result of this was
that the police were to some degree restrained from their harassment
of London's queer community of cross-dressers, which, although the
evidence is uneven, appears to have had a history going as far back
as the mollies of the early eighteenth century, if not before.[41] It is
important to note that Boulton and Park dressed suspiciously even
when not in women's clothing. Their tight trousers, open-necked
shirts and rouged cheeks at such times were seemingly more disturbing than the drag which 'seemed the proper uniform for effeminacy'.[42]
This is how a real-life, Irish, male prostitute is described in a privately
printed volume, *The Sins of the Cities of the Plain, or Recollections of a
Mary-Ann, with Short Essays on Sodomy and Tribadism* (1881):

> an effeminate, but very good-looking young fellow … looking in
> shop-windows from time to time, and now and then looking round
> as if to attract attention.
>   Dressed in tight-fitting clothes, which set off his Adonis-like
> figure to the best advantage, especially about what snobs call the
> fork of his trousers.[43]

This is Jack Saul, and the rest of the book purports to be his auto-
biography. The volume includes a scene in which he spies through a
keyhole at Boulton in drag as Stella. 'I would rather have had Boulton
than anyone. His make-up was so sweetly pretty that I longed to have
him, and him have me.'[44] These are unreliable memoirs if they are
not simply someone else's erotic fantasy, but they do indicate clearly
that there was no precise division between the markets for male and
female prostitution.[45] Youth and a good figure were the main indicators of marketability, together with an ability to dress well.

16 A Wildean figure narcissistically reclines by a pond. George Du Maurier, *A Love Agony. Design by Maudle*, in *Punch* 78, 5 June 1880.

The trial of Boulton and Park in May 1871 appears to have been on the mind of the Scottish writer Robert Buchanan when he attacked what he termed the 'Fleshly School of Poetry' in *The Contemporary Review* in October of the same year. He singled out the poet A.C. Swinburne as an 'intellectual hermaphrodite' who cloaked nastiness in beautiful words.[46] The Pre-Raphaelite painter Simeon Solomon was then disgraced in 1873 as a result of his arrest for a same-sex transgression. It was, therefore, not a coincidence that George Du Maurier's *A Love Agony. Design by Maudle* (1880; FIG. 16), showing the young poet 'Jellaby Postlethwaite' in Pre-Raphaelite style, was accompanied by a pastiche of verses by Swinburne.[47] The character of Postlethwaite had evolved in his many appearances in *Punch* to take on various characteristics of Wilde, but then so had that of Maudle the supposed painter.

Inversion was a theory of homosexuality that became favoured by various doctors around the turn of the nineteenth century. It explained male homosexuality by the notion that a women's mind or soul might, as an occasional medical aberration, exist within a man's body and vice versa. This idea was not new. An article in 1870 had analysed what it termed 'Inverted Relations' in which female inverts consorted with men as equals and male inverts wished only to be like women: 'he is dull and vicious in the company of men. His whole sympathies go with women and their occupations, and nothing pleases him more than to be the only man in a roomful of women.'[48] Such a creature wishes only to concern himself with domestic adornment and has no interest in politics just like the man in Du Maurier's 'Intellectual Epicures' who collects Georgian periodicals but 'never reads a newspaper'.[49]

A piece entitled 'A Double Evolution', published in the *Daily News* in August 1891, alleged that young men were becoming physically shorter than their female counterparts as well as mentally similar. This is not all bad, since they drink less and do not collect 'coarse and suggestive pictures… Whither are all these changes tending? Twenty years hence, will the stalwart girl and ladylike youth have completely changed places?'[50] These changes, however tongue-in-cheek the reportage, were couched in biological terms. The title of this piece implied that what was then termed 'the future of the race' was understood to be at stake. Cartoons about androgynous youth became increasingly frequent and, on the part of the right-wing media, snide. An example is *Evolution*, which was published in *Judy*, a more conservative alternative to *Punch*, in 1894. This shows a man and woman with the latter posed in an authoritative way with hands on her hips. The man says, 'I shall turn over a new leaf and be a new man'. She replies, 'if you mean that you are going to turn woman, you've been effeminate enough for a very long time.'[51]

The New Woman was identified with those who rejected many of the gendered expectations of their mothers by refusing an early marriage and seeking increased independence. The more radical types embraced dress reform and sought out higher education and a professional job. They were closely associated with the various campaigns for women's suffrage. The New Woman and New Man were understood as complementary types, although the misogynist logic of the time meant that the latter was regarded with more scorn than the former. Since men were widely held to be superior it seemed more logical for a woman to want to be like a man than it was for a man to be like a woman. It was the supposedly sickly abdication of masculine control that associated the New Man with decadence.[52] This idea was picked up by certain New Women such as Ella Hepworth Dixon, who, in *The Story of a Modern Woman* (1894), looked forward to a new age of relations between men and women. She was, however, wary of dandies such as Wilde since she suspected them of narcissistic self-absorption and of lacking a serious interest in reform.[53]

If men were taking on female qualities, it might appear to reformers that they had picked the worst ones such as an obsession with appearance. Traditionalists were equally unimpressed and were also appalled at the queer implications when they read in the papers that 'it is an absolute fact that a large number of young men get themselves up. The rouge-pot and the powder-puff find a place on their toilet table. Their eyebrows are darkened; their hair is often crimped or curled, and sometimes even dyed; and their figures are trained and artificially improved.'[54] It was alleged that the masculin-ized New Women as mother would birth a race of emasculated New Men, who with 'no mind... [and] as much muscle as a sawdust doll' would be unable to keep the females of the future in their supposedly natural place.[55] Such nonentities were already widespread since it was observed that 'there are so many effeminate men peacocking about society who don't desire to be anything else.'[56]

The older generation was presented as struck with incomprehension at what was taking place before their very eyes. In *The New Woman*, a cartoon published in *Fun* in 1894, an elderly couple think that one of the young women in front of them is not a masculine New Woman but an effeminate New Man (FIG. 17).[57] In this case both of the women in the foreground have identically curved figures, but the one on the right has adopted the upright pose expected of the dandy along with elements of his dress. It is notable, however, that in this cartoon, which was published in a relatively liberal periodical, the older couple are not depicted as authoritative. This should alert us to something that the satirical representations tend to obscure: namely, that the New Man and Woman were often seen as alluringly modern and fashionable.

By the early 1890s Wilde habitually wore a richly fur-trimmed coat, but this would not have been thought at all effeminate at the time.[58] Moreover, he had always been rather thickset and grew more so over time. He could not have been described as a physically delicate flower by anyone who knew him personally. What did startle the public was his strategic use of flowers, from the lilies and sunflowers of the early 1880s onwards.[59] The macaronis had been noted for their nosegays – presumably as a mark of their attention to beauty and intolerance of bad smells. Flowers were associated with the arts of feminine love and their extravagant use by men was increasingly read as queer. Homosexual men might find themselves referred to as 'horticultural lads'.[60] On 5 March 1892 the *Star* reported that Wilde was present with a 'suite of young gentlemen all wearing the vivid dyed carnation which has superseded the lily and the sunflower'. This had taken place at the opening of the play *The Kiss* by Théodore de Banville, which had been translated by John Gray, another of Wilde's lovers.[61]

Creating a sensation on an opening night was a favourite tactic of Wilde, who was nothing if not an attention-seeker. He gained immense publicity when he appeared onstage smoking at the premier of *Lady Windermere's Fan* (1892) and was duly depicted by Alfred Bryan in the *Footlights Annual* (1894) cross-dressed as Lady Windermere herself.[62] He was to draw Wilde as a 'Flower Merchant' wearing a vast carnation in the lapel of his long fur-collared coat in October of the same year. The queer element of this unnatural flower did not go unnoticed. In March 1892 Violet Harris, who was a fan of Wilde, published a story entitled 'The Green Carnation' in which the flower became a *gage d'amour* ('pledge of love') between Billy and an older man, Mr Dacre.[63] A range of suggestions for the origins of the flower

THE NEW WOMAN.
Short-sighted Old Lady [*in audible tones*].—" What a very effeminate young fellow that is with that young lady."
(*Miss Upter Date feels immensely flattered.*)

17 A New Woman is mistaken for a New Man. George Gatcombe, *The New Woman*, in *Fun*, 2 October 1894.

appeared in the press. One was that it had happened by accident in Paris – where else? – when white carnations had been put in a glass filled with green ink. The resulting flower, which exhibited a metallic, artificial blue-green hue, was duly taken up by the fast set.[64] Some suggested that Wilde himself had invented it.[65] One commentator, taking a turn as a ventriloquist, said in the persona of Wilde that 'when I'm in the front row with my big collar on and green carnation in my coat, the rest of the audience don't count for much in my opinion'.[66]

The media frenzy intensified with the anonymous publication of a novel, *The Green Carnation*, in 1894. Written by Robert Hichens, this was an obvious satire on the relationship between Wilde and Douglas, who appeared, respectively, in the characters of Esmé Amarinth and Lord Reggie Hastings: 'Reggie was very frank. When he could not be witty, he often told the naked truth; and truth, without any clothes on, frequently passes for epigram. It is daring, and so it seems clever... Society smiled and murmured that it was a pose.'[67] Although Amarinth was married (as, of course, was Wilde), he argued that 'marriage is a sort of forcing house. It brings strange sins to fruit.'[68] Reggie's green carnation has a fascinating effect on boys such as Jimmy Stubbs: 'it appeared to mesmerise him, and to render him unaware of outward things. Whenever it moved his eyes moved too, and he even forgot to blush as he lost himself in its astonishing green fascinations.'[69] To many members of the reading public the daring flippancy of the novel's contents made up for its lack of literary merit. Wilde wrote to the press to associate himself with the flower but to deny, on grounds of quality, that he was the author of that 'middle-class and mediocre book'.[70]

Gossip about the sexually queer nature of Wilde and his circle mounted steadily, egged on by a series of increasingly unambiguous cartoons by Alfred Bryan in *Judy*. The magazine's theatre columnist 'Call Boy' (i.e. the stagehand who alerts actors to their entrances) recorded in February 1895 that 'I saw such sights in the audience'. It was the first night of Wilde's *The Importance of Being Ernest*. Many New Men were there, sitting in ladylike fashion. One camp couple was observed as they 'slapped each other playfully, the one saying the other was a naughty fellow for thinking so much about appearances, and the specimen thus giddily admonished replying that it was *too* unkind of him to say so, although he would forgive him on account of the lovely box of chocolates he sent him on St. Valentine's day'.[71]

Prints such as *Fashionable Ties* (1810) had long insinuated that the dandy was only a short step away from a criminal conviction (see PLATE 15). It was, therefore, perhaps not surprising that Oscar Wilde's conviction and disgrace had been imagined long before its actual occurrence. In 1883 the *Illustrated Sporting and Dramatic News* presented him in prison uniform in a cartoon showing the 'frightful foreshadowing of our Oscar's future' should he 'resume the knee breeches'.[72] The year before Wilde's trials Max Beerbohm wrote in jest to Reggie Turner to say that 'Oscar has at last been arrested for certain kinds of crime' in the Café Royal. Alfred Douglas escaped by running but Oscar, now grown corpulent, was less nimble.[73] Earlier that year Lord Queensberry, Douglas's father, had written to his son saying 'to my mind to pose as a thing is as bad as to be it. With my own eyes I saw you both in the most loathsome and disgusting relationship as expressed by your manner of expression. Never in my experience have I ever seen such a sight as that in your horrible features. No wonder people are talking as they are.'[74] In February 1895 Queensberry left a card at the Albermarle Club – a kind of latter-day Almack's in that it was so daring as to admit both men and women – addressed 'to Wilde posing sodomite' (or 'posing as a sodomite', as was subsequently claimed).

It is hard to think about the three trials of Oscar Wilde in 1895 without the benefit of hindsight. We know that Queensberry was right in his estimation of Wilde and, therefore, that the ensuing libel case was a risky undertaking. We also know that after two criminal trials Wilde was sentenced to two years' imprisonment with hard labour; that this broke his health and that he was to die a few years later as a poverty-stricken exile in Paris. Yet Alfred Douglas, for one, anticipated success, and various of Wilde's friends exchanged flippant gossip about the proceedings.[75] Douglas's father had a bad public reputation and many people thought that Wilde had been dragged into an unpleasant family feud. All that notwithstanding, Wilde's enthusiasm for literary decadence primed many of those in court to see him as not just a dandy, and therefore contemptible, but also a danger on the widest moral grounds. His conviction meant that dandyism itself became very visibly associated with homosexuality. Just as Wilde had sensationalized the appearances and homes of decadent aesthetes in his novel *The Picture of Dorian Gray* (1890), so he, the objects he valued and the places he frequented were scrutinized for the signs of unnatural vice.[76] When, in due course, Wilde was bankrupted and his effects put up for sale, the public discovered that the contents of his house in Tite Street were not particularly outré.[77] During the trials, by contrast, the dandified but not otherwise extraordinary figure in the dock was written about in terms of disgust and monstrosity.[78] One of the sensational pamphlets sold to a fascinated public related that 'Mr. Oscar Wilde as witness looked ponderous and fleshy, his face a dusky red, and his hair brushed away from a middle-parting in smooth waves.'[79] His circle of associates had also noticed this aspect of his appearance. Max Beerbohm had written to Reggie Turner a couple of years earlier to say that Wilde 'has deteriorated very much in appearance: his cheeks being quite a dark purple'.[80]

Wilde had in truth put on a considerable amount of weight in recent years and his skin was likely flushed as a result of heavy drinking. But if he bore some responsibility for not having retained the patina of self-control expected of a nineteenth-century British dandy, so did certain of his friends for having delightedly seized on that fact. Max Beerbohm should be singled out. He enjoyed an ambivalent friendship with Wilde and his visual caricatures grew more savage as he lost confidence in his associate.[81] One such cartoon was published in *Pick-Me-Up* in 1894 (FIG. 18).[82] It combines grossness with effete detailing, as shown in the extraordinary hand which reminds one of Leigh Hunt's description of Byron as discussed in the previous chapter.[83] Wilde's clothing is hardly represented and it looks as if his body is bursting out before our horrified eyes.[84] The bloated Wilde was also a source of amusement for Aubrey Beardsley, who

18 Wilde caricatured as a decadent freak of fashion. Max Beerbohm, *Oscar Wilde*, in *Pick-Me-Up*, 22 September 1894.

depicted him thus as 'The Woman in the Moon' in his illustrations for *Salomé*.[85]

Beerbohm commented on the effect of the passing years in a piece entitled 'Oscar Wilde' that appeared in the *Anglo-American Times* in March 1893. Gone was the bohemian youth 'in face and figure most thin'. The man is now 'not only immensely tall, but in proportion fat'. His coat, flowers, gemstones, and 'many little gold chains which insinuate themselves from one pocket to another … proclaim in unison a dandy of the type most elaborate and voluptuous'.[86] In 1911 Beerbohm wrote to Christopher Millard, who was a pioneering scholar of Wilde, enclosing a better drawing. The previous one had 'showed only the worse side of his nature. … I hardly realized what a cruel thing it was; I only realized that after Oscar's tragedy and downfall. … This caricature I am sending you shows Oscar in a light that won't pain posterity, and is … much more really true.'[87] Beerbohm's original aim may have been to emphasize and, therefore, to celebrate Wilde's queerness but it had tragic results. In 1953 Beerbohm told the writer Samuel Behrman that he had visited the office of the police inspector who had arrested Oscar Wilde, hoping for some positive news, and saw this drawing hung up amid a 'grisly collection' of weapons and other criminal souvenirs 'as though it were evidence'.[88] Wilde's lack of self-discipline, literally embodied in fat, meant that he was rocking the boat for his more discreet fellow-travellers. He thus appeared sinking the end of the punt that he shared with the feather-light (and cross-dressed) Douglas in *A Dream of Decadence on the Cherwell*, a cartoon published by students at Oxford in May 1893 (FIG. 19).[89]

Beerbohm was himself a dandy, but one in the tradition of Brummell rather than of D'Orsay. His style 'reduced male dress to a few essentials: buttonhole, shoes, cane, hat', all of which were chosen with great care.[90] He is almost like a character in one of Wilde's comedies who, 'operating almost entirely through ties, waistcoats

19 Wilde and Lord Alfred Douglas (1870–1945) go punting in Oxford. JCR Spider [pseud.], *A Dream of Decadence on the Cherwell*, in *New Rattle*, vol. 4, no. 20, May 1893.

and those all-important buttonholes', takes pleasure from fashion but also enjoys laughing at its superficiality.[91] Beerbohm set himself up as an amused observer of the social scene in both his visual and verbal satires. His essay 'The Incomparable Beauty of Modern Dress' was published in *Spirit Lamp* when that Oxford student publication was edited by Alfred Douglas. This celebrates, with considerable irony, the spread of the masculine dress of his own native land across the world: 'It is very strange that, of all nations, England should have done this great service for the beauty of nations.'[92] The essay also records the putting on trial of a case of 'excessive foppery' on the part of 'one of those who try to realize the ideal man by combining in themselves whatever seems best in either sex'. It also comments, of *The Picture of Dorian Gray*, that 'foppishness is woven, with exquisite effect, through the very fabric of the work'.[93]

Beerbohm kept his own sexuality studiously unclear. It has been suggested that although he subsequently married he may have been homosexual and celibate.[94] In January 1895 he cautioned Robert Ross that he feared that Douglas would prove 'fatal' to Reggie Turner and cause him to 'fall an entire victim to the love that dares not tell its name. You are a person of far stronger character and it doesn't affect you in the way it would affect him.'[95] Beerbohm, in other words, adhered to the Brummellian dandy's ethos of self-control both in public and in private. Yet his caricatures of Wilde were so overtly queer that they threatened to implicate the artist himself in scandal. In 1894 an anonymous critic declared that 'one is beginning to dread the coming around of the quarters of the year. Not because they mark the flight of time, but because they announce the coming of *The Yellow Book*.' The latest edition contained 'Aubrey Beardsley's and Max Beerbohm's agonized vulgarities. In their efforts to attract attention with the current issue of their Quarterly, the editors have stepped over the boundary line of decency... Mr. Beardsley's "Wagnerites" and Mr. Beerbohm's "George IV" are more indecent than any "living pictures" [i.e. nude *poses plastiques*] that were ever exhibited in a public hall.'[96] The latter drawing looked more like Beerbohm's caricatures of Oscar Wilde than it did the king.[97] In his 1896 article 'Dandies and Dandies' Beerbohm praised Brummell as an artist.[98] By contrast he commented in his essay on George IV that once, when in Brighton, 'I fancied I saw the shade of a swaying figure and a wine-red face'.[99] The Regent was depicted as a wit, a scholar and a drunkard but as nothing more remarkable than that. The implication was that the same could be said of Wilde.

Dandyism had never been easy otherwise it would have quickly lost its aura of exclusivity, but it was becoming more difficult to stand out and be appreciated. As the population became wealthier more people had access to clothes that fit well. The twentieth century was to see the acceleration of trends that had begun under the Regency and continued during the reign of Queen Victoria. The challenge was not only to wear the perfect costume but also to possess the ideal body.[100] *The Picture of Dorian Gray* was a fantasy in which an aesthetic dandy was able to indulge all his bodily appetites and yet remain physically perfect. Wilde's fall from grace in 1895 reinforced the popular stereotype that effete dandyism contained within it the seeds of its own destruction as a result of self-indulgence. Before Wilde dandies had often been represented as antithetical to British values, but their behaviour had never been displaced as a vital component of the country's conversation about male probity. The reflex after 1895 was to deny the continued existence of the dandy in all his queerness and ambivalence. Dandyism became publicly tainted by homo-sexuality and, in the twentieth century, was to emerge as an increasingly countercultural position removed from the inner conversations of the Establishment. To be accused of posing, after the elaborate discussion of that term during Wilde's trials, was to be identified as an Oscar.[101]

Fashion and scandal in the twentieth century

From the eighteenth century to the twentieth the mainstay of men's formal clothing was the three-piece suit. This was composed of coat, waistcoat and breeches (and later trousers). It did not alter in its fundamentals until the widespread abandonment of the waistcoat in the later twentieth century.[1] Perhaps the most important change was not in the form of the suit but in the way in which it was made and sold. The arrival of the ready-to-wear suit made the garment far more affordable, and prestige was now associated less with the material with which it was made than with the precision with which it fitted. Only the wealthy could afford made-to-measure garments. The arrival of the modern mass market in menswear ushered in an age when a 'range of differing styles could be consumed with an almost fetishistic attention to detail'.[2] Rising incomes among the working classes led to the prominence of mashers who combined upper-class styles of dandified deportment with a predatory sexuality.[3] This meant that those who wished to stand out for their excellence in attire were forced to contend with changes in popular taste so as always to appear superior. Dandyism in the Victorian age, therefore, took a variety of forms. Sometimes it was loud and colourful, while at other times it darkened into what has been termed 'stove-pipe severity'.[4] Its various forms were criticized as evidence of aristocratic decadence and even as evidence of racial degeneration at a time when popular taste encouraged the adoption of the more informal lounge suit for country and sporting activities.[5]

This produced a paradoxical situation at the start of the twentieth century. The new consumerism meant that more people than ever before could afford to impersonate a dandified aristocrat.[6] But, as a result, the art of individualistic distinction had become more challenging.[7] The world of work, or the ostentatious denial of it, remained fertile ground on which to establish one's dandyism as a state of being rather than of doing.[8] Gender transgression provided both opportunities and dangers. Society valorized prettiness as a female attribute, seen in contradistinction to masculine strength and fortitude. To aspire to be a pretty man was, therefore, perceived as a perversion of gender. Creative play with personal attractiveness could, however, enable tacit statements to be made about queer desire as a 'species of ugliness'.[9]

The Wildean position of dandyism as a mask that revealed the truth about its wearer outlived its creator, who died in Paris in November 1900. Moreover, it not only endured but became a cliché. When Walter Pater appears in Tom Stoppard's play *The Invention of Love* (1997) we know instantly from his costume that he is a homosexual poseur who is not to be taken seriously: 'In the young Raphael, in the sonnets of Michaelangelo, in Correggio's lily-bearer in the cathedral at Parma, and ever so faintly in my necktie, we feel the touch of a, what shall I say? ... the touch of a refined and comely paganism.'[10] In the aftermath of Wilde's trials of 1895 dandyism became popularly associated with behaviour that was not simply unmanly but also un-British. In W.K. Haselden's *Coming and Going of the 'Dandy'*, published in the *Daily Mirror* in February 1906, an etiolated poseur is kicked out of a window by John Bull, who is proclaiming that 'there's no room for you in this century' (FIG. 20).[11] Haselden played an important role in establishing the popularity of

20 Edwardian dandyism was denounced in the press as unmanly and un-British. W.K. Haselden, *The Coming and Going of the 'Dandy'*, *Daily Mirror*, 9 February 1906.

the newspaper and achieved this partly through his attacks on New Men and New Women, suffragists and other such types.[12] The figure of John Bull as the embodiment of Englishness was intended to be read as referring to the 'common sense' of a popular mainstream of opinion.[13] It will be recalled that dandy types were typically caricatured as unduly thin or unduly fat. At this stage extreme thinness was regarded as a suspiciously unhealthy and androgynous quality in both men and women, as can be seen in Lewis Baumer's cartoon *The Sex Question*, which was published in *Punch* in 1911.[14] Both man and woman wear the tightest of coats, and his bowler hat is almost indistinguishable from her cloche hat. These looks would become mainstream in the 1920s but were startling a decade earlier.

Not all dandies were bachelors and not all bachelors dandies, but the two categories significantly overlapped. The middle-class expectation was that a man would not get married until he had enough income to support a wife and children. Furthermore, because the numbers in higher education were tiny, a large proportion of the workforce was composed of young men in their teens and twenties. Other men moved to towns and sent money to their families back home. All of this produced what has been termed, on both sides of the Atlantic, a 'bachelor subculture', which was sustained by concepts of manliness and male solidarity.[15] The family home, seen from this perspective, was regarded a part of women's domain and one which could potentially prove unduly feminine for boys growing up there.[16] There was, therefore, nothing necessarily strange or queer about sharing bachelor chambers after the manner of Sherlock Holmes and John Watson in Arthur Conan Doyle's detective stories.

There were homosexual bachelors who employed dandified dress and decor to signal their difference from others of their gender. Just as great care might be taken over costume, so the queer domestic interior could be carefully styled with attention paid to the smallest of details. Ostentatious shopping for exquisite curios and art objects had been denounced by Max Nordau (Simon Südfeld) in his influential diatribe *Degeneration* (*Entartung*) (1892–93).[17] Interior decoration emerged as a profession that was thought to be peculiarly populated by androgynes, homosexual men and lesbians. The writer and humourist Dorothy Parker (née Rothschild) depicted the camp figure of Alastair St Cloud in her article 'Interior Desecration' which was published in American *Vogue* in 1917: "'it took me two weeks to arrange that fruit", he said, "and now you have upset it" … Alistair had persuaded some Futurist friend of his to paint a frieze of lifesize

21 The ballet dancer Vaslav Nijinsky (1889–1950) became established as a model for male physicality and sex appeal. Nijinksy in *L'Après-midi d'un faune*, Paris, 1913.

nude figures – the nudest nudes I have ever seen ... [alongside] various divans, leopard skins and a bronze statue of "L'Après midi d'un faune".[18] The statue is a reference to the *succès de scandale* that Vaslav Nijinsky had achieved in the ballet of the same name that had premiered in Paris in 1912. His body swiftly become established as a model for male physicality and sex appeal (FIG. 21).

When homosexuality became widely talked about in public discourse during the interwar period there was a rapid decline in older models of bachelordom and the eclipse of ideals of non-sexual 'romantic friendship' between men.[19] To be an unmarried man became slightly suspect, particularly after the stock-market crash of 1929, when family cohesion and economic survival rather than individualistic consumerism became seen as imperative.[20] Never-theless, all through the Depression there remained a market for escapist glamour. This sustained the career of Noël Coward – dandy, homosexual and celebrity bachelor (PLATE 27).[21] The appeal of his plays and cinematic appearances has been explained as the result of his having 'offered English audiences a suggestion of the risqué and the fashionable combined with the reassurance of conventionality'.[22] He impersonated aristocratic glamour and provided a model for the self-made man.[23] He became so well known that his dress, style and form of speech became both widely copied and mocked: 'for the first time since Oscar Wilde, a writer's appearance seemed as important as what he wrote'.[24] In 1938 *Vogue* gave away a 'Noël Coward paper doll' that could be dressed in a range of fashionable garments.[25]

The British stage in the 1920s was not notably radical and some of Coward's plays, such as *Design for Living* (1932), which centred on a relationship between two men and one woman, were 'once deemed too ambisextrous for London'.[26] The term 'gay', which generally meant happy and fun, had started to come into use in urban sub-cultures as a code for homosexuality. A party was more likely to be 'gay' for queer men if they were not in a small minority. Coward made discreet but significant use of the word in song lyrics such as those of 'Bright Young People' (1931):

Gay to the utmost degree. We play funny jokes
On more dignified folks
And laugh with extravagant glee.
We give lovely parties that last through the night,
I dress as a woman and scream with delight,
We wake up at lunchtime and find we're still tight.[27]

Coward was, as the critic Alan Sinfield put it, able to 'hold homosexuality poised at the brink of public visibility'.[28] In 'Bachelor's Bounce', an article published in *Harper's Bazaar* in 1932, a host of fashionable queer men – including the writer Beverley Nichols, the celebrity photographer Cecil Beaton, Noël Coward and Robert Byron, who was the magazine's theatre columnist – are discussed without the issue of sexuality being addressed. The accompanying cartoon shows them packed into the boxes at a theatre admiring a woman on stage.[29] This suggests the world of the homosexual closet that gay liberation campaigners were to condemn later in the century. But it should be recalled that the aim of this closet was to enable living a fashionable life in an age when sex between men remained criminalized.[30]

The nineteenth-century dandy, it should be recalled, was often noted for his lack of interest in women without that necessarily being read as a queer characteristic. Decadent New Men were, by contrast, often discussed with progressive women as part of a new social and sexual phenomenon.[31] Ellen Moers even argued in her influential book *The Dandy: Brummell to Beerbohm* (1960) that the arrival of the New Women, with 'a cigarette, a bicycle and a will of her own', pushed the dandy 'from the centre of the stage'.[32] The story of women's liberation was to be a central element of the cultural life of the twentieth century, but the male dandy did not instantly lose all his share of the limelight. Interwar dandies, such as Coward, still enjoyed considerable popular attention. However, although they were sometimes homosexual, they were typically depicted in the company of the opposite sex. For some of them, such as Beaton, women were their clients. Others, such as Coward, were able to use female characterization on the stage to explore queer desire for men. Meanwhile, publicly associating with women lured the press away from revelations of same-sex scandal.

It was also in the later 1920s that female same-sex desire became much more widely recognized and discussed. Attacks on allegedly masculine women before 1914 had focused on issues of gender transgression rather than of deviant sexuality, although the journalist Harry J. Birnstingl, writing in *Freewoman* magazine in 1912, did suggest a link between 'uranians' (sexual 'inverts' who supposedly combined a man's mentality with a woman's body) and suffragists.[33] Some of those with whom Coward was depicted were lesbian friends who also wore tailored jackets and had their hair similarly cropped. The art historian John Potvin has referred to these androgynous

22 The 'man-woman' was just too modern for the mainstream. George Belcher, *Man–Woman*, 'In the Old Days I Never Paid More Than Sixpence for a Haircut', in *Punch* 189, 1925.

pairings as 'perverse double-portraits'.[34] Perhaps the most widely recognized British lesbian from this period was the novelist Radclyffe Hall (PLATE 28).[35] Her public fame was largely the result of the obscenity trial that led to the banning of her novel *The Well of Loneliness* (1928) in Britain.[36] She has been referred to as a 'kindred spirit' of Noël Coward.[37] A figure similar to Hall appears as a 'man-woman' in a cartoon published in *Punch* in 1925.[38] Now that the short haircut had become fashionable for women she has to pay for her crop at women's prices rather than getting the cheaper men's cut as she had been accustomed to do (FIG. 22). An androgynous woman also featured in a *Punch* cartoon of 1930 in which a guest at a party objected to what he termed "'futurist bric-à-brac'". "'But I must put something on my walls'", says the fashionable hostess. "'Ah, I was speaking of what you put on the carpet'", replies the guest with reference to his fellow attendees, who include a woman in jacket and monocle.[39]

Just as the initial reviews of Hall's book had been positive so responses to lesbianism were by no means always negative. Sappho, the poet from ancient Greece who was famous – or infamous to bigots – for her celebration of lesbian desire, featured as one of the 'Famous Women in History' in the magazine *Britannia and Eve* in 1929. The article explained that there were legends that she killed herself for love of a young man, or that she was really a nice, respectable wife, mother and schoolmistress, but that we need to see her differently: 'the Greeks had a different morality: they even allowed "friendship" to be passionate. ... For it was in later ages than theirs that the limits of friendship came, no doubt for the good of the world, to be more strictly drawn.'[40] The article further informed the reader that 'it must have been an exciting business to belong to Sappho's House of the Muses: there was a great deal of emotion about... the little island became a centre of that cult of beauty which was somehow innate in the Greek character. If anyone had this love of beauty it was Sappho. Like Michelangelo, she was most susceptible to it when she saw it in her own sex.'[41]

The British dandy has been presented in this book as a male phenomenon that arose because of the problematization of male sartorial splendour. Some individuals had been identified as 'female macaronies' in the later eighteenth century or 'dandyzettes' in the early nineteenth. Female dandyism had been discussed in nineteenth-century France but more in connection with spectacular individuals rather than as a widespread social type.[42] However, feminist scholars have defended the notion that women too could be dandies, such as by appropriating male dandy styles in order to assert empowerment and individuality.[43] 'Female masculinity' has taken a wide range of forms, some with more liberatory potential than others. What such women wore in the interwar period influenced male styles and, therefore, had an impact on the history of masculinity.[44] An example of the resulting gender complexity is provided by the bisexual actress and singer Marlene Dietrich. In 1933 *Sketch* magazine ran an article headlined 'Marlene Sets the Trouser Fashion'. Readers were told that she wore suits all the time in Hollywood and that she had ten of them as well as a dinner jacket.[45] Unlike Stephen Gordon, the hero/ine of *The Well of Loneliness*, Dietrich did not appear to be an invert – a

AN INDUCEMENT.

Swedish Exercise Instructress. "Now, LADIES, IF YOU WILL ONLY FOLLOW MY DIRECTIONS CAREFULLY, IT IS QUITE POSSIBLE THAT YOU MAY BECOME EVEN AS I AM!"

23 Some men held that sport had masculinizing effects on the female physique. Arthur Wallis Mills, *An Inducement*, in *Punch* 130, 1906.

man in a woman's body – but as 'always fully feminine and fully masculine'.[46]

This was a remarkable act to carry off, since, as *Vogue* commented in 1927 at the height of the fashion for short hair for women, 'the severely tailored suit is much harder to wear, it reveals every line of the figure and is inclined to be harsh to the woman who is not especially feminine looking'.[47] But even Hall – 'magnificent and freakish, primitive and modern' – had not initially been publicly read as a transgressor of sexual boundaries because the appropriation of masculine style had become a well-established feature of women's fashion.[48] The increasing popularity of sports for women had hitherto generated ribald (male) satire on the masculinizing effects of activity on the female physique. An example of this was a cartoon by Arthur Wallis Mills in *Punch* in 1906 (FIG. 23). This featured a gym mistress who looked like a man in a dress, complete with cropped hair, saying to her bored feminine pupils, 'Now, ladies, if you will only follow my directions carefully, it is quite possible that you may become even as I am!'[49]

By the 1920s the New Woman had evolved into the Modern Girl and the Masculine Woman, and 'experimentation in clothing and gender bending was so pervasive that one could speak of an entire culture as, in a sense, cross-dressing.'[50] According to historian of sexuality Lorna Doan, Radclyffe Hall 'did not invent the mannish lesbian so much as embrace sexological theories of inversion and develop an existing style made possible by the startling degree of toleration and experimentation, of dizzying permutations of sartorial play and display'.[51] Rather than the gender-crossing that opponents often alleged it to be, this behaviour can be understood as 'gender stretching'.[52] These women did not become men. They stretched what a woman could be. Another example is provided by the case of Lilias Barker, who married in 1918 and bore two children. From 1923, however, she took the name of Colonel Leslie Barker and then had various relationships with women. Such a life does not map neatly onto our categories of bisexuality, cross-dressing or trans identities. Her/his own preferred term was 'masquerade'.[53]

A review of G. Sheila Donisthorpe's novel on the subject of lesbian lives, *The Loveliest of Friends* (1931), commented that 'while not a few have some acquaintance with such a word as homosexual very few could give a feminine counterpart.'[54] In the press female cross-dressing, which after all had been a popular act on the music-hall stage, only slowly became associated with lesbianism, whereas 'by the 1930s it was increasingly evident that [discussion of] men's effeminacy and cross-dressing was a euphemism for homosexuality.'[55] The relative slowness with which female dandyism was attacked as evidence of sexual transgression arguably allowed it to maintain the social cachet – without which the dandy was nothing – that the public scandal over male homosexuality threatened to deny to men.[56]

The insouciant pose of the interwar male dandy was often a cover for insecurity and private shame.[57] When Coward met Cecil Beaton for the first time at sea in April 1930 he lectured him for being 'flabby, floppy and affected, with an undulating walk, exaggerated clothes and voice both too high and too precise'.[58] Beaton had basically been told that he was too camp. As the 1920s gave way to the 1930s there was a reaction against gender radicalism.[59] Those who wanted men and women to remain in their traditional roles strove to reinforce the conceptual division between normality, on the one hand, and queerness, on the other.[60] Yet even as the fashionability of queer, indeterminate style waned there rose a vogue for attending nightclubs at which entertainment was provided by queer performers. This 'pansy craze' was named after an originally American derogative term which, like 'fairy', was applied to effeminate homosexual men. In 1931 an edition of the British high-society magazine *Sketch* featured a cover photograph showing a bed of the plants in full bloom captioned 'The Origin of the Fairies! A Crowd of Pansy Faces'.[61] In New York *Weekly Variety* said that 'reports are around that Broadway during the new season will have nite [*sic*] places with "pansies" as the prime draw'.[62] This had the effect of exhibiting queers as a marginalized group, and many in the audience would have gone away more convinced than ever of their own heterosexual 'normality'.[63]

This scene developed in several major cities. The Paris equivalent was captured by the photographer Brassaï (born Gyula Halásc).[64] He focused, as did the police, on the butchest of the women and the most feminine of the men as visual spectacles.[65] Many of these photographs were not published until the appearance of *The Secret Paris of the 30s* in 1976. Of the scene at a drag ball in 1933 the book acidly records that 'of course most of them were in dressmaking, lacemaking, furs, hairdressing – creators of hats, ribbons, embroidery, fabrics, laces... Almost all of them had devoted their lives to dressing, beautifying, deifying women, making them seductive and attractive for others to love – for they certainly didn't.'[66] After this the location shifts to the scenes in an opium den. The viewpoint, therefore, is explicitly judgemental and voyeuristic. Such fashionable 'slumming' was, arguably, 'becoming the ultimate mark of cosmopolitan sophistication' in the early 1930s but it also reinforced stereotypical expectations of queer gender non-conformity.[67] The stereotyped 'pansy' might dress in imitation of a beautiful woman but he could never be a truly handsome man. *Variety Weekly* provided guidance on such matters to its readers in an article from 1930 on the subject of 'Hollywood's Male Magnolias'. A stately magnolia tree, unlike a common little pansy, simply represented 'good guys gone gorgeous'.[68]

The effect of this was to undermine the social status of dandyism by associating it with déclassé urban subcultures rather than with aristocratic elites. In the process the stereotypes of the effete and ridiculous homosexual man and the rough and aggressive lesbian became ingrained in popular culture. This makes it hard to appreciate that when the queer artistic polymath Jean Cocteau was drawn in a *Vanity Fair* cartoon with his hand camply on his hip in

1924 he was not being mocked for his sexuality but celebrated for his dandified individualism.[69] The rise of the pansy and the decline in the status of queer dandies can be charted in the illustrations that Anna Zinkeisen drew to accompany the Mariegold in Society column in *Sketch* magazine. This was, in essence, a high-class gossip column, but the cartoons by Zinkeisen parodied the life of a fashionable young woman about town in a light and humorous vein. Smart young men accompany her in raids on bastions of stuffiness such as gentlemen's clubs: 'to permit the entry of the sedate wives of … elderly members was *one* thing; but that Mariegold should … [enter] the premises with her bevy of gay young friends – should sit on the arms of chairs and chatter, while drinking *cocktails* – that was something no one had bargained for, and was positively *indecent!*'[70] Mariegold commissioned her clothes from a proletarian queer man, as illustrated in a series of cartoons depicting 'Marie-gold's Dress Designer'. This included 'an exclusive and charming portrait of Madame Jamais, who in private life is Mr. Pimpskin Pottle'.[71]

24 Did the so-called pansy represent the future of the race? Anna Zinkeisen in Mariegold [pseud.], 'Mariegold Broadcasts', *Sketch*, 26 April 1933.

25 The United Kingdom has produced many queens. *Quentin Crisp Taken Near His Home in Fulham* by Simon Dack, 1980.

Zinkeisen subsequently drew a similar pansy in a characteristic costume of tight jacket and floppy hat (FIG. 24) to illustrate one of a series of cartoons that despaired of modern forms of masculinity in the age of Hitler and Mussolini: '*Soon – it may not matter much – / "Do away with men – as such!"*'[72]

In the interwar period the police became obsessed with looking for the supposed signs of male homosexuality such as the powder puff.[73] It had not been that long since the use of cosmetics by women had been regarded as morally dubious, so it is perhaps not surprising that their employment by men was viewed with great suspicion. There had, indeed, long been an urban subculture in London of 'queens' (the British equivalent of the fairy) who sometimes used make-up or even cross-dressed. Some of this community were sex workers. The wit and raconteur Quentin Crisp was a sometime member of this group and became famous not only because of his memoir *The Naked Civil Servant* (1968) but because he never gave up this style of dress (FIG. 25).[74]

In order to be taken seriously, queer artists and left-wing intellectuals distanced themselves from decorative dandyism in the 1930s. One of the leading aesthetes of the time, Harold Acton, found himself dismissed as a mere 'decorative dilettante':

> the astute younger generation had decided quite rightly that they had a better chance of a public hearing by grafting political messages onto T.S. Eliot's technique. Their cantos, interlarded with music-hall ditties, the puns of Joyce, pedantic jokes, and passages of bisexual sentiment, were riveted with pink slogans and hoisted on Red flags. Through terse obscurities they were groping towards a creed, through the clowning of the Marx brothers, they were approaching Father [Karl] Marx.[75]

In the words of the queer literary critic Gregory Woods, the 1920s had seen the rise to prominence of the 'affluent and whimsical queen, dedicated to aestheticism and leisure, with a wandering eye for a burly sportsman. As this type went out of fashion in the 1930s he was replaced by the more masculine and politicized artist, espouser of causes and befriender of workers.'[76]

The path from aestheticism to communism in the 1930s was satirized by the critic Cyril Connolly in his essay 'Where Engels Fears to Tread' (1937). Connolly was heterosexual, although he had had experience of same-sex love at Eton, his public school, and was friends with a wide range of queer men and women.[77] The article purports to be a review of *From Oscar to Stalin: A Progress* by Christian de Clavering. This fictional character's mother was a social climber and his father a turf accountant. Sent to Eton, he presented himself as if he were from old money. He was expelled from school and then from Oxford University for doing no work. His father then lost his money, and the son, reduced to poverty, discovered the beauty of the working classes. Looking forward to a new age he changed his name to Cris Clay and imagined himself back on top of the social heap. The whole was written in the camp, epigrammatic style of the queer aesthete Ronald Firbank.

> An impression, above all, of arches, my dears, each with its handsome couple ... and the naughtiest elms! While the battle of Waterloo was being fought all around me, I just sat still and watched my eyelashes grow... The boys of course took up most of my time... London at last. The 'twenties. Parties. Parties. Parties. And behind them all an aching feeling – was it worth it? What is it all for? Futility... It was then that I saw the light. One day I wandered into a little book-shop near Red Lion Square. It was full of slim volumes by unfamiliar names – who were Stephen [Spender], Wystan [Hugh Auden], Cecil [Day-Lewis], and Christopher [Isherwood]... One quatrain in particular haunted me.
> M is for Marx
> And Movement of Masses
> And Massing of Arses
> And Clashing of Classes.
> It was new. It was vigorous. It was real. It was chic![78]

When the Oxford Union voted in 1933 in favour of the motion 'That this House would under no circumstances fight for its King and country', the reaction in the right-wing press was that this was the work of 'woolly-minded communists, practical jokers and sexual in-determinates'.[79] In the 1930s accusations of dandified effeminacy were hurled from one side of the political spectrum to the other as Britain became embroiled in what has come to be spoken of as the politics of appeasement.[80] Pacifism had become associated with queer men as early as World War I, as in the novel *Despised and Rejected* (1918) by Rose Allatini (who may have been bisexual), which appeared under a pseudonym. This featured the anti-hero Dennis, a homosexual

26 The queerness of the conscientious objector. Ian Fenwick, in J.B. Morton, 'Conscription for Young Pacifists', in *Everyman: The World News Weekly* 247 (NS, no. 4), 13 October 1933.

conscientious objector, who was masculine but marked by a female physical trait: 'his mouth alone, curved and sensitive above the firm chin, betrayed a nature in which such a longing, and others equally freakish, might hold their sway.'[81]

The periodical *Everyman: The World News Weekly* swung editorially to the right in the politically significant year of 1933. It published a pacifist article by the homosexual author Beverley Nichols but also a retort to this by J.B. Morton, who was widely known for his 'Beachcomber' column in the *Daily Express*.[82] Morton's article, 'Conscription for Young Pacifists', was accompanied by a cartoon of a pansy disdaining to hold a gun by Ian Fenwick, who would serve as a major during World War II (FIG. 26).[83] Morton accused Nichols of having 'hysterics in public' and displaying attitudes typical of 'emotional young people to-day. He writes, or used to write, exactly as they talk, in a high, shrill voice.' Among such circles 'the normal man who loathes war but believes in honour is held up to ridicule'.[84] So it was his 'voice' that gave him away as abnormal – Nichols wrote like a woman. Another queer writer, Jocelyn Brooke, described the voice of the 1920s in his novel *The Military Orchid* (1948) as 'half revealing (like the voice of M. de Charlus) behind its ill-assumed masculinity a whole bevy of *jeunes filles en fleurs*'.[85] This is a reference to one of Proust's characters, who was presented as a closeted but obvious homosexual. Conscientious objectors were popularly pilloried as self-indulgent, effeminate cowards. They were, like the macaronis before them, allegedly pleasure-obsessed, foreign-loving and mentally enfeebled.[86]

During the twentieth century attention shifted away from dressy men and focused increasingly on the role of women in society. As in many ways a declassé figure, the dandy, whether queer or otherwise, slowly ceased to be central to debates over core British values. But for the heirs of Oscar Wilde, whatever their sexuality, this was not necessarily a problem, as the American cultural critic Susan Sontag explained in her influential essay 'Notes on "Camp"' (1964). Wilde did not merely valorize stylistic excellence; he also celebrated the vulgarities of mass culture. In drawing attention to 'the necktie, the boutonniere, the chair, Wilde was anticipating the democratic esprit of Camp'.[87] The culture of mass commodities is, however, globalized and far less influenced by British taste than was the case in the eighteenth and nineteenth centuries. None of which is to say that dandies have ceased to exist, even though dandyism is no longer central to the cultural politics of Britain, and the world it influenced, in the way it has been for several centuries. Perhaps that is why some more recent expressions of dandyism, such as the styles of the 1950s working-class Teddy Boys, display nostalgia for a time when the precise cut of a man's suit was a matter for public drama and scandal.

Notes

ONE

1. John Berger, *Ways of Seeing*, Penguin, Harmondsworth, 1972, pp. 147–8.
2. Elizabeth Amann, *Dandyism in the Age of Revolution: The Art of the Cut*, University of Chicago Press, Chicago IL, 2015, p. 13.
3. Charles Baudelaire, *Selected Writings in Art and Literature*, Penguin, London, 1992, p. 420.
4. Ellen Moers, *The Dandy: Brummell to Beerbohm*, Secker & Warburg, London, 1960, p. 13.
5. Dominic Janes, *Oscar Wilde Prefigured: Queer Fashioning and British Caricature*, University of Chicago Press, Chicago IL, 2016, pp. 171–90.
6. John Cook, after unknown artist, *George Brummell*, 1844, line engraving, published by Richard Bentley, London, 18.2 × 11.8 cm; National Portrait Gallery, London, NPG D1125.
7. Joanna Bourke, 'The Great Male Renunciation: Men's Dress Reform in Inter-War Britain', *Journal of Design History*, vol. 9, no. 1, 1996, p. 30.
8. J.C. Flügel, *The Psychology of Clothes*, Hogarth Press, London, 1930, pp. 110–13.
9. John Harvey, *Men in Black*, Reaktion, London, 1995, p. 27.
10. Aileen Ribeiro, *Fashion and Fiction: Dress in Art and Literature in Stuart England*, Yale University Press, New Haven CT, 2005, p. 191.
11. Harvey, *Men in Black*, p. 120; Ribeiro, *Fashion and Fiction*, p. 199.
12. Harvey, *Men in Black*, pp. 140–44.
13. David Kuchta, *The Three-Piece Suit and Modern Masculinity: England, 1550–1850*, University of California Press, Berkeley CA, 2002, p. 125.
14. Laura Lunger Knoppers, 'The Politics of Portraiture: Oliver Cromwell and the Plain Style', *Renaissance Quarterly*, vol. 51, no. 4, 1998, p. 1289.
15. Kuchta, *The Three-Piece Suit and Modern Masculinity*, p. 82.
16. Peter McNeil, *Pretty Gentlemen: Macaroni Men and the Eighteenth-Century Fashion World*, Yale University Press, New Haven CT, 2018, p. 13.
17. Joseph Addison, untitled, *Spectator*, 24 April 1711, p. 1.
18. Horace Walpole, letter to Lord Hertford, 6 February 1764, in Walpole, *The Yale*

Edition of Horace Walpole's Correspondence, 48 vols, ed. W.S. Lewis, Yale University Press, New Haven CT, 1937–83, vol. 38, p. 306.

19. Venetia Murray, *High Society: A Social History of the Regency Period, 1788–1830*, Viking, London, 1998, p. 24.

20. Thomas Gainsborough, *William Wade*, 1771, oil on canvas, 234.3 × 153 cm; Victoria Art Gallery, Bath and North East Somerset Council.

21. Richard Cosway, *Self-Portrait*, c. 1770–75, paint on ivory, 5 × 4.2 cm; Metropolitan Museum of Art, New York, 62.49. See McNeil, *Pretty Gentlemen*, p. 106; Stephen Lloyd, *Richard and Maria Cosway: Regency Artists of Taste and Fashion*, Scottish National Portrait Gallery, Edinburgh, 1995.

22. Aileen Ribeiro, 'Portraying the Fashion, Romancing the Past: Dress and the Cosways', in Stephen Lloyd, Roy Porter and Aileen Ribeiro (eds), *Richard and Maria Cosway: Regency Artists of Taste and Fashion*, Scottish National Portrait Gallery, Edinburgh, 1995, pp. 101–5.

23. McNeil, *Pretty Gentlemen*, p. 107.

24. Anon., 'The History of Captain H——, a Macaroni', *Macaroni and Theatrical Magazine*, October 1772, pp. 1–5.

25. Linda Colley, 'Britishness and Otherness: An Argument', *Journal of British Studies*, vol. 31, no. 4, 1992, p. 327; see also Linda Colley, *Britons: Forging the Nation, 1707–1837*, Yale University Press, New Haven CT, 2005.

26. Aileen Ribeiro, *Clothing Art: The Visual Culture of Fashion, 1600–1915*, Yale University Press, New Haven CT, 2017, p. 1; compare with Andrew Stephenson, '"But the Coat Is the Picture": Issues of Masculine Fashioning, Politics and Sexual Identity in Portraiture in England, c. 1890–1905', in Justine de Young (ed.), *Fashion in European Art: Dress and Identity, Politics and the Body 1775–1925*, I.B. Tauris, London, 2017, pp 178–206.

27. Kuchta, *The Three-Piece Suit*, p. 174.

28. Harvey, *Men in Black*, p. 147.

TWO

1. Daniel Roche, *The Culture of Clothing: Dress and Fashion in the Ancien Régime*, trans. Jean Birrell, Cambridge University Press, Cambridge, 1996, p. 44.

2. Christopher Breward, *The Culture of Fashion: A New History of Fashionable Dress*, Manchester University Press, Manchester, 1995, p. 140; Clare A. Lyons, 'Mapping an Atlantic Sexual Culture: Homoeroticism in Eighteenth-Century Philadelphia', *William and Mary Quarterly*, vol. 60, no. 1, 2003, p. 142; John Styles, *The Dress of the People: Everyday Fashion in Eighteenth-Century England*, Yale University Press, New Haven CT, 2007, p. 52.

3. Madeleine Delpierre, *Dress in France in the Eighteenth Century*, trans. Caroline Beamish, Yale University Press, New Haven CT, 1997, pp. 58–68.

4. Kimberly Chrisman, 'Unhoop the Fair Sex: The Campaign Against the Hoop Petticoat in Eighteenth-Century England', *Eighteenth-Century Studies*, vol. 30, no. 1, 1996, p. 13.

5. Jennifer M. Jones, 'Repackaging Rousseau: Femininity and Fashion in Old Regime France', *French Historical Studies*, vol. 18, no. 4, 1994, p. 155.

6. Thomas Laqueur, *Making Sex: Body and Gender from the Greeks to Freud*, Harvard University Press, Cambridge MA, 1990, p. 149.
7. Ibid., p. 194.
8. Michael McKeon, 'Historicizing Patriarchy: The Emergence of Gender Difference in England, 1660–1760', *Eighteenth Century Studies*, vol. 28, no. 3, 1995, p. 300.
9. Randolph Trumbach, *Sex and the Gender Revolution*, Volume 1: *Heterosexuality and the Third Gender in Enlightenment London*, University of Chicago Press, Chicago IL, 1998, p. 9.
10. Chrisman, 'Unhoop the Fair Sex', p. 7.
11. Jean-Honoré Fragonard, *Les Hasards heureux de l'escarpolette* [*The Happy Accidents of the Swing*], 1767, oil on canvas, 81 × 64 cm, Wallace Collection, London, P430; Chrisman, 'Unhoop the Fair Sex', p. 17.
12. David Kunzle, *Fashion and Fetishism: Corsets, Tight Lacing and Other Forms of Body-Sculpture*, Sutton, Stroud, 2004, p. 65.
13. Delpierre, *Dress in France*, p. 29.
14. Michael Kwass, 'Big Hair: A Wig History of Consumption in Eighteenth-Century France', *American Historical Review*, vol. III, no. 3, 2006, p. 631; see also Amelia Rauser, 'Hair, Authenticity, and the Self-Made Macaroni', *Eighteenth-Century Studies*, vol. 38, no. 1, 2004, pp. 101–17.
15. Kunzle, *Fashion and Fetishism*, p. 69.
16. Chrisman, 'Unhoop the Fair Sex', p. 21.
17. Aileen Ribeiro, *Dress in Eighteenth-Century Europe, 1715–1789*, rev. edn, Yale University Press, New Haven CT, 2002, p. 6.
18. Christoph Heyl, 'The Metamorphosis of the Mask in Seventeenth- and Eighteenth-Century London', in Efrat Tseëlon (ed.), *Masquerade and Identities: Essays on Gender, Sexuality and Marginality*, Routledge, London, 2003, p. 119.
19. Aileen Ribeiro, *The Art of Dress: Fashion in England and France, 1750–1820*, Yale University Press, New Haven CT, 1995, p. 224; Ribeiro, *Dress in Eighteenth-Century Europe*, pp. 266–72.
20. David Porter, 'Monstrous Beauty: Eighteenth-Century Fashion and the Aesthetics of the Chinese Taste', *Eighteenth-Century Studies*, vol. 35, no. 3, 2002, p. 404.
21. Terry Castle, *Masquerade and Civilization: The Carnivalesque in Eighteenth-Century English Culture and Fiction*, Stanford University Press, Stanford CA, 1986, p. 7.
22. Mark Booth, '*Campe-Toi!* On the Origins and Definitions of Camp', in Fabio Cleto (ed.), *Camp: Queer Aesthetics and the Performing Subject: A Reader*, Edinburgh University Press, Edinburgh, 1999, pp. 66–7; Pierre Zoberman, 'Queer(ing) Pleasure: Having a Gay Old Time in the Culture of Early-Modern France', in Greg Forter and Paul Allen Miller (eds), *The Desire of the Analysts*, State University of New York Press, Albany NY, 2008, pp. 225–52.
23. School of Pierre Mignard, *Philippe de France, duc d'Orléans, prés du portrait de sa fille aînée, Marie-Louise d'Orléans* [*Philippe de France, Duke of Orleans, With the Portrait of His Daughter Marie-Louise*], c. 1670, oil on canvas; Château de Versailles, MV2161.
24. Roche, *The Culture of Clothing*, p. 116.
25. Porter, 'Monstrous Beauty', p. 399.

26. Jessica Munns and Penny Richards (eds), *The Clothes that Wear Us: Essays on Dressing and Transgressing in Eighteenth-Century Culture*, University of Delaware Press, Newark DE, 1999, p. 23.

27. David Kuchta, *The Three-Piece Suit and Modern Masculinity: England, 1550–1850*, University of California Press, Berkeley CA, 2002, p. 125.

28. John Harvey, *Men in Black*, Reaktion, London, 1995, p. 120; Laura Lunger Knoppers, 'The Politics of Portraiture: Oliver Cromwell and the Plain Style', *Renaissance Quarterly*, vol. 51, no. 4, 1998, p. 1289.

29. Aileen Ribeiro, *Fashion and Fiction: Dress in Art and Literature in Stuart England*, Yale University Press, New Haven CT, 2005, p. 191.

30. Kuchta, *The Three-Piece Suit*, p. 1.

31. Christopher Breward, *The Suit: Form, Function and Style*, Reaktion, London, 2016, p. 17.

32. Quoted in David Kuchta, '"Graceful Virile and Useful": The Origins of the Three-Piece Suit', in Andrew Reilly and Sarah Cosbey (eds), *Men's Fashion Reader*, Fairchild, New York, 2008, p. 500.

33. Breward, *The Suit*, p. 88.

34. Kutcha, *The Three-Piece Suit*, p. 101.

35. Hannah Greig, *The Beau Monde: Fashionable Society in Georgian London*, Oxford University Press, Oxford, 2013, p. 241.

36. Ibid., p. 234.

37. Overview in Thomas A. King, *The Gendering of Men, 1600–1750*, Volume 2: *Queer Articulations*, University of Wisconsin Press, Madison WI, 2008, pp. xix–xxii.

38. Ibid., p. 87; Erin Mackie, *Rakes, Highwaymen, and Pirates: The Making of the Modern Gentleman in the Eighteenth Century*, Johns Hopkins University Press, Baltimore MD, 2009, p. 183.

39. D.A. Coward, 'Attitudes to Homosexuality in Eighteenth-Century France', *Journal of European Studies* 10, 1980, p. 245.

40. Dorothy Noyes, 'La Maja Vestida: Dress as Resistance to Enlightenment in Late-18th-Century Madrid', *Journal of American Folklore*, vol. III, no. 40, 1998, p. 199.

41. Felicity A. Nussbaum, *The Limits of the Human: Fictions of Anomaly, Race and Gender in the Long Eighteenth Century*, Cambridge University Press, Cambridge, 2003, pp. 72–3; see also Susan C. Shapiro, '"Yon Plumed Dandebrat": Male Effeminacy in English Satire and Criticism', *Review of English Studies*, vol. 39, no. 155, 1988, pp. 400–412.

42. Kristina Straub, 'Actors and Homophobia', in J. Douglas Cranfield and Deborah C. Payne (eds), *Cultural Readings of Restoration and Eighteenth-Century English Theater*, University of Georgia Press, Athens GA, 1995, p. 273; see also Kristina Straub, *Sexual Suspects: Eighteenth-Century Players and Sexual Ideology*, Princeton University Press, Princeton NJ, 1992.

43. David L. Orvis, '"Old Sodom" and "Dear Dad": Vanbrugh's Celebration of the Sodomitical Subject in *The Relapse*', *Journal of Homosexuality*, vol. 57, no. 1, 2009, pp. 140–62.

44. Tobias Smollett, *The Adventures of Roderick Random*, 2 vols, Osborn, London, 1748,

vol. 1, p. 306; see also George Haggerty, 'Smollett's World of Masculine Desire in *The Adventures of Roderick Random*', *Eighteenth Century*, vol. 53, no. 3, 2012, p. 318.

45. Randolph Trumbach, 'Sodomitical Assaults, Gender Role, and Sexual Development in Eighteenth-Century London', *Journal of Homosexuality*, vol. 16, no. 1–2, 1988. On mollies, see also Castle, *Masquerade and Civilization*, p. 46; Tanya Cassidy, 'People, Place, and Performance: Theoretically Revisiting Mother Clap's Molly House', in Chris Mounsey and Caroline Gonda (eds), *Queer People: Negotiations and Expressions of Homosexuality, 1700–1800*, Bucknell University Press, Lewisburg PA, 2007, pp. 99–113; Netta Goldsmith, 'London's Homosexuals in the Eighteenth-Century: Rhetoric Versus Practice', in Mounsey and Gonda (eds), *Queer People*, p. 186; Mackie, *Rakes, Highwaymen, and Pirates*, p. 117.

46. Trumbach, 'Sodomitical Assaults', pp. 408–9.

47. Rictor Norton (ed.), 'The He-Strumpets, 1707–10', in *Homosexuality in Eighteenth-Century England: A Sourcebook*, 1 December 1999, updated 15 June 2008; www.rictornorton.co.uk/eighteen/dunton.htm.

48. Susan Staves, 'A Few Kind Words for the Fop', *Studies in English Literature, 1500–1900*, vol. 22, no. 3, 1982, p. 428.

49. Philip Carter, *Men and the Emergence of Polite Society, Britain, 1660–1800*, Longman, Harlow, 2001, p. 156.

50. John Brewer, *The Pleasures of the Imagination: English Culture in the Eighteenth Century*, HarperCollins, London, 1997, p. 81.

51. Lorna Hutson, 'Liking Men: Ben Jonson's Closet Opened', *ELH*, vol. 71, no. 4, 2004, p. 1086; Thomas A. King, *The Gendering of Men, 1600–1750*, Volume 1: *The English Phallus*, University of Wisconsin Press, Madison WI, 2004, p. 246; Emma K. Atwood, 'Fashionably Late: Queer Temporality and the Restoration Fop', *Comparative Drama*, vol. 47, no. 1, 2013, p. 85.

52. Terry Castle, 'Matters Not Fit to Be Mentioned: Fielding's *The Female Husband*', *ELH*, vol. 49, no. 3, 1982, pp. 602–22.

53. Gary Kates, 'The Transgendered World of the Chevalier/Chevalière d'Eon', *Journal of Modern History*, vol. 67, no. 3, 1995, p. 584.

54. Lisa F. Cody, 'Sex, Civility, and the Self: Du Coudray, D'Eon, and Eighteenth-Century Conceptions of Gendered, National, and Psychological Identity', *French Historical Studies*, vol. 24, no. 3, 2001, p. 403.

55. Anna Clark, 'The Chevalier D'Eon and Wilkes: Masculinity and Politics in the Eighteenth Century', *Eighteenth-Century Studies*, vol. 32, no. 1, 1998, p. 34.

56. Anon., 'Mademoiselle de Beaumont, or the Chevalier d'Eon', *London Magazine* 46, 1777, p. 443, Lewis Walpole Library, Yale University, 777.09.00.01 Impression 1 (lwlpr04221); Clark, 'The Chevalier D'Eon', p. 37.

57. Kates, 'The Transgendered World', p. 590; J.M.J. Rogister, 'D'Éon de Beaumont, Charles Geneviève Louis Auguste André Timothée, Chevalier D'Éon in the French Nobility (1728–1810)', *Oxford Dictionary of National Biography*, Oxford University Press, Oxford, 2004, www.oxforddnb.com/view/article/7523.

58. Roche, *The Culture of Clothing*, p. 101.

59. Harvey, *Men in Black*, p. 128.

60. Karen Harvey, 'The Century of Sex? Gender, Bodies, and Sexuality in the

Long Eighteenth Century', *Historical Journal*, vol. 45, no. 4, 2002, pp. 899–916; Julie Park, *The Self and It: Novel Objects in Eighteenth-Century England*, Stanford University Press, Stanford CA, 2010, p. 59.

61. Valerie Steele, *Fetish: Fashion, Sex and Power*, Oxford University Press, Oxford, 1996, p. 12; Dominic Janes, *Victorian Reformation: The Fight over Idolatry in the Church of England, 1840–1860*, Oxford University Press, Oxford, 2009, pp. 16–18.

62. David Dabydeen, *Hogarth's Blacks: Images of Blacks in Eighteenth Century English Art*, Dangaroo Press, Kingston-upon-Thames, 1985, pp. 37–9; Catherine Molineux, 'Hogarth's Fashionable Slaves: Moral Corruption in Eighteenth-Century London', *ELH*, vol. 72, no. 2, 2005, pp. 495–520; compare with the colonial contexts discussed in Rebecca Earle, '"Two Pairs of Pink Satin Shoes!!" Race, Clothing and Identity in the Americas (17th–19th Centuries)', *History Workshop Journal*, vol. 52, no. 1, 2001, p. 184.

63. *A Mungo Macaroni*, 10 September 1772, M. Darly, London; Lewis Walpole Library, Yale University, Folio 72 771 D37 v.4 Plate 14 (lwlpro3458).

64. Monica L. Miller, *Slaves to Fashion: Black Dandyism and the Styling of Black Diasporic Identity*, Duke University Press, Durham NC, 2009, pp. 58–9.

65. Tita Chico, *Designing Women: The Dressing Room in Eighteenth-Century English Literature and Culture*, Bucknell University Press, Lewisburg PA, 2005, p. 27.

66. Ibid., p. 44.

67. Mimi Hellman, 'Interior Motives: Seduction by Decoration in Eighteenth-Century France', in Harold Koda and Andrew Bolton (eds), *Dangerous Liaisons: Fashion and Furniture in the Eighteenth Century*, Yale University Press, New Haven CT, 2006, p. 23.

68. Gillian Perry and Michael Rossington (eds), *Femininity and Masculinity in Eighteenth-Century Art and Culture*, Manchester University Press, Manchester, 1994, p. 7.

69. *The Bum-Bailiff Outwitted, or, The Convenience of Fashion*, 6 May 1786, S.W. Fores, London; Lewis Walpole Library, Yale University 786.05.06.01 (lwlpro5966).

70. Kuchta, *The Three-Piece Suit*, p. 176.

THREE

1. John Cooke, *The Macaroni Jester, and Pantheon of Wit; Containing All that Has Lately Transpired in the Regions of Politeness, Whim, and Novelty*, John Cooke, London, *c.* 1773, p. 108.

2. Ibid., p. 7.

3. Anon., '*The Macaroni*' [review], *Critical Review, or, Annals of Literature* 36, 1773, p. 235, Huntington Library, Larpent Collection MSS LA 34; with thanks to Dr David O'Shaughnessy.

4. Anon., 'Ferdinand Twigem', *The Macaroni: A Satire*, G. Allen, London, 1773, p. 12.

5. Ibid., p. 13.

6. Netta Goldsmith, 'London's Homosexuals in the Eighteenth-Century: Rhetoric Versus Practice', in Chris Mounsey and Caroline Gonda (eds), *Queer People: Negotiations and Expressions of Homosexuality, 1700–1800*, Bucknell University Press, Lewisburg PA, 2007, p. 186; Erin Mackie, *Rakes, Highwaymen, and Pirates: The*

Making of the Modern Gentleman in the Eighteenth Century, Johns Hopkins University Press, Baltimore MD, 2009, p. 117.

7. George Rousseau, *Perilous Enlightenment: Pre- and Post-Modern Discourses – Sexual, Historical,* Manchester University Press, Manchester, 1991, p. 28; Tanya Cassidy, 'People, Place, and Performance: Theoretically Revisiting Mother Clap's Molly House', in Mounsey and Gonda (eds), *Queer People,* pp. 99–113.

8. Terry Castle, *Masquerade and Civilization: The Carnivalesque in Eighteenth-Century English Culture and Fiction,* Stanford University Press, Stanford CA, 1986, p. 46.

9. Kristina Straub, *Sexual Suspects: Eighteenth-Century Players and Sexual Ideology,* Princeton University Press, Princeton NJ, 1992, pp. 47–68.

10. Anon., 'News', *Gazetteer and New Daily Advertiser,* 27 October 1764.

11. Kristina Straub, 'Actors and Homophobia', in J. Douglas Cranfield and Deborah C. Payne (eds), *Cultural Readings of Restoration and Eighteenth-Century English Theater,* University of Georgia Press, Athens GA, 1995, p. 273.

12. Felicity A. Nussbaum, *The Limits of the Human: Fictions of Anomaly, Race and Gender in the Long Eighteenth Century,* Cambridge University Press, Cambridge, 2003, pp. 72–3.

13. Emma K. Atwood, 'Fashionably Late: Queer Temporality and the Restoration Fop', *Comparative Drama,* vol. 47, no. 1, 2013, p. 85; Kimberly C. Campbell, 'The Face of Fashion: Milliners in Eighteenth–Century Visual Culture', *British Journal for Eighteenth–Century Studies,* vol. 25, no. 2, 2002, pp. 157–72.

14. Mark Hallett, *The Spectacle of Difference: Graphic Satire in the Age of Hogarth,* Yale University Press, New Haven CT, 1999, p. 187.

15. John Caspar Lavater, *Essays on Physiognomy,* trans. H. Hunter, 3 vols, John Murray, London, 1789–98, vol. 3, pt 1, p. 213.

16. Johan Zoffany, *David Garrick in Vanbrugh's 'The Provoked Wife',* Theatre Royal, Drury Lane, 1763–65, oil on canvas, 99.1 × 124.5 cm; Wolverhampton Art Gallery.

17. James Roberts, *Mr Garrick in the Character of Sir John Brute,* 1 June 1776, Bell, London, British Museum, Department of Prints and Drawings, Ee,3.164; Beth H. Friedman-Romell, 'Breaking the Code: Toward a Reception Theory of Theatrical Cross-Dressing in Eighteenth-Century London', *Theatre Journal,* vol. 47, no. 4, 1995, p. 465.

18. Peter McNeil, 'Dissipation and Extravagance: Ageing Fops', UTS E-Press, Sydney, 2007, p. 91, http://epress.lib.uts.edu.au/research/handle/10453/3030.

19. Leslie Ritchie, 'Garrick's Male-Coquette and Theatrical Masculinities', in Shelley King and Yaël Schlick (eds), *Refiguring the Coquette: Essays on Culture and Coquetry,* Bucknell University Press, Lewisburg PA, 2008, p. 187 n41.

20. David Garrick, *The Fribbleriad,* Coote, London, 1761, p. 11.

21. Peter McNeil, *Pretty Gentlemen: Macaroni Men and the Eighteenth-Century Fashion World,* Yale University Press, New Haven CT, 2018, pp. 155, 204.

22. Proust quoted and discussed in Eve Kosofsky Sedgwick, *Epistemology of the Closet,* University of California Press, Berkeley CA, 2008, p. 228.

23. Tim Hitchcock, *English Sexualities, 1700–1800,* Palgrave Macmillan, Basingstoke, 1997, pp. 58–75.

24. George Parker, *A View of Society and Manners in High and Low Life,* 2 vols, Printed for the author, London, 1781, vol. 2, pp. 87–8.

25. William Kenrick, *Love in the Suds: A Town Eclogue, Being the Lamentation of Roscius for the Loss of His NYKY*, Wheble, London, 1772.

26. Ibid., p. 7.

27. Hannah Smith and Stephen Taylor, 'Hephaestion and Alexander: Lord Hervey, Frederick, Prince of Wales, and the Royal Favourite in England in the 1730s', *English Historical Review*, vol. 124, no. 507, 2009, p. 311.

28. Randolph Trumbach, 'Sodomy Transformed: Aristocratic Libertinage, Public Reputation and the Gender Revolution of the 18th Century', *Journal of Homosexuality*, vol. 19, no. 2, 1990, p. 119; Andrew Elfenbein, *Romantic Genius: The Prehistory of a Homosexual Role*, Columbia University Press, New York, 1999, p. 22.

29. Alexander Pope, *An Epistle from Mr. Pope, to Dr. Arbuthnot*, Printed by J. Wright for Lawton Gilliver, London, 1734, p. 21.

30. Alexander Pope, *The Works of Alexander Pope, Esq*, 6 vols, Printed for Lawton Gilliver, London, 1735, vol. 2, p. 21; emphasis in original.

31. Jill Campbell, 'Politics and Sexuality in Portraits of John, Lord Hervey', *Word and Image*, vol. 6, no. 4, 1990, p. 283.

32. Peter Leach, 'John Chute (1701–1776)', *Oxford Dictionary of National Biography*, Oxford University Press, Oxford, 2020, https://doi.org/10.1093/ref:odnb/37285; Timothy Mowl, *Horace Walpole: The Great Outsider*, John Murray, London, 1996, p. 116.

33. Gabriel Mathias, *John Chute*, 1758; National Trust, The Vyne.

34. Silver satin suit, *c.*1765; National Trust, The Vyne.

35. Daniel Claro, 'Historicizing Masculine Appearance: John Chute and the Suits at The Vyne, 1740–76', *Fashion Theory*, vol. 9, no. 2, 2005, pp. 159, 166.

36. Rousseau, *Perilous Enlightenment*, p. 189. See also Andrew Wilton and Ilaria Bignamini (eds), *Grand Tour: The Lure of Italy in the Eighteenth Century*, Tate, London, 1996; Jeremy Black, *Italy and the Grand Tour*, Yale University Press, New Haven CT, 2003.

37. Michèle Cohen, 'The Grand Tour: Constructing the English Gentleman in Eighteenth–Century France', *History of Education*, vol. 21, no. 3, 1992, p. 255; Black, *Italy and the Grand Tour*, pp. 118–31.

38. Anon., 'The New Fable of the Bees', in Anon., *Crazy Tales*, Thomas Ewing, Dublin, 1772, p. 31.

39. Black, *Italy and the Grand Tour*, p. 126.

40. Quoted in Hugh Belsey, 'Mann, Sir Horatio, First Baronet (*bap.* 1706, *d.* 1786)', *Oxford Dictionary of National Biography*, Oxford University Press, Oxford, 2004; online edn, May 2009, www.oxforddnb.com/view/article/17945.

41. George Haggerty, *Horace Walpole's Letters: Masculinity and Friendship in the Eighteenth Century*, Bucknell University Press, Lanham MD, 2011, p. 122.

42. Horace Walpole, letter to Richard West, 24 January 1740, in Horace Walpole, *The Yale Edition of Horace Walpole's Correspondence*, 48 vols, ed. W.S. Lewis, Yale University Press, New Haven CT, 1937–83, vol. 13, p. 199.

43. Johan Zoffany, *The Tribuna of the Uffizi*, 1772–77, oil on canvas; Royal Collection Trust, RCIN 406983.

44. Quoted in Martin Postle (ed.), *Johan Zoffany RA: Society Observed*, Yale University Press, New Haven CT, 2011, p. 232.

45. Eve Kosofsky Sedgwick, *Between Men: English Literature and Male Homosocial Desire*, Columbia University Press, New York, 1993, p. 92.

46. Rousseau, *Perilous Enlightenment*, p. 176.

47. Mowl, *Horace Walpole*, p. 78.

48. George Haggerty, 'Queering Horace Walpole', *Studies in English Literature*, vol. 46, no. 3, 2006, p. 560.

49. Horace Walpole, letter to Lord Hertford, 6 February 1764, in Walpole, *Correspondence*, vol. 38, p. 306.

50. McNeil, *Pretty Gentlemen*, p. 95.

51. Hanneke Grootenboer, *Treasuring the Gaze: Intimate Vision in Late Eighteenth-Century Eye Miniatures*, University of Chicago Press, Chicago IL, 2012, p. 87.

52. McNeil, *Pretty Gentlemen*, p. 33.

53. Anon., 'Origins of Macaronism', *Morning Post*, 26 September 1827.

54. Ben Rogers, *Beef and Liberty: Roast Beef, John Bull and the English Nation*, Vintage, London, 2004, p. 68.

55. William Hogarth, *O the Roast Beef of Old England*, or *The Gate of Calais*, 1748, oil on canvas, 80 x 96 cm; Tate Gallery, London, N01464.

56. Ronald Paulson, 'Smollett and Hogarth: The Identity of Pallet', *Studies in English Literature, 1500–1900*, vol. 4, no. 3, 1964, pp. 351–9.

57. Tobias Smollett, *The Adventures of Peregrine Pickle*, 4 vols, Wilson, London, 1751, vol. 2, p. 89.

58. Dominic Janes, 'Unnatural Appetites: Sodomitical Panic in Hogarth's *The Gate of Calais*, or *O the Roast Beef of Old England (1748)*', *Oxford Art Journal*, vol. 35, no. 1, 2012, pp. 19–31.

59. Anon., 'Newmarket Races', *Owen's Weekly Chronicle and Westminster Journal*, 4–11 May 1765.

60. Album collected by Horace Walpole, 2 vols, vol. 1, pt 2, p. 2; Lewis Walpole Library, Yale University, fol. 49/3563/v1.2.

61. Jane Rendell, *The Pursuit of Pleasure: Gender, Space and Architecture in Regency London*, Athlone, London, 2002, pp. 92–6; Rendell, 'Almack's Assembly Rooms – a Site of Sexual Pleasure', *Journal of Architectural Education*, vol. 55, no. 3, 2002, pp. 136–49; Cheryl A. Wilson, 'Almack's and the Silver-Fork Novel', *Women's Writing: The Elizabethan to Victorian Period*, vol. 16, no. 2, 2009, p. 241.

62. Oscar Wilde, *The Picture of Dorian Gray*, ed. Joseph Bristow, Oxford University Press, Oxford, 2006, p. 6.

63. Amelia Rauser, *Caricature Unmasked: Irony, Authenticity and Individualism in Eighteenth-Century English Prints*, University of Delaware Press, Newark DE, 2008, p. 76.

64. Shearer West, 'The Darly Macaroni Prints and the Politics of "Private Man"', *Eighteenth-Century Life*, vol. 25, no. 2, 2001, p. 176.

65. Horace Walpole, *Clotworthy Skeffington*, c.1765, pen and ink, 11.2 × 6.6 cm; Lewis Walpole Library, Yale University, SH Contents W218 no. 5 Box 120 (lwlpr15045).

66. Horace Walpole, letter to George Selwyn, 12 January 1766, in Walpole, *Correspondence*, vol. 30, p. 211.

67. Anon, 'Lord —— [Grandison] or the Nosegay Macaroni', *Macaroni and Theatrical Magazine*, February 1773, p. 193.

68. *Macaroni Dresses for 1740 and 1776*, in *New Lottery Magazine*, *c.* 1776; Lewis Walpole Library, Yale University, 776.00.00.08 (lwlpro3998).

69. John Blatchly, 'Matthias Darly and the Macaroni Print Shop', *Bookplate Journal*, vol. 9, no. 1, 2011, p. 18 n1.

70. Edward Topham, *The Macaroni Print Shop*, Darly, London, 14 July 1772; Lewis Walpole Library, Yale University, 772.07.14.02 Impression 1 (lwlpro3416).

71. Mary Dorothy George, *Catalogue of Political and Personal Satires Preserved in the Department of Prints and Drawings in the British Museum*, Volume 5: *1771–1783*, British Museum, London, 1935, p. xxviii; Mary Dorothy George, *English Political Caricature to 1792: A Study of Opinion and Propaganda*, Oxford University Press, Oxford, 1959, pp. 147–8.

72. On the issue of body shapes, see Constance C. McPhee and Nadine M. Orenstein, *Infinite Jest: Caricature and Satire from Leonardo to Levine*, Metropolitan Museum of Art, New York, 2011, p. 46, no. 26.

73. John Smith, *Miss Macaroni and Her Gallant at a Print-Shop*, John Bowles, London, 2 April 1773; Lewis Walpole Library, Yale University, 773.04.02.01+ (lwlpro3645).

74. Eirwen E.C. Nicholson, 'Consumers and Spectators: The Public of the Political Print in Eighteenth–Century England', *History*, vol. 81, no. 261, 1996, pp. 5–21.

75. Robert Dighton, *The Macaroni Painter, or Billy Dimple Sitting for His Picture*, 25 September 1772; Lewis Walpole Library, Yale University, 772.09.25.01.1+ Impression 1 (lwlpro3463).

76. McNeil, *Pretty Gentlemen*, pp. 174–5.

77. McNeil, 'Dissipation and Extravagance'.

78. *The Paintress of Maccaroni's*, Carington Bowles, London, 13 April 1772; Lewis Walpole Library, Yale University, 772.04.13.01.2+ (Lwlpro3301).

79. Peter McNeil, 'Conspicuous Waist: Queer Dress in the "Long Eighteenth Century"', in Valerie Steele (ed.), *A Queer History of Fashion: From the Closet to the Catwalk*, Fashion Institute of Technology, New York, 2013, p. 94.

80. Susan C. Shapiro, '"Yon Plumed Dandebrat": Male Effeminacy in English Satire and Criticism', *Review of English Studies*, vol. 39, no. 155, 1988, p. 409; Amelia Rauser, 'Hair, Authenticity, and the Self-Made Macaroni', *Eighteenth-Century Studies*, vol. 38, no. 1, 2004, p. 101.

81. Peter McNeil, '"That Doubtful Gender": Macaroni Dress and Male Sexualities', *Fashion Theory: The Journal of Dress, Body and Culture*, vol. 3, no. 4, 1999, p. 418; emphasis in original.

82. McNeil, *Pretty Gentlemen*, p. 214.

83. *How d'Ye Like Me?*, 18 November 1772, Carington Bowles, London; Lewis Walpole Library, Yale University, 772.11.19.02+ (lwlpro3503). See also McNeil, '"That Doubtful Gender"', pp. 424–5.

84. Emma Donoghue, 'Imagined More than Women: Lesbians as Hermaphrodites, 1671–1766', *Women's History Review*, vol. 2, no. 2, 1993, pp. 199–216; Cathy McClive, 'Masculinity on Trial: Penises, Hermaphrodites and the Uncertain Male Body in Early Modern France', *History Workshop Journal*, vol. 68, no. 1, 2009, pp. 45–68.

85. British Museum, Department of Prints and Drawings, 1877,1013.837 and 1935,0522.1.119.

86. Margaret K. Powell and Joseph R. Roach, 'Big Hair', *Eighteenth-Century Studies*, vol. 38, no. 1, 2004, pp. 79–99.

87. Lynn M. Festa, 'Personal Effects: Wigs and Possessive Individualism in the Long Eighteenth Century', *Eighteenth-Century Life*, vol. 29, no. 2, 2005, p. 82.

88. McNeil, *Pretty Gentlemen*, p. 48.

89. Philip Dawe, *The Macaroni: A Real Character at the Late Masquerade*, John Bowles, London, 3 July 1773; Lewis Walpole Library, Yale University, 773,07.03.01.2+ (lwlpr03715).

90. David Porter, 'Monstrous Beauty: Eighteenth-Century Fashion and the Aesthetics of the Chinese Taste', *Eighteenth-Century Studies*, vol. 35, no. 3, 2002, p. 404.

91. Tita Chico, *Designing Women: The Dressing Room in Eighteenth-Century English Literature and Culture*, Bucknell University Press, Lewisburg PA, 2005, p. 44.

92. Mimi Hellman, 'Interior Motives: Seduction by Decoration in Eighteenth-Century France', in Harold Koda and Andrew Bolton (eds), *Dangerous Liaisons: Fashion and Furniture in the Eighteenth Century*, Yale University Press, New Haven CT, 2006, p. 23.

93. Rauser, *Caricature Unmasked*, p. 60.

94. Horace Walpole, letter to William Hamilton, 22 February 1774, in Walpole, *Correspondence*, vol. 35, p. 419.

95. Christoph Heyl, 'The Metamorphosis of the Mask in Seventeenth- and Eighteenth-Century London', in Efrat Tseëlon (ed.), *Masquerade and Identities: Essays on Gender, Sexuality and Marginality*, Routledge, London, 2003, p. 119.

96. Diana Donald, *Followers of Fashion: Graphic Satires from the Georgian Period, Prints from the British Museum*, Hayward Gallery Publishing, London, 2002, p. 35.

97. McNeil, *Pretty Gentlemen*, p. 74.

98. Robert W. Jones, 'Notes on *The Camp*: Women, Effeminacy and the Military in Late Eighteenth-Century Literature', *Textual Practice*, vol. 11, no. 3, 1997, p. 464; Matthew McCormack, *Embodying the Militia in Georgian England*, Oxford University Press, Oxford, 2015, p. 61.

99. After Henry Bunbury, *The Relief*, 1781, William Dickinson, London; British Museum, Department of Prints and Drawings, J,6.48.

100. Anon., 'News', *Morning Herald and General Advertiser*, 21 July 1781.

101. Richard St George Mansergh, *Refin'd Taste*, c. May 1773, M. Darly, London; Lewis Walpole Library, Yale University, Folio 724 776D (lwlpr 37109b). See also McNeil, 'Dissipation and Extravagance', p. 102.

102. Quoted in Rictor Norton (ed.), 'The First Public Debate about Homosexuality in England: The Case of Captain Jones, 1772', *Homosexuality in Eighteenth-Century England: A Sourcebook*, 2007, http://rictornorton.co.uk/eighteen/jones1.htm.

103. Anon., 'News', *Morning Chronicle and London Advertiser*, 8 August 1772.

104. Anon., 'News', *London Evening News*, 6 August 1772.

105. Anon., 'News', *Bingley's London Journal*, 12–19 September 1772.

106. Letter, 4 November 1772, in Anon., 'Juvenis', letter to the printer, *Middlesex Journal, or Universal Evening Post*, 7–10 November 1772; emphasis in original.

107. Jody Greene, 'Public Secrets: Sodomy and the Pillory in the Eighteenth Century and Beyond', *Eighteenth Century*, vol. 44, no. 2–3, 2003, p. 225.

108. *Ganymede and Jack-Catch*, 1771, M. Darly, London; Lewis Walpole Library, Yale University, Folio 724 776D (lwlpr37112a).
109. Anon., 'Punch', 'A Card', *Morning Chronicle and London Advertiser*, 7 August 1772; emphasis in original.
110. Anon., *The Vauxhall Affray; or, the Macaronies Defeated*, J. Williams, London, 1773; Miles Ogborn, 'Locating the Macaroni: Luxury, Sexuality and Vision in Vauxhall Gardens', *Textual Practice*, vol. 11, no. 3, 1997, pp. 445–61.
111. Anon., *The Vauxhall Affray*, p. 14.
112. Quoted in Rictor Norton (ed.), 'The Macaroni Club: Newspaper Items', *Homosexuality in Eighteenth-Century England: A Sourcebook*, 2005, www.rictornorton. co.uk/eighteen/macaroni.htm.
113. West, 'The Darly Macaroni Prints', p. 172.
114. Michèle Cohen, 'The Grand Tour: Language, National Identity and Masculinity', *Changing English*, vol. 8, no. 2, 2001, p. 130; McNeil, *Pretty Gentlemen*, p. 98.
115. Peter Mandler, *Aristocratic Government in the Age of Reform: Whigs and Liberals, 1830–1852*, Oxford University Press, Oxford, 1990, p. 16.
116. Hannah Greig, *The Beau Monde: Fashionable Society in Georgian London*, Oxford University Press, Oxford, 2013, p. 236.
117. Overview in Thomas A. King, *The Gendering of Men, 1600–1750*, Volume 2: *Queer Articulations*, University of Wisconsin Press, Madison WI, 2008, pp. xix–xxii.
118. Mackie, *Rakes, Highwaymen, and Pirates*, p. 183.
119. D.A. Coward, 'Attitudes to Homosexuality in Eighteenth-Century France', *Journal of European Studies* 10, 1980, p. 245.
120. Karen Harvey, 'The History of Masculinity, circa 1650–1800', *Journal of British Studies*, vol. 44, no. 2, 2005, p. 309.
121. Michèle Cohen, '"Manners" Make the Man: Politeness, Chivalry, and the Construction of Masculinity, 1750–1830', *Journal of British Studies*, vol. 44, no. 2, 2005, p. 313.
122. Leslie G. Mitchell, *Charles James Fox*, Oxford University Press, Oxford, 1992, p. 92.
123. Anna Clark, 'The Chevalier d'Eon, Rousseau, and New Ideas of Gender, Sex and the Self in the Late Eighteenth Century', in Simon Burrows, Jonathan Conlin, Russell Goulbourne and Valerie Mainz (eds), *The Chevalier d'Eon and His Worlds: Gender, Espionage and Politics in the Eighteenth Century*, Continuum, London, 2010, p. 190.
124. Henry Mackenzie, *The Man of Feeling*, T. Cadell, London, 1771.
125. Dror Wahrman, *The Making of the Modern Self: Identity and Culture in Eighteenth-Century England*, Yale University Press, New Haven CT, 2004, p. 38.
126. Laura J. Rosenthal, 'The Sublime, the Beautiful, "The Siddons"', in Jessica Munns and Penny Richards (eds), *The Clothes that Wear Us: Essays on Dressing and Transgressing in Eighteenth-Century Culture*, Associated University Presses, Cranbury NJ, 1999, p. 61.
127. George Haggerty, '*O Lachrymarum Fons*: Tears, Poetry and Desire in Gray', *Eighteenth-Century Studies* 30, 1996, p. 83. See also Philip Carter, "An 'Effeminate' or an 'Efficient' Nation? Masculinity and Eighteenth-Century Social

Documentary', *Textual Practice*, vol. 11, no. 3, 1997, p. 439; G.J. Barker-Benfield, *The Culture of Sensibility: Sex and Society in Eighteenth-Century Britain*, University of Chicago Press, Chicago IL, 1992, pp. 340–42; Michael Rowland, 'Shame and Futile Masculinity: Feeling Backwards in Henry Mackenzie's *Man of Feeling*', *Eighteenth-Century Fiction*, vol. 31, no. 3, 2019, pp. 529–48.

128. Joseph Wright, *Sir Brooke Boothby*, 1781, oil on canvas, 148.6 × 207.6 cm; Tate Gallery, London, N04132.

129. Jacques [also spelt Sjaak] Zonneveld, *Sir Brooke Boothby: Rousseau's Roving Baronet Friend*, De Jacques Nieuwe Haagsche, Voorburg, 2004, p. 161.

130. Jean-Jacques Rousseau, *Dialogues*, Jackson, Lichfield, 1780.

131. Richard A. Etlin, *In Defense of Humanism: Value in the Arts and Letters*, Cambridge University Press, Cambridge, 1996, p. 153.

132. Judy Egerton, *Wright of Derby*, Tate, London, 1990, pp. 116–18.

133. Joseph Wright, *Thomas Day*, 1770, oil on canvas, 121.9 × 97.8 cm; National Portrait Gallery, London, NPG 2490.

134. Joshua Reynolds, *Horace Walpole*, 1756–57, oil on canvas, 127.2 × 101.8 cm, National Portrait Gallery, London, NPG 6520; David Mannings, *Sir Joshua Reynolds: A Complete Catalogue of His Paintings*, 2 vols, Yale University Press, New Haven CT, 2000, vol. 1, pp. 458–9.

135. Henry Bunbury, *Front, Side View, and Back of a Modern Fine Gentleman*, 24 March 1783, in *Etchings by Henry William Bunbury, Esq; and After His Designs*, vol. 2, p. 16, Lewis Walpole Library, Yale University, Folio 49 3563 2; John Carter, *Horace Walpole After Breakfast, Before Dinner and After Dinner*, 1788, drawing, watercolour, Lewis Walpole Library, Yale University, Folio 33 30 Copy 22 (Oversize) (lwlpr 16676).

136. This material is explored in detail in Dominic Janes, *Oscar Wilde Prefigured: Queer Fashioning and British Caricature, 1750–1900*, University of Chicago Press, Chicago IL, 2016, pp. 55–85.

137. William Guthrie, *A Reply to the Counter Address*, W. Nicoll, London, 1764, p. 7.

138. Horace Walpole, letter to Henry Conway, 1 September 1764, in Walpole, *Correspondence*, vol. 38, p. 437.

139. John Brewer, *The Pleasures of the Imagination: English Culture in the Eighteenth Century*, HarperCollins, London, 1997, p. 81; Philip Carter, *Men and the Emergence of Polite Society, Britain, 1660–1800*, Longman, Harlow, 2001, p. 156.

140. Thomas A. King, *The Gendering of Men, 1600–1750*, Volume 1: *The English Phallus*, University of Wisconsin Press, Madison WI, 2004, p. 246; emphasis in original.

141. Vic Gatrell, *City of Laughter: Sex and Satire in Eighteenth-Century London*, Atlantic, London, 2006, p. 111.

142. David M. Robinson, *Closeted Writing and Lesbian and Gay Literature: Classical, Early Modern, Eighteenth Century*, Ashgate, Aldershot, 2006, p. 69; Michael S. Kimmel, 'Masculinity as Homophobia: Fear, Shame and Silence in the Construction of Gender Identity', in Mary M. Gergen and Sara N. Davis (eds), *Toward a New Psychology of Gender*, Routledge, Florence KY, 1997, p. 240.

FOUR

1. Hester Lynch Thrale, undated diary entry *c.*late March/early April 1778, in *Thraliana: The Diary of Mrs. Hester Lynch Thrale (Later Mrs. Piozzi) 1776–1809*, ed. Katharine C. Balderston, 2 vols, Clarendon Press, Oxford, 2nd edn, 1951, vol. 1, pp. 246–7; see also Rictor Norton (ed.), 'Mrs Piozzi's Reminiscences, 1770s-1790s', *Homosexuality in Eighteenth-Century England: A Sourcebook*, 20 April 2003, http://rictornorton.co.uk/eighteen/piozzi.htm.

2. Thrale, diary entry, 30 October 1781, in *Thraliana*, vol. 1, p. 517.

3. Thrale, diary entry, 29 March 1794, in *Thraliana*, vol. 2, pp. 874–5.

4. Dror Wahrman, '"Percy's Prologue": From Gender Play to Gender Panic in Eighteenth-Century England', *Past and Present* 159, May 1998, pp. 113–60.

5. Arthur N. Gilbert, 'Sexual Deviance and Disaster during the Napoleonic Wars', *Albion*, vol. 9, no. 1, 1977, pp. 98–113.

6. *Macaronies Drawn After the Life*, 1 December 1773, M. Darly, London; Lewis Walpole Library, Yale University, 773.12.01.02.1 (lwlpr03758).

7. *Fashionable Ties or Modern Neckcloths*, 1810, n.pub.; Lewis Walpole Library, Yale University, 810.00.00.83+ (lwlpr36241).

8. Ian McCormick, 'Sex, Sodomy, and Death Sentences in the Long Eighteenth Century', in Jolene Zigarovich (ed.), *Sex and Death in Eighteenth-Century Literature*, Routledge, New York, 2013, p. 292.

9. Keith Thomas, 'Afterword', in Karen Harvey (ed.), *The Kiss in History*, Manchester University Press, Manchester, 2005, pp. 193–4.

10. Isaac Cruikshank, *A New French Bussing Match, or, More Cursing and Swearig* [sic] *for the Assembly*, S.W. Fores, London, 16 July 1790; Lewis Walpole Library, Yale University, 792.07.16.01.1 (lwlpr07516).

11. Quoted in Dror Wahrman, *The Making of the Modern Self: Identity and Culture in Eighteenth-Century England*, Yale University Press, New Haven CT, 2004, p. 65; see also Christopher Breward, *The Suit: Form, Function and Style*, Reaktion, London, 2016, pp. 41–3.

12. Thomas Moore [pseud. Thomas Brown], *Replies to the Letters of the Fudge Family in Paris*, Pinnock and Maunder, London, 1818, p. 162; emphasis in original.

13. Anon., *Fashion. Dedicated to All the Town. By the Author of the Greeks. – The Pigeons. – Modern Belles. – Fashionable Anecdotes, &c. Illustrated* [by George Cruikshank], 5th edn, Stockdale, London, 1818, p. 50.

14. Douglas Fordham and Adrienne Albright, 'The Eighteenth-Century Print: Tracing the Contours of a Field', *Literature Compass*, vol. 9, no. 8, 2012, p. 517.

15. Isaac Cruikshank, *The Knowing Crops*, *c.* 12 May 1794, Laurie and Whittle, London; Lewis Walpole Library, Yale University, 794.05.12.55 (lwlpr08314). See also Edward J. Nygren, *Isaac Cruikshank and the Politics of Parody: Watercolors in the Huntingdon Collection*, Huntingdon Library Press, San Marino CA, 1994, p. 34, no. 14; Elizabeth Amann, *Dandyism in the Age of Revolution: The Art of the Cut*, University of Chicago Press, Chicago IL, 2015, p. 185.

16. James Gillray, *'Monstrosities' of 1799: Scene, Kensington Gardens*, 25 June 1799, Hannah Humphrey, London; Lewis Walpole Library, Yale University, 799.06.25.03+ (lwlpr 09512).

17. Robert Godfrey, *James Gillray: The Art of Caricature*, Tate, London, 2001, p. 213, Fig. 197.

18. Anon., *Modern Bloods, or, Acoat-ation*, 22 September 1803, Laurie and Whittle, London; Lewis Walpole Library, Yale University, 803.09.22.01 (lwlpr10430).

19. Nygren, *Isaac Cruikshank*, p. 156, no. 117.

20. George Cruikshank, *Money Hunting Deigned [sic] by an Amature*, 10 January 1823, G. Humphrey, London; Lewis Walpole Library, Yale University, 823.01.10.01 (lwlpr12482).

21. Saul David, *Prince of Pleasure: The Prince of Wales and the Making of the Regency*, Little, Brown, London, 1998, p. 284.

22. Amann, *Dandyism*, p. 196.

23. Ellen Moers, *The Dandy: Brummell to Beerbohm*, Secker & Warburg, London, 1960, p. 26.

24. Ian Kelly, *Beau Brummell: The Ultimate Dandy*, Hodder & Stoughton, London, 2005, p. 299.

25. Jane Rendell, 'Displaying Sexuality: Gendered Identities and the Early Nineteenth-Century Street', in Nicholas R. Fyfe (eds), *Images of the Street: Planning, Identity, and Control in Public Space*, Routledge, London, 1998, p. 80.

26. Thorsten Botz-Bornstein, 'Rule-Following in Dandyism: "Style" as an Overcoming of "Rule" and "Structure"', *Modern Language Review*, vol. 90, no. 2, 1995, p. 289.

27. Lisa O'Connell, 'The Libertine, the Rake and the Dandy: Personae, Styles, and Affects', in E.L. McCallum and Mikko Tuhkanen (eds), *The Cambridge History of Gay and Lesbian Literature*, Cambridge University Press, Cambridge, 2014, p. 233.

28. William Jesse, *The Life of George Brummell, Esq., Commonly Called Beau Brummell*, Clarke & Beeton, London, 1854 (1844), p. 32.

29. Moers, *The Dandy*, p. 154,

30. Fred Kaplan, *Thomas Carlyle: A Biography*, Cambridge University Press, Cambridge, 1983, pp. 157–60; William J.F. Keenan, 'Introduction: *Sartor Resartus* Restored: Dress Studies in Carlylean Perspective', in Keenan (ed.), *Dressed to Impress: Looking the Part*, Berg, Oxford, 2001, p. 33.

31. Thomas Carlyle, *Sartor Resartus: The Life and Opinions of Herr Teufelsdröckh in Three Books*, Chapman & Hall, London, 1869, p. 70.

32. Michael Carter, 'Thomas Carlyle and *Sartor Resartus*', in Peter McNeil and Vicki Karaminas (eds), *The Men's Fashion Reader*, Berg, Oxford, 2009, pp. 78–81.

33. Jane Welsh Carlyle, letter 13 April 1845, in *A New Selection of Her Letters*, ed. Trudy Bliss, Victor Gollancz, London, 1949, p. 159, quoted and discussed in Christopher Breward, 'Masculine Pleasures: Metropolitan Identities and the Commercial Sites of Dandyism, 1790–1840', *London Journal*, vol. 28, no. 1, 2003, p. 60.

34. George Cruikshank, *Ancient Military Dandies of 1450... Modern Military Dandies of 1819*, 8 February 1819, G. Humphrey, London; Lewis Walpole Library, Yale University, 819.02.08.01+ (lwlpr12051).

35. Christopher Hibbert, *George IV: Regent and King, 1811–1830*, Allen Lane, London, 1973, pp. 120–31.

36. Mary Dorothy George, *Catalogue of Political and Personal Satires Preserved in the*

Department of Prints and Drawings in the British Museum, Volume 9: *1811–19*, British Museum, London, 1949, pp. 654–6, no. 12749. On corsets for men, see Valerie Steele, *The Corset: A Cultural History*, Yale University Press, New Haven CT, 2001, p. 38; Sean Cole, *The Story of Men's Underwear*, Parkstone, London, 2010, pp. 46–7.

37. Robert L. Patten, 'Signifying Shape in Pan-European Caricature', in Todd Porterfield (ed.), *The Efflorescence of Caricature, 1759–1838*, Ashgate, Farnham, 2011, p. 147.

38. Anon., 'The Late Emperor of China, Kien Long', *Morning Herald*, 27 December 1799.

39. William Hone, *The Man in the Moon: or, the 'Devil to Pay'. With Thirteen Cuts* [by George Cruikshank], William Hone, London, 1820; Robert L. Patten, *George Cruikshank's Life, Times, and Art*, Volume 1: *1792–1835*, Lutterworth, London, 1992, pp. 163–9.

40. Patten, *George Cruikshank's Life*, p. 60.

41. Ibid., p. 75.

42. Robert L. Patten, 'Cruikshank, (Isaac) Robert (1789–1856)', *Oxford Dictionary of National Biography*, Oxford University Press, Oxford, 2004, www.oxforddnb.com/view/article/6845.

43. Blanchard Jerrold, *The Life of George Cruikshank: In Two Epochs*, 2 vols, Chatto & Windus, London, 1882, vol. 1, pp. 49–54.

44. Patten, *George Cruikshank's Life*, p. 209.

45. Ibid., p. 217; Frank Palmeri, 'Cruikshank, Thackeray, and the Victorian Eclipse of Satire', *SEL Studies in English Literature 1500–1900*, vol. 44, no. 4, 2004, pp. 753–7.

46. George Soames Layard, *George Cruikshank's Portraits of Himself*, W.T. Spencer, London, 1897, pp. 14–15.

47. Attributed to Alfred Henry Forrester/Daniel Maclise, *George Cruikshank*, 1833, pencil, 30.8 × 23.8 cm; National Portrait Gallery, London, NPG 5170. See also Dominic Janes, *Oscar Wilde Prefigured: Queer Fashioning and British Caricature, 1750–1900*, University of Chicago Press, Chicago IL, 2016, pp. 107–8.

48. Adam Chill, 'Boundaries of Britishness: Boxing, Minorities, and Identity in Late-Georgian Britain', Ph.D. dissertation, Boston College, 2007, p. 49.

49. George Smeeton (ed.), *Doings in London; or, Day and Night Scenes of the Frauds, Frolics, Manners, and Depravities of the Metropolis*, 7th edn, O. Hodgson, London, c. 1840 (1828), p. 195.

50. George Cruikshank, *The Boxers Arms*, c. 1819, watercolour with pencil, pen and ink, 38 × 26.6 cm; Lewis Walpole Library, Yale University, Drawings C889 no. 6 Box D115 (lwlpr12113). This image was the basis for a print with the same title published by George Humphrey, London, 1819.

51. George Cruikshank, *The Dandies Coat of Arms*, c. 1819, watercolour with pencil, pen and ink, 37.5 × 25.5 cm; Lewis Walpole Library, Yale University, Drawings C889 no. 6 Box D115 (lwlpr12064). This image was the basis for a print with the same title published by Thomas Tegg, London, 1819.

52. Compare Catherine Molineux, 'Hogarth's Fashionable Slaves: Moral Corruption in Eighteenth-Century London', *ELH*, vol. 72, no. 2, 2005, pp. 495–520.

53. William Makepeace Thackeray, *The Four Georges*, Harper, New York, 1860, p. 185.
54. David Kurnick, 'Thackeray's Theater of Interiority', *Victorian Studies*, vol. 48, no. 2, 2006, p. 258.
55. George, *Catalogue of Political and Personal Satires*, vol. 9, p. 975, no. 13395.
56. Isaac Robert Cruikshank, *A Dandy Fainting, or, An Exquisite in Fits: Scene a Private Box Opera*, 11 December 1818, G. Humphrey, London, Lewis Walpole Library, Yale University, 818.12.11.01+ (lwlpr 11990); see George, *Catalogue of Political and Personal Satires*, vol. 9, p. li.
57. Diana Donald, *Followers of Fashion: Graphic Satires from the Georgian Period, Prints from the British Museum*, Hayward Gallery Publishing, London, 2002, p. 70.
58. Alfred Henry Forrester, *Beauties of Brighton*, 1825, pen, ink and wash, 22.4 × 32.9 cm, Victoria and Albert Museum, London, P.6–1932; George Cruikshank, after Alfred Henry Forrester, *Beauties of Brighton*, 1 March 1826, S. Knight, London, 25 × 35.2 cm, British Museum, Department of Prints and Drawings, 1859, 0316.189.
59. Shaun Regan, '"Pranks, Unfit for Naming": Pope, Curll, and the "Satirical Grotesque"', *Eighteenth Century*, vol. 46, no. 1, 2005, pp. 37–57.
60. Anon., *The Dandies' Ball; or, High Life in the City. Embellished with Sixteen Coloured Engravings* [by Robert Cruikshank], John Marshall, London, 1819; Gregory Dart, *Metropolitan Art and Literature 1810–1840: Cockney Adventures*, Cambridge University Press, Cambridge, 2012, p. 121.
61. Miranda Gill, 'The Myth of the Female Dandy', *French Studies*, vol. 61, no. 2, 2007, p. 173.
62. Pierce Egan, *Boxiana; or, Sketches of Antient [sic] and Modern Pugilism*, Smeeton, London, 1812.
63. William Makepeace Thackeray, *An Essay on the Genius of George Cruikshank, with Numerous Illustrations of His Works (from the 'Westminster Review', no. LXVI)*, Henry Hooper, London, 1840, p. 24.
64. Ibid., p. 17.
65. Jerrold, *Life of George Cruikshank*, vol. 1, pp. 124–5.
66. Patten, *George Cruikshank's Life*, p. 223.
67. Isaac Robert and George Cruikshank, *Jerry in Training for a 'Swell'*, 31 August 1820, London, Sherwood, Neely and Jones, Lewis Walpole Library, Yale University, 820.08.31.02 (lwlpr 12210); Pierce Egan, *Life in London; or, the Day and Night Scenes of Jerry Hawthorne, Esq., and His Elegant Friend Corinthian Tom, Accompanied by Bob Logic, the Oxonian, in Their Rambles and Sprees Through the Metropolis*, Sherwood, Neely and Jones, London, 1821, opposite p. 146.
68. Egan, *Life in London*, p. 146; emphases in original.
69. Ibid., opposite p. 252.
70. Ibid., opposite p. 250.
71. Ibid., p. 146 n15; emphasis in original.
72. Andrew Elfenbein, 'Byronism and the Work of Homosexual Performance in Early Victorian England', *Modern Language Quarterly*, vol. 54, no. 4, 1993, p. 544.
73. Quoted in Elfenbein, 'Byronism', p. 544; emphasis in original.
74. Laura George, 'The Emergence of the Dandy', *Literature Compass*, vol. 1, no. 1, 2004, p. 10; emphasis in original.

75. Thomas Phillips, *George Gordon, Lord Byron in Albanian Dress, c.*1835, based on a work of 1813, oil on canvas, 76.5 × 63.9 cm; National Portrait Gallery, London, NPG 142.

76. Louis Crompton, *Byron and Greek Love: Homophobia in 19th-Century England*, Faber & Faber, London, 1985, pp. 185, 404.

77. Emily A. Bernhard Jackson, 'Least Like Saints: The Vexed Issue of Byron's Sexuality', *Byron Journal* 38, 2010, p. 34.

78. Quoted and discussed in Elfenbein, 'Byronism', p. 559; see also David S. Neff, 'Bitches, Mollies, and Tommies: Byron, Masculinity, and the History of Sexualities', *Journal of the History of Sexuality*, vol. 11, no. 3, 2002, p. 407.

79. Peter Drucker, 'Byron and Ottoman Love: Orientalism, Europeanisation and Same-Sex Sexualities in the Early Nineteenth-Century Levant', *Journal of European Studies*, vol. 42, no. 2, 2012, p. 145.

80. Michael Eberle-Sinatra, 'A Revaluation of Leigh Hunt's *Lord Byron and Some of His Contemporaries*', *Byron Journal* 29, 2001, pp. 17–26.

81. Leigh Hunt, *Lord Byron and Some of His Contemporaries*, Henry Colburn, London, 1828, p. 88.

82. Ibid., p. 141.

83. Ibid., p. 91.

84. Andrew Elfenbein, 'Byron: Gender and Sexuality', in Drummond Bone (ed.), *The Cambridge Companion to Byron*, Cambridge University Press, Cambridge, 2004, p. 57.

85. Neff, 'Bitches, Mollies, and Tommies', p. 430.

86. William Kuhn, *Disraeli: The Politics of Pleasure*, Free Press, London, 2006, pp. 153–55; Robert O'Kell, *Disraeli: The Romance of Politics*, University of Toronto Press, Toronto ON, 2013, p. 146.

87. Attributed to Alfred Henry Forrester/Daniel Maclise, *Benjamin Disraeli*, early 1830s, pen and ink, 25.2 × 20.1 cm, National Portrait Gallery, London, NPG D34564; Judith Law Fisher, '"In the Present Famine of Anything Substantial": Fraser's "Portraits" and the Construction of Literary Celebrity; or, "Personality, Personality is the Appetite of the Age"', *Victorian Periodicals Review*, vol. 39, no. 2, 2006, p. 111.

88. George Cruikshank, *Monstrosities of 1788 and 1823*, 1 January 1823, George Humphrey, London; British Museum, Department of Prints and Drawings, 1859,0316.163.

89. Jane Rendell, *The Pursuit of Pleasure: Gender, Space and Architecture in Regency London*, Athlone, London, 2002, p. 53.

90. Vic Gatrell, *City of Laughter: Sex and Satire in Eighteenth-Century London*, Atlantic, London, 2006, p. 155.

91. J. Bisset, *Dandyism Displayed, or the Follies of the Ton*, Duncombe, London, n.d., p. 7.

92. Laura George, 'Byron, Brummell, and the Fashionable Figure', *Byron Journal* 24, 1996, p. 33.

93. Fisher, '"In the Present Famine"', p. 112.

94. Robert B. Brough, 'Resemblances', *Lloyd's Weekly Newspaper*, 17 April 1859, p. 8.

95. Moe Meyer, 'The Signifying Invert: Camp and the Performance of Nineteenth–Century Sexology', *Text and Performance Quarterly*, vol. 15, no. 4, 1995, p. 265,

discussing J. Redding Ware, *Passing English of the Victorian Era: A Dictionary of Heterodox English, Slang and Phrase*, George Routledge, London, 1909, p. 61.

96. Meyer, 'The Signifying Invert', p. 276.

97. Jules-Amédée Barbey d'Aurevilly, *Du Dandysme et de George Brummell*, Privately printed, Caen, 1845; George Walden, *Who Is a Dandy? On Dandyism and Beau Brummell*, Gibson, London, 2002.

98. Moers, *The Dandy*, p. 309; Walden, *Who Is a Dandy?*, pp. 45, 148.

99. Lauren Gillingham, 'The Novel of Fashion Redressed: Bulwer-Lytton's *Pelham* in a 19th-Century Context', *Victorian Review*, vol. 32, no. 1, 2006, p. 80.

FIVE

1. Henry Stephen Ludlow, *Athletics v. Aesthetics*, in *Illustrated London News*, 17 March 1883, p. 377; see also Merlin Holland, *The Wilde Album*, Fourth Estate, London, 1997, p. 50.

2. Anon., *The New Aesthete-Athlete Era*, in *Funny Folks*, 6 April 1881, p. 116.

3. Brent Shannon, 'Refashioning Men: Fashion, Masculinity, and the Cultivation of the Male Consumer in Britain, 1860–1914', *Victorian Studies*, vol. 46, no. 4, 2004, p. 625.

4. George L. Mosse, *The Image of Man: The Creation of Modern Masculinity*, Oxford University Press, Oxford, 1996, p. 52; Christopher Breward, *The Hidden Consumer: Masculinities, Fashion and City Life, 1860–1914*, Manchester University Press, Manchester, 1999, p. 172.

5. Shannon, 'Refashioning Men', p. 627 n8; Peter K. Andersson, '"High Collars and Principles": The Late–Victorian World of the Masher', *Gender and History*, vol. 31, no. 2, 2019, pp. 422–43.

6. James Eli Adams, *Dandies and Desert Saints: Styles of Victorian Manhood*, Cornell University Press, Ithaca NY, 1995, p. 174.

7. Ellen Moers, *The Dandy: Brummell to Beerbohm*, Secker & Warburg, London, 1960, pp. 273, 281.

8. Rhonda K. Garelick, *Rising Star: Dandyism, Gender, and Performance in the Fin de Siècle*, Princeton University Press, Princeton NJ, 1998, p. 38.

9. Linda C. Dowling, 'The Aesthetes and the Eighteenth Century', *Victorian Studies*, vol. 20, no. 4, 1977, p. 373; see also Francis O'Gorman and Katherine Turner (eds), *The Victorians and the Eighteenth Century: Reassessing the Tradition*, Ashgate, Aldershot, 2004.

10. Eugenia Zuroski Jenkins, *A Taste for China: English Subjectivity and the Prehistory of Orientalism*, Oxford University Press, Oxford, 2013.

11. George Du Maurier, *Intellectual Epicures*, in *Punch* 70, 5 February 1876, p. 33.

12. Anon., 'The Japanese Ambassadors at North Seaton Colliery', *Liverpool Mercury*, 30 May 1862.

13. Anne Anderson, '"Fearful Consequences ... of Living Up to One's Teapot": Men, Women and "Cultcha" in the English Aesthetic Movement, *c.* 1870–1900', *Victorian Literature and Culture*, vol. 37, no. 1, 2009, p. 243.

14. James Hadley, *Aesthetic Teapot*, 1882, Museum of Royal Worcester, 2561; Anderson, '"Fearful Consequences"', p. 220, Fig. 220.

15. J.B. Bullen, *The Pre-Raphaelite Body: Fear and Desire in Painting, Poetry and Criticism*, Oxford University Press, Oxford, 1998, p. 212.

16. Janice Nadelhaft, '*Punch* and the Syncretics: An Early Victorian Prologue to the Aesthetic Movement', *Studies in English Literature, 1500–1900*, vol. 15, no. 4, 1975, pp. 627–40; Anon., '*Punch's* literature', *Punch* 1, 5 September 1841, p. 86.

17. George Du Maurier, *A Love Agony. Design by Maudle*, in *Punch* 78, 5 June 1880, p. 254. See also Michael Hatt, 'Space, Surface, Self: Homosexuality and the Aesthetic Interior', *Visual Culture in Britain*, vol. 8, no. 1, 2007, p. 106; Dennis Denisoff, '"Men of My Own Sex": Genius, Sexuality, and George Du Maurier's Artists', in Richard Dellamora (ed.), *Victorian Sexual Dissidence*, University of Chicago Press, Chicago IL, 1999, pp. 147–69.

18. Jonathan H. Grossman, 'The Mythic Svengali: Anti-Aestheticism in *Trilby*', *Studies in the Novel*, vol. 28, no. 4, 1996, p. 527; Talia Schaffer, 'Fashioning Aestheticism by Aestheticizing Fashion: Wilde, Beerbohm, and the Male Aesthetes' Sartorial Codes', *Victorian Literature and Culture*, vol. 28, no. 1, 2000, p. 49.

19. George Du Maurier, *Nincompoopiana*, in *Punch* 77, 20 December 1879, p. 282; Dennis Denisoff, *Aestheticism and Sexual Parody, 1840–1940*, Cambridge University Press, Cambridge, 2001, p. 81.

20. George Du Maurier, *Maudle on the Choice of a Profession*, in *Punch* 80, 12 February 1881, p. 62; emphasis in original. See also Anne Anderson, 'The Mutual Admiration Society, or Mr Punch Against the Aesthetes', *Popular Narrative Media*, vol. 2, no. 1, 2009, p. 80; Heather Marcovitch, *The Art of the Pose: Oscar Wilde's Performance Theory*, Peter Lang, Bern, 2010, p. 54.

21. Anon., 'The Man in the Street', *Funny Folks*, 4 February 1882, p. 34.

22. Andrew Elfenbein, *Byron and the Victorians*, Cambridge University Press, Cambridge, 1995, pp. 206–46.

23. Anon., 'News', *Funny Folks*, 19 March 1881, p. 82.

24. Dominic Janes, 'Frederick Rolfe's Christmas Cards: Popular Culture and the Construction of Queerness in Late Victorian Britain', *Early Popular Visual Culture*, vol. 10, no. 2, 2012, pp. 105–24; Jamie Horrocks, 'Asses and Aesthetes: Ritualism and Aestheticism in Victorian Periodical Illustration', *Victorian Periodicals Review*, vol. 46, no. 1, 2013, pp. 1–36.

25. Quoted and discussed in Carolyn Williams, 'Parody and Poetic Tradition: Gilbert and Sullivan's *Patience*', *Victorian Poetry*, vol. 46, no. 4, 2008, p. 381.

26. George Cruikshank, *Ancient Military Dandies of 1450…*, 8 February 1819, G. Humphrey, London, Lewis Walpole Library, Yale University, 819.02.08.01+ (lwlpr12051); Anon., 'Shirl', *Guy-ing Him*, in *Funny Folks*, 10 March 1883, p. 77.

27. Charles Ross, 'The Only Jones', *Judy*, 27 April 1881, p. 195.

28. Anon., 'The Man about Town', *Country Gentleman*, 16 May 1885, p. 617.

29. Anon., 'The Man about Town', *Country Gentleman*, 24 February 1883, p. 205; Anon., 'Did Sarony Invent Oscar Wilde?', *Photographic Times*, vol. 13, no. 156, December 1883, pp. 658–9.

30. Anon., *Ye Soul Agonies in ye Life of Oscar Wilde*, n.pub., New York, 1882, p. 12.

31. Anon., 'Essence of Parliament', *Punch* 84, 19 May 1883, p. 240. Note that Benson's wife and children had a wide range of queer relationships, on which

see Simon Goldhill, *A Very Queer Family Indeed: Sex, Religion, and the Bensons in Victorian Britain*, University of Chicago Press, Chicago IL, 2016.

32. R.G. Harper Pennington, *Oscar Wilde*, 1884, oil on canvas; William Andrews Clark Memorial Library, University of California, Los Angeles.

33. Alfred Douglas, *Oscar Wide and Myself*, Duffield, New York, 1914, p. 51.

34. Anon., 'Plain Dress', *Boy's Herald*, 6 July 1878, p. 15.

35. Such as Jonathan Shirland, '"A Singularity of Appearance Counts Doubly in a Democracy of Clothes": Whistler, Fancy Dress and the Camping of Artists' Dress in the Late Nineteenth Century', *Visual Culture in Britain*, vol. 8, no. 1, 2007, p. 27, Fig. 9, cartoon, *c.* 1894.

36. Anon., 'Flashes from the Footlights', *Licensed Victuallers' Mirror*, 10 December 1889, p. 550.

37. Waleska Schwandt, 'Oscar Wilde and the Stereotype of the Aesthete: An Investigation into the Prerequisites of Wilde's Aesthetic Self-Fashioning', in Uwe Böker, Richard Corballis and Julie Hibbard (eds), *The Importance of Reinventing Oscar: Versions of Wilde during the Last 100 Years*, Rodopi, Amsterdam, 2002, p. 91.

38. Anon., 'The Charge of Personating Women', *Morning Post*, 14 May 1870, p. 6; see also Jeffrey Weeks, 'Inverts, Perverts, and Mary-Annes: Male Prostitution and the Regulation of Homosexuality in England in the Nineteenth and Early Twentieth Centuries', in Martin Duberman, Martha Vicinus and George Chauncey (eds), *Hidden from History: Reclaiming the Gay and Lesbian Past*, Penguin, Harmondsworth, 1991, pp. 195–211.

39. *The Queen v. Boulton and Others Before the Lord Chief Justice and a Special Jury: Proceedings on the Trial of the Indictment*, National Archives, DPP 4/6, quoted and discussed in Neil McKenna, *Fanny and Stella: The Young Men Who Shocked Victorian England*, Faber & Faber, London, 2013, p. 331.

40. Charles Upchurch, 'Forgetting the Unthinkable: Cross-Dressers and British Society in the Case of the Queen vs. Boulton and Others', *Gender and History*, vol. 12, no. 1, 2000, p. 149.

41. Ari Adut, 'A Theory of Scandal: Victorians, Homosexuality, and the Fall of Oscar Wilde', *American Journal of Sociology*, vol. 111, no. 1, 2005, p. 243.

42. Laurence Senelick, *The Changing Room: Sex, Drag and Theatre*, Routledge, Abingdon, 2000, p. 306.

43. Anon., *The Sins of the Cities of the Plain, or The Recollections of a Mary-Ann, with Short Essays on Sodomy and Tribadism*, 2 vols, Privately printed, London, 1881, vol. 1, pp. 7–8.

44. Anon., *The Sins*, vol. 1, p. 102.

45. McKenna, *Fanny and Stella*, pp. 216, 230–34.

46. Robert Buchanan, 'The Fleshly School of Poetry', *Contemporary Review* 18, October 1871, p. 335; see also Thaïs E. Morgan, 'Victorian Effeminacies', in Richard Dellamora (ed.), *Victorian Sexual Dissidence*, University of Chicago Press, Chicago IL, 1999, pp. 109–26.

47. Du Maurier, *A Love Agony*, p. 254; see also Jason Edwards, *Alfred Gilbert's Aestheticism: Gilbert amongst Whistler, Wilde, Leighton, Pater and Burne-Jones*, Ashgate, Aldershot, 2006, p. 39.

48. Anon., 'Inverted Relations', *Pall Mall Gazette*, 29 June 1870.

49. Du Maurier, *Intellectual Epicures*, p. 33.
50. Anon., 'A Double Evolution', *Daily News*, 26 August 1891.
51. Anon., *Evolution*, in *Judy*, 24 October 1894, p. 202; see also Richard Scully, 'William Henry Boucher (1837–1906): Illustrator and *Judy* cartoonist', *Victorian Periodicals Review*, vol. 46, no. 4, 2013, p. 445.
52. Linda C. Dowling, 'The Decadent and the New Woman in the 1890s', *Nineteenth-Century Fiction*, vol. 33, no. 4, 1979, pp. 434–53; Emma Churchman Hewitt, 'The "New Woman" in Her Relation to the "New Man"', *Westminster Review*, vol. 147, no. 3, 1897, pp. 335–7.
53. Tara MacDonald, 'Doctors, Dandies and the New Man: Ella Hepworth Dixon and Late-Victorian Masculinities', *Women's Writing: The Elizabethan to Victorian Period*, vol. 19, no. 1, 2012, p. 44.
54. Anon., 'Young Men Who Are Got Up', *Huddersfield Daily Chronicle*, 4 April 1893, p. 4.
55. Anon., 'Human Novelties', *Hearth and Home*, 26 July 1894, p. 379.
56. Ibid.
57. George Gatcombe, 'The New Woman', *Fun*, 2 October 1894, p. 140.
58. Eva Thienpont, 'Visibly Wild(e): A Re-evaluation of Oscar Wilde's Homosexual Image', *Irish Studies Review*, vol. 13, no. 3, 2005, p. 295.
59. Joel H. Kaplan and Sheila Stowell, *Theatre and Fashion: Oscar Wilde to the Suffragettes*, Cambridge University Press, Cambridge, 1994. p. 12.
60. Alison Syme, *A Touch of Blossom: John Singer Sargent and the Queer Flora of Fin-de-Siècle Art*, Pennsylvania State University Press, University Park PA, 2010, p. 46; see also Dominic Janes, '*The Catholic Florist*: Flowers and Deviance in the Mid-Nineteenth-Century Church of England', *Visual Culture in Britain*, vol. 12, no. 1, 2011, pp. 77–96.
61. Karl Beckson, 'Oscar Wilde and *The Green Carnation*', *English Literature in Transition, 1880–1920*, vol. 42, no. 4, 2000, p. 388.
62. Anon., 'Manners Maketh the Man', *Hearth and Home*, 3 March 1892, p. 479; Merlin Holland, 'Biography and the Art of Lying', in Peter Raby (ed.), *The Cambridge Companion to Oscar Wilde*, Cambridge University Press, Cambridge, 1997, p. 13; Holland, *The Wilde Album*, p. 141.
63. Beckson, 'Oscar Wilde', p. 389.
64. Anon., 'The Man about Town', *Country Gentleman*, 5 March 1892, p. 334.
65. Anon., 'Current Carols; or Ditties in Doselets up to Date', *Fun*, 16 March 1892, p. 114.
66. Anon., 'Through the Opera Glass', *Pick-Me-Up*, 21 July 1894, p. 246.
67. Robert Hichens, *The Green Carnation*, William Heinemann, London, 1894, p. 3.
68. Ibid., p. 25.
69. Ibid., p. 105.
70. Quoted and discussed in Kaplan and Stowell, *Theatre and Fashion*, p. 187 n14.
71. Anon., 'The Call Boy', *Judy*, 20 February 1895, p. 88.
72. *Illustrated Sporting and Dramatic News*, 21 July 1883, discussed in Holland, *The Wilde Album*, p. 101.
73. Letter, Max Beerbohm to Reggie Turner, 12 August 1894, in Max Beerbohm, *Letters to Reggie Turner*, ed. Rupert Hart-Davis, Hart-Davis, London, 1964, p. 97.

74. Quoted in Dennis Denisoff, 'Posing a Threat: Queensberry, Wilde and the Portrayal of Decadence', in Liz Constable, Dennis Denisoff and Matthew Potolsky (eds), *Perennial Decay: On the Aesthetics and Politics of Decadence*, University of Pennsylvania Press, Philadelphia PA, 1999, p. 83.
75. Letter, Max Beerbohm to Reggie Turner, postmark 3 May 1895, in Beerbohm, *Letters to Reggie Turner*, pp. 102–4.
76. Oscar Wilde, *The Picture of Dorian Gray*, ed. Joseph Bristow, Oxford University Press, Oxford, 2006; John Potvin, 'The Aesthetics of Community: Queer Interiors and the Desire for Intimacy', in Jason Edwards and Imogen Hart (eds), *Rethinking the Interior, c. 1867–1896: Aestheticism and Arts and Crafts*, Ashgate, Farnham, 2010, pp. 178–9.
77. Peter Calloway, 'Wilde and the Dandyism of the Senses', in Peter Raby (ed.), *The Cambridge Companion to Oscar Wilde*, Cambridge University Press, Cambridge, 1997, p. 50.
78. David Schulz, 'Redressing Oscar: Performance and the Trials of Oscar Wilde', *TDR*, vol. 40, no. 2, 1996, p. 54.
79. Anon., *The Life of Oscar Wilde Prosecutor and Prisoner*, The proprietors, 43 Stanhope St, London, 1895, p. 4.
80. Letter, Max Beerbohm to Reggie Turner, postmark 12 April 1893, in Beerbohm, *Letters to Reggie Turner*, p. 35.
81. John M. Hall, *Max Beerbohm: A Kind of a Life*, Yale University Press, New Haven CT, 2002, p. 201.
82. Max Beerbohm, 'Oscar Wilde', *Pick-Me-Up*, 22 September 1894, p. 390.
83. Leigh Hunt, *Lord Byron and Some of His Contemporaries*, Henry Colburn, London, 1828, p. 91.
84. Katherine Stern, 'What is Femme? The Phenomenology of the Powder Room', *Women: A Cultural Review*, vol. 8, no. 2, 1997, p. 186; Schaffer, 'Fashioning Aestheticism', p. 48.
85. Robert Schweik, 'Congruous Incongruities: The Wilde-Beardsley "Collaboration"', *English Literature in Transition, 1880–1920*, vol. 37, no. 1, 1994, pp. 17–18; Linda Gertner Zatlin, 'Wilde, Beardsley, and the Making of *Salomé*', *Journal of Victorian Culture*, vol. 5, no. 2, 2000, p. 354.
86. Max Beerbohm, *Oscar Wilde*, in *Anglo-American Times*, 25 March 1893, in Beerbohm, *Letters to Reggie Turner*, p. 286.
87. Rupert Hart-Davis (ed.), *A Catalogue of the Caricatures of Max Beerbohm*, Macmillan, London, 1972, p. 158.
88. John M. Hall, *Max Beerbohm Caricatures*, Yale University Press, New Haven CT, 1997, p. 19; Hall, *Max Beerbohm*, pp. 34–5.
89. JCR Spider [pseud.], *A Dream of Decadence on the Cherwell*, in *New Rattle*, vol. 4, no. 20, May 1893, supplement; Holland, *The Wilde Album*, p. 141.
90. Schaffer, 'Fashioning Aestheticism', p. 47.
91. Kaplan and Stowell, *Theatre and Fashion*, p. 12.
92. Max Beerbohm, 'The Incomparable Beauty of Modern Dress', *Spirit Lamp*, vol. 4, no. 2, 6 June 1893, p. 98.
93. Ibid., p. 90.
94. Hall, *Max Beerbohm Caricatures*, p. 11.

95. Letter, Max Beerbohm to Robert Ross, 27 January 1895, in Max Beerbohm, *Letters of Max Beerbohm, 1892–1956*, ed. Rupert Hart-Davis, John Murray, London, 1988, p. 7.

96. Anon., [review, *Yellow Book*, vol. 3] 'A Yellow Bore', *Critic*, 10 November 1894, p. 316; see also Anon., 'A Phalse Note on George the Fourth', *Punch* 107, 27 October 1894, p. 204.

97. Max Beerbohm, 'George the Fourth', *Yellow Book*, vol. 3, October 1894, p. 245.

98. Max Beerbohm, *The Incomparable Max*, Heinemann, London, 1962, p. 2.

99. Ibid., p. 41.

100. Christopher Breward, *The Hidden Consumer: Masculinities, Fashion and City Life, 1860–1914*, Manchester University Press, Manchester, 1999, p. 252.

101. Ed Cohen, 'Posing the Question: Wilde, Wit and the Ways of Man', in Elin Diamond (ed.), *Performance and Cultural Politics*, Routledge, London, 1996, p. 45.

SIX

1. Christopher Breward, *The Culture of Fashion: A New History of Fashionable Dress*, Manchester University Press, Manchester, 1995, p. 117.

2. Ibid., p. 174.

3. Brent Shannon, *The Cut of His Coat: Men, Dress, and Consumer Culture in Britain, 1860–1914*, Ohio University Press, Athens OH, 2006, p. 158.

4. Christopher Breward, *The Hidden Consumer: Masculinities, Fashion and City Life, 1860–1914*, Manchester University Press, Manchester, 1999, pp. 29, 260.

5. Shannon, *The Cut of His Coat*, p. 190.

6. Philip Mann, *The Dandy at Dusk: Taste and Melancholy in the Twentieth Century*, Head of Zeus, London, 2017, p. 79.

7. J.A. Mangan and J. Walvin (eds), *Manliness and Morality: Middle-Class Masculinity in Britain and America, 1800–1940*, Manchester University Press, Manchester, 1987.

8. Mann, *The Dandy at Dusk*, p. 23.

9. Elizabeth Wilson, *Adorned in Dreams: Fashion and Modernity*, I.B. Tauris, London, 2003, p. 132.

10. Tom Stoppard, *The Invention of Love*, 2nd edn, Faber & Faber, London, 1997, ebook, n.pag.

11. W.K. Haselden, *Coming and Going of the 'Dandy'*, in *Daily Mirror*, 9 February 1906, p. 7.

12. Carolyn Tilghman, 'Staging Suffrage: Women, Politics, and the Edwardian Theater', *Comparative Drama*, vol. 45, no. 4, 2011, p. 347.

13. Miles Taylor, 'John Bull and the Iconography of Public Opinion in England c. 1712–1929', *Past and Present* 134, 1992, p. 118.

14. Lewis Baumer, *The Sex Question*, in *Punch* 140, 1911, p. 235.

15. Howard P. Chudacoff, *The Age of the Bachelor: Creating an American Subculture*, Princeton University Press, Princeton NJ, 1999, p. 19.

16. John Tosh, *A Man's Place: Masculinity and the Middle-Class Home in Victorian England*, Yale University Press, New Haven CT, 1999.

17. Discussed in John Potvin, *Bachelors of a Different Sort: Queer Aesthetics, Material Culture and the Modern Interior in Britain*, Manchester University Press, Manchester, 2014, p. 57.

18. Dorothy Rothschild, 'Interior Desecration', *Vogue*, 1 May 1917, pp. 28, 62.

19. Martin Taylor (ed.), *Lads: Love Poetry of the Trenches*, Constable, London, 1989, p. 29.

20. Chudacoff, *The Age of the Bachelor*, p. 253.

21. Dorothy Wilding, *Noël Coward*, 1951, chlorobromide print, 29 × 21.8 cm; National Portrait Gallery, London, NPG x6936.

22. Martin Pugh, *We Danced All Night: A Social History of Britain Between the Wars*, Bodley Head, London, 2008, p. 345.

23. Stephen Gundle, *Glamour: A History*, Oxford University Press, Oxford, 2008, p. 167.

24. Philip Hoare, *Noël Coward: A Biography*, Sinclair-Stevenson, London, 1995, p. 140.

25. Anon., 'The Noel Coward Paper Doll', *Vogue*, March 1938, p. 68.

26. Nicholas De Jongh, *Not in Front of the Audience: Homosexuality on Stage*, Routledge, London, 1992, p. 20; Penny Farfan, 'Noël Coward and Sexual Modernism: *Private Lives* as Queer Comedy', *Modern Drama*, vol. 48, no. 4, 2005, p. 35; John Potvin, *Bachelors of a Different Sort: Queer Aesthetics, Material Culture and the Modern Interior in Britain*, Manchester University Press, Manchester, 2014, p. 234.

27. Quoted and discussed in Alan Sinfield, 'Private Lives/Public Theater: Noël Coward and the Politics of Homosexual Representation', *Representations* 36, Autumn 1991, p. 55.

28. Ibid., p. 58.

29. Kate O'Niall, 'Bachelor's Bounce', *Harper's Bazaar*, May 1932, p. 9.

30. Potvin, *Bachelors of a Different Sort*, p. 240; Hugh David, *On Queer Street: A Social History of British Homosexuality, 1895–1995*, HarperCollins, London, 1997, p. 91.

31. Rhonda K. Garelick, *Rising Star: Dandyism, Gender, and Performance in the Fin de Siècle*, Princeton University Press, Princeton NJ, 1998, pp. 43, 128–53.

32. Ellen Moers, *The Dandy: Brummell to Beerbohm*, Secker & Warburg, London, 1960, p. 308.

33. Deborah Cohler, *Citizen, Invert, Queer: Lesbianism and War in Early Twentieth-Century Britain*, University of Minnesota Press, Minneapolis MN, 2010.

34. Terry Castle, *Noël Coward and Radclyffe Hall: Kindred Spirits*, Columbia University Press, New York, 1996, pp. 26–7; Potvin, *Bachelors of a Different Sort*, p. 215.

35. Karl August Büchel, *Radclyffe Hall*, 1918, oil on canvas, 91.4 × 71.1 cm; National Portrait Gallery, London, NPG 4347.

36. Radclyffe Hall, *The Well of Loneliness*, Jonathan Cape, London, 1928; Laura Doan, *Fashioning Sapphism: The Origins of a Modern Lesbian Culture*, Columbia University Press, New York, 2001, p. xii.

37. Castle, *Noël Coward*, pp. 107–9; Farfan, 'Noël Coward', p. 678.

38. George Belcher, *Man–Woman*. 'In the Old Days I Never Paid More Than Sixpence for a Haircut', in *Punch* 189, 1925, p. 9.

39. Lewis Baumer, 'Well, What Do You Think of My New Flat, Uncle John?', in *Punch* 178, 1930, p. 216.

40. Kenneth Bell, 'Famous Women from History, no. 5: Sappho', *Britannia and Eve*, vol. 1, no. 5, September 1929, p. 46.

41. Ibid., p. 47.

42. Miranda Gill, 'The Myth of the Female Dandy', *French Studies*, vol. 61, no. 2,

2007, p. 180; see also Senem Yazan, 'The Black Princess of Elegance: The Emergence of the Female Dandy', *Critical Studies in Fashion and Beauty*, vol. 3, no. 1–2, 2012, pp. 101–15.

43. Susan Fillin-Yeh, 'Introduction: New Strategies for a Theory of Dandies', in Fillin-Yeh (ed.), *Dandies: Fashion and Finesse in Art and Culture*, New York University Press, New York, 2001, p. 20.

44. Jack [Judith] Halberstam, *Female Masculinity*, Duke University Press, Durham NC, 1998, p. 46.

45. Anon., 'Marlene Sets the Trouser Fashion', *Sketch*, 22 February 1933, p. 247.

46. Doan, *Fashioning Sapphism*, p. 141; Rebecca Kennison, 'Clothes Make the (Wo)man: Marlene Dietrich and "Double Drag"', *Journal of Lesbian Studies*, vol. 6, no. 2, 2002, p. 150.

47. Anon., 'The Fur Scarf and the Tailored Suit', *Vogue*, March 1927, p. 70.

48. Elisa Glick, *Materializing Queer Desire: Oscar Wilde to Andy Warhol*, State University of New York Press, Albany NY, 2009, p. 72; see also Esther Newton, 'The Mythic Mannish Lesbian: Radclyffe Hall and the New Woman', *Signs*, vol. 9, no. 2, 1984, pp. 557–75.

49. Arthur Wallis Mills, *An Inducement*, in *Punch* 130, 1906, p. 261.

50. Doan, *Fashioning Sapphism*, p. xxii.

51. Ibid., p. xv.

52. Laura Doan, *Disturbing Practices: History, Sexuality, and Women's Experience of Modern War*, University of Chicago Press, Chicago IL, 2013, p. 111.

53. James Vernon, '"For Some Queer Reason": The Trials and Tribulations of Colonel Barker's Masquerade in Interwar Britain', *Signs*, vol. 26, no. 1, 2000, p. 58.

54. Anon., review, 'The Loveliest of Friends', by G.S. Donisthorpe, *Aberdeen Journal*, 23 June 1931, p. 2; see also Neil Pearson, *Obelisk: A History of Jack Kahane and the Obelisk Press*, Liverpool University Press, Liverpool, 2007, pp. 351–2.

55. Alison Oram, *Her Husband Was a Woman! Women's Gender-Crossing in Modern British Popular Culture*, Routledge, London, 2007, p. 83.

56. Marjorie Garber, *Vested Interests: Cross-Dressing and Cultural Anxiety*, Routledge, New York, 1992, p. 152.

57. Potvin, *Bachelors of a Different Sort*, p. 240.

58. Noël Coward, *The Noël Coward Diaries*, ed. Graham Payn and Sheridan Morley, Weidenfeld & Nicolson, London, 1982, p. 38 n2; Hoare, *Noël Coward*, p. 201; Potvin, *Bachelors of a Different Sort*, p. 257.

59. Dominic Janes, *Freak to Chic: 'Gay' Men in and out of Fashion after Oscar Wilde*, Bloomsbury, London, 2021.

60. Rebecca Jennings, 'From "Woman-Loving Woman" to "Queer": Historiographical Perspectives on Twentieth–Century British Lesbian History', *History Compass*, vol. 5, no. 6, 2007, pp. 1901–20.

61. C.N [pseud.], 'The Origin of the Fairies! A Crowd of Pansy Faces', *Sketch*, 3 August 1931, cover.

62. Anon., '"Pansy" Palaces on Broadway', *Weekly Variety*, vol. 100, no. 9, 10 September 1930, p. 1.

63. Chad Heap, *Slumming: Sexual and Racial Encounters in American Nightlife, 1885–1940*, University of Chicago Press, Chicago IL, 2009, p. 232.
64. Christopher Reed, *Art and Homosexuality: A History of Ideas*, Oxford University Press, Oxford, 2011, p. 111.
65. Frances E. Hutchins, 'The Pleasures of Discovery: Representations of Queer Space by Brassaï and Colette', in Renate Günther and Wendy Michallat (eds), *Lesbian Inscriptions in Francophone Society and Culture*, University of Durham, Durham, 2007, p. 198.
66. Brassaï, *The Secret Paris of the 30s*, trans. Richard Miller, Thames & Hudson, London, 1976, n.pag.
67. Heap, *Slumming*, p. 237.
68. 'Hollywood's Male Magnolias', *Variety Weekly*, 4 October 1930, p. 1.
69. Georges de Zayas, 'Jean Cocteau', in Clive Bell, 'Jean Cocteau: A Master Modernist', *Vanity Fair*, January 1924, p. 52.
70. Anna Zinkeisen in Mariegold [pseud.], 'Mariegold in Society', *Sketch*, 15 January 1930, p. 88; emphasis in original.
71. Anna Zinkeisen in Mariegold, 'Mariegold in Society', *Sketch*, 12 January 1927, p. 56.
72. Anna Zinkeisen in Mariegold, 'Mariegold Broadcasts', *Sketch*, 26 April 1933, p. 145; emphasis in original.
73. Matt Houlbrook, '"The Man with the Powder Puff" in Interwar London', *Historical Journal*, vol. 50, no. 1, 2007, pp. 149, 165; see also Matt Houlbrook, 'Queer Things: Men and Make-Up Between the Wars', in Hannah Greig, Jane Hamlett and Leonie Hannan (eds), *Gender and Material Culture in Britain since 1600*, Palgrave Macmillan, Basingstoke, 2016, pp. 120–37.
74. *Quentin Crisp Taken Near His Home in Fulham*, 1980, 34 × 25 cm; Simon Dack Archive/Alamy Stock Photo, D10G4N.
75. Harold Acton, *Memoirs of an Aesthete*, Methuen, London, 1948, pp. 163–4.
76. Gregory Woods, 'British Homosexuality, 1920–1939', in Tony Sharpe (ed.), *W.H. Auden in Context*, Cambridge University Press, Cambridge, 2013, p. 90.
77. Florence Tamagne, *A History of Homosexuality in Europe: Berlin, London, Paris, 1919–1939*, Algora, New York, 2006, pp. 124–5.
78. Cyril Connolly, *The Condemned Playground*, Routledge, London, 1945, pp. 138, 139, 146, 150; first published in Leonard Russell (ed.), *Press Gang: Crazy World Chronicle*, Hutchinson, London, 1937.
79. Quoted in Sean O'Connor, *Straight Acting: Popular Gay Drama from Wilde to Rattigan*, Cassell, London, 1998, p. 131.
80. D.J. Dutton, 'Power Brokers or Just "Glamour Boys"? The Eden Group, September 1939–May 1940', *English Historical Review*, vol. 118, no. 476, 2003, pp. 412–24; Julie V. Gottlieb, *'Guilty Women', Foreign Policy, and Appeasement in Inter-War Britain*, Palgrave Macmillan, Basingstoke, 2015.
81. Rose Allatini [pseud. 'A.T. Fitzroy'], *Despised and Rejected*, C.W. Daniel, London, 1918, p. 31.
82. Beverley Nichols, 'The Devil and Disarmament', *Everyman: The World News Weekly* 246 (NS no. 3), 20 October 1933, p. 16.

83. J.B. Morton, 'Conscription for Young Pacifists', *Everyman: The World News Weekly* 247 (NS no. 4), 13 October 1933, p. 11.

84. Ibid.

85. Jocelyn Brooke, *The Military Orchid*, Bodley Head, London, 1948, p. 67.

86. Mark Hussey, 'Clive Bell, "a Fathead and Voluptuary": Conscientious Objection and British Masculinity', in Brenda Helt and Madelyn Detloff (eds), *Queer Bloomsbury*, Edinburgh University Press, Edinburgh, 2016, pp. 244, 255 n11.

87. Susan Sontag, 'Notes on "Camp"', *Partisan Review*, vol. 31, no. 4, 1964, p. 528.

Bibliography

Many of the news stories and periodical entries below were found via *British Newspapers, 1600–1950* (Gale), which is a digitized collection of British library holdings. Unfortunately the database does not always supply details of volume and page numbers and some of the originals are too fragile to be checked in hard copy.

Acton, Harold, *Memoirs of an Aesthete*, Methuen, London, 1948.

Adams, James Eli, *Dandies and Desert Saints: Styles of Victorian Manhood*, Cornell University Press, Ithaca NY, 1995.

Adut, Ari, 'A Theory of Scandal: Victorians, Homosexuality, and the Fall of Oscar Wilde', *American Journal of Sociology*, vol. III, no. 1, 2005, pp. 213–48.

Allatini, Rose [pseud. 'A.T. Fitzroy'], *Despised and Rejected*, C.W. Daniel, London, 1918.

Amann, Elizabeth, *Dandyism in the Age of Revolution: The Art of the Cut*, University of Chicago Press, Chicago IL, 2015.

Anderson, Anne, '"Fearful Consequences … of Living Up to One's Teapot": Men, Women and "Cultcha" in the English Aesthetic Movement, *c.* 1870–1900', *Victorian Literature and Culture*, vol. 37, no. 1, 2009, pp. 219–54.

——— , 'The Mutual Admiration Society, or Mr Punch Against the Aesthetes', *Popular Narrative Media*, vol. 2, no. 1, 2009, pp. 69–88.

Andersson, Peter K., '"High Collars and Principles": The Late-Victorian World of the Masher', *Gender and History*, vol. 31, no. 2, 2019, pp. 422–43.

Anon., 'News', *Gazetteer and New Daily Advertiser*, 27 October 1764.

——— , 'Newmarket Races', *Owen's Weekly Chronicle and Westminster Journal*, 4–11 May 1765.

——— , *Crazy Tales*, Ewing, Dublin, 1772.

——— , 'The History of Captain H ——— , a Macaroni', *Macaroni and Theatrical Magazine*, October 1772, pp. 1–5.

——— , 'News', *Bingley's London Journal*, 12–19 September 1772.

——— , 'News', *London Evening News*, 6 August 1772.

——— , 'News', *Morning Chronicle and London Advertiser*, 8 August 1772.

——— , *The Vauxhall Affray; or, the Macaronies Defeated*, J. Williams, London, 1773.

————, 'Lord —— [Grandison] or the Nosegay Macaroni', *Macaroni and Theatrical Magazine*, February 1773, p. 193.

————, [review] *'The Macaroni'*, *Critical Review, or, Annals of Literature* 36, 1773, p. 235.

————, 'Mademoiselle de Beaumont, or the Chevalier d'Eon', *London Magazine* 46, 1777, p. 443.

————, 'News', *Morning Herald and General Advertiser*, 21 July 1781.

————, 'The Late Emperor of China, Kien Long', *Morning Herald*, 27 December 1799.

————, *Fashion. Dedicated to All the Town. By the Author of the Greeks. – The Pigeons. – Modern Belles. – Fashionable Anecdotes, &c. Illustrated* [by George Cruikshank], 5th edn, Stockdale, London, 1818.

————, *The Dandies' Ball; or, High Life in the City. Embellished with Sixteen Coloured Engravings* [by Robert Cruikshank], John Marshall, London, 1819.

————, 'Origins of Macaronism', *Morning Post*, 26 September 1827.

————, *'Punch's Literature'*, *Punch*, vol. 1, 5 September 1841, p. 86.

————, 'The Japanese Ambassadors at North Seaton Colliery', *Liverpool Mercury*, 30 May 1862.

————, 'The Charge of Personating Women', *Morning Post*, 14 May 1870, p. 6.

————, 'Inverted Relations', *Pall Mall Gazette*, 29 June 1870.

————, 'Plain Dress', *Boy's Herald*, 6 July 1878, p. 15.

————, 'News', *Funny Folks*, 19 March 1881, p. 82.

————, 'The New Aesthete-Athlete Era', *Funny Folks*, 6 April 1881, p. 116.

————, *The Sins of the Cities of the Plain, or the Recollections of a Mary-Ann, with Short Essays on Sodomy and Tribadism*, 2 vols, Privately printed, London, 1881.

————, 'The Man in the Street', *Funny Folks*, 4 February 1882, p. 34.

————, 'The Man about Town', *Country Gentleman*, 25 March 1882, p. 318.

————, *Ye Soul Agonies in ye Life of Oscar Wilde*, n.pub., New York, 1882.

————, 'The Man about Town', *Country Gentleman*, 24 February 1883, p. 205.

————, 'Essence of Parliament', *Punch* 84, 19 May 1883, p. 240.

————, 'Did Sarony Invent Oscar Wilde?' *Photographic Times* 156, December 1883, pp. 658–9.

————, 'The Man about Town', *Country Gentleman*, 16 May 1885, p. 617.

————, 'Flashes from the Footlights', *Licensed Victuallers' Mirror*, 10 December 1889, p. 550.

————, 'A Double Evolution', *Daily News*, 26 August 1891.

————, 'Manners Maketh the Man', *Hearth and Home*, 3 March 1892, p. 479.

————, 'The Man about Town', *Country Gentleman*, 5 March 1892, p. 334.

————, 'Current Carols; or Ditties in Doselets up to Date', *Fun*, 16 March 1892, p. 114.

————, 'Young Men Who Are Got Up', *Huddersfield Daily Chronicle*, 4 April 1893, p. 4.

————, 'Through the Opera Glass', *Pick-Me-Up*, 21 July 1894, p. 246.

————, 'Human Novelties', *Hearth and Home*, 26 July 1894, p. 379.

————, 'Evolution', *Judy*, 24 October 1894, p. 202.

————, 'A Phalse Note on George the Fourth', *Punch*, 27 October 1894, p. 204.

————, [review, *Yellow Book*, vol. 3] 'A Yellow Bore', *Critic*, 10 November 1894, p. 316.

————, *The Life of Oscar Wilde Prosecutor and Prisoner*, The proprietors, 43 Stanhope St, London, 1895.

————, 'The Call Boy', *Judy*, 20 February 1895, p. 88.

————, 'The Fur Scarf and the Tailored Suit', *Vogue*, March 1927, p. 70.

————, '"Pansy" Palaces on Broadway', *Weekly Variety*, vol. 100, no. 9, 10 September 1930, p. 1.

————, 'Hollywood's Male Magnolias', *Variety Weekly*, 4 October 1930, pp. 1–2.

———— [review] 'The Loveliest of Friends', by G.S. Donisthorpe, *Aberdeen Journal*, 23 June 1931, p. 2.

————, 'Marlene Sets the Trouser Fashion', *Sketch*, 22 February 1933, p. 247.

————, 'The Noel Coward Paper Doll', *Vogue*, March 1938, p. 68.

Atwood, Emma K., 'Fashionably Late: Queer Temporality and the Restoration Fop', *Comparative Drama*, vol. 47, no. 1, 2013, pp. 85–111.

Barbey d'Aurevilly, Jules-Amédée, *Du Dandysme et de George Brummell*, Privately printed, Caen, 1845.

Baumer, Lewis, 'The Sex Question', *Punch* 140, 1911, p. 235.

————, '"Well, What Do You Think of My New Flat, Uncle John?"', *Punch* 178, 1930, p. 216.

Beckson, Karl, 'Oscar Wilde and *The Green Carnation*', *English Literature in Transition, 1880–1920*, vol. 42, no. 4, 2000, pp. 387–97.

Beerbohm, Max, 'The Incomparable Beauty of Modern Dress', *Spirit Lamp*, vol. 4, no. 2, 6 June 1893, pp. 90–98.

————, 'George the Fourth', *Yellow Book* 3, October 1894, p. 245.

————, *The Incomparable Max*, Heinemann, London, 1962.

————, *Letters to Reggie Turner*, ed. Rupert Hart-Davis, Hart-Davis, London, 1964.

————, *Letters of Max Beerbohm, 1892–1956*, ed. Rupert Hart-Davis, John Murray, London, 1988.

Belcher, George, *'Man-Woman. "In the Old Days I Never Paid More Than Sixpence for a Haircut"'*, *Punch* 189, 1925, p. 9.

Bell, Clive, 'Jean Cocteau: A Master Modernist', *Vanity Fair*, January 1924, pp. 52, 82.

Bell, Kenneth, 'Famous Women from History, no. 5: Sappho', *Britannia and Eve*, vol. 1, no. 5, September, 1929, pp. 44–7, 162.

Belsey, Hugh, 'Mann, Sir Horatio, First Baronet (*bap.* 1706, *d.* 1786)', *Oxford Dictionary of National Biography*, Oxford University Press, Oxford, 2004; online edn, May 2009, www.oxforddnb.com/view/article/17945.

Berberich, Christine, *The Image of the English Gentleman in Twentieth-Century Literature: Englishness and Nostalgia*, Routledge, London, 2016.

Bernhard Jackson, Emily A., 'Least Like Saints: The Vexed Issue of Byron's Sexuality', *Byron Journal* 38, 2010, pp. 29–37.

Bisset, J., *Dandyism Displayed, or the Follies of the Ton*, Duncombe, London, n.d.

Black, Jeremy, *Italy and the Grand Tour*, Yale University Press, New Haven CT, 2003.

Blatchly, John, 'Matthias Darly and the Macaroni Print Shop', *Bookplate Journal*, vol. 9, no. 1, 2011, pp. 15–28.

Booth, Mark, *'Campe-Toi!* On the Origins and Definitions of Camp', in Fabio Cleto (ed.), *Camp: Queer Aesthetics and the Performing Subject: A Reader*, Edinburgh University Press, Edinburgh, 1999, pp. 66–79.

Botz-Bornstein, Thorsten, 'Rule-Following in Dandyism: "Style" as an Overcoming of "Rule" and "Structure"', *Modern Language Review*, vol. 90, no. 2, 1995, pp. 285–95.

Bourke, Joanna, 'The Great Male Renunciation: Men's Dress Reform in Inter-War Britain', *Journal of Design History*, vol. 9, no. 1, 1996, pp. 23–34.

Brassaï, *The Secret Paris of the 30s*, trans. Richard Miller, Thames & Hudson, London, 1976.

Breward, Christopher, *The Culture of Fashion: A New History of Fashionable Dress*, Manchester University Press, Manchester, 1995.

——— , *The Hidden Consumer: Masculinities, Fashion and City Life, 1860–1914*, Manchester University Press, Manchester, 1999.

——— , 'Masculine Pleasures: Metropolitan Identities and the Commercial Sites of Dandyism, 1790–1840', *London Journal*, vol. 28, no. 1, 2003, pp. 60–72.

——— , *The Suit: Form, Function and Style*, Reaktion, London, 2016.

Brewer, John, *The Pleasures of the Imagination: English Culture in the Eighteenth Century*, HarperCollins, London, 1997.

Brooke, Jocelyn, *The Military Orchid*, Bodley Head, London, 1948.

Brough, Robert B., 'Resemblances', *Lloyd's Weekly Newspaper*, 17 April 1859, p. 8.

Buchanan, Robert, 'The Fleshly School of Poetry', *Contemporary Review* 18, October 1871, pp. 334–50.

Bullen, J.B., *The Pre-Raphaelite Body: Fear and Desire in Painting, Poetry and Criticism*, Oxford University Press, Oxford, 1998.

Calloway, Peter, 'Wilde and the Dandyism of the Senses', in Peter Raby (ed.), *The Cambridge Companion to Oscar Wilde*, Cambridge University Press, Cambridge, 1997, pp. 34–54.

Campbell, Jill, 'Politics and Sexuality in Portraits of John, Lord Hervey', *Word and Image*, vol. 6, no. 4, 1990, pp. 281–97.

Campbell, Kimberly C., 'The Face of Fashion: Milliners in Eighteenth–Century Visual Culture', *British Journal for Eighteenth–Century Studies*, vol. 25, no. 2, 2002, pp. 157–72.

Carlyle, Jane Welsh, *A New Selection of Her Letters*, ed. Trudy Bliss, Victor Gollancz, London, 1949.

Carlyle, Thomas, *Sartor Resartus: The Life and Opinions of Herr Teufelsdröckh in Three Books*, Chapman & Hall, London, 1869.

Carter, Michael, 'Thomas Carlyle and *Sartor Resartus*', in Peter McNeil and Vicki Karaminas (eds), *The Men's Fashion Reader*, Berg, Oxford, 2009, pp. 72–83.

Carter, Philip, 'An "Effeminate" or an "Efficient" Nation? Masculinity and Eighteenth-Century Social Documentary', *Textual Practice*, vol. 11, no. 3, 1997, pp. 429–43.

——— , *Men and the Emergence of Polite Society, Britain, 1660–1800*, Longman, Harlow, 2001.

Cassidy, Tanya, 'People, Place, and Performance: Theoretically Revisiting Mother Clap's Molly House', in Chris Mounsey and Caroline Gonda (eds), *Queer People: Negotiations and Expressions of Homosexuality, 1700–1800*, Bucknell University Press, Lewisburg PA, 2007, pp. 99–113.

Castle, Terry, 'Matters Not Fit to Be Mentioned: Fielding's *The Female Husband*', *ELH*, vol. 49, no. 3, 1982, pp. 602–22.
———, *Masquerade and Civilization: The Carnivalesque in Eighteenth-Century English Culture and Fiction*, Stanford University Press, Stanford CA, 1986.
———, *Noël Coward and Radclyffe Hall: Kindred Spirits*, Columbia University Press, New York, 1996.
Chico, Tita, *Designing Women: The Dressing Room in Eighteenth-Century English Literature and Culture*, Bucknell University Press, Lewisburg PA, 2005.
Chill, Adam, 'Boundaries of Britishness: Boxing, Minorities, and Identity in Late-Georgian Britain', Ph.D. dissertation, Boston College, 2007.
Chrisman, Kimberly, 'Unhoop the Fair Sex: The Campaign Against the Hoop Petticoat in Eighteenth-Century England', *Eighteenth-Century Studies*, vol. 30, no. 1, 1996, pp. 5–23.
Chudacoff, Howard P., *The Age of the Bachelor: Creating an American Subculture*, Princeton University Press, Princeton NJ, 1999.
Clark, Anna, 'The Chevalier D'Eon and Wilkes: Masculinity and Politics in the Eighteenth Century', *Eighteenth-Century Studies*, vol. 32, no. 1, 1998, pp. 19–48.
———, 'The Chevalier d'Eon, Rousseau, and New Ideas of Gender, Sex and the Self in the Late Eighteenth Century', in Simon Burrows, Jonathan Conlin, Russell Goulbourne and Valerie Mainz (eds), *The Chevalier d'Eon and His Worlds: Gender, Espionage and Politics in the Eighteenth Century*, Continuum, London, 2010, pp. 187–200.
Claro, Daniel, 'Historicizing Masculine Appearance: John Chute and the Suits at The Vyne, 1740–76', *Fashion Theory*, vol. 9, no. 2, 2005, pp. 147–74.
C.N. [pseud.], 'The Origin of the Fairies! A Crowd of Pansy Faces', *Sketch*, 3 August 1931, cover.
Cody, Lisa F., 'Sex, Civility, and the Self: Du Coudray, D'Eon, and Eighteenth-Century Conceptions of Gendered, National, and Psychological Identity', *French Historical Studies*, vol. 24, no. 3, 2001, pp. 379–407.
Cohen, Ed, 'Posing the Question: Wilde, Wit and the Ways of Man', in Elin Diamond (ed.), *Performance and Cultural Politics*, Routledge, London, 1996, pp. 35–47.
Cohen, Michèle, 'The Grand Tour: Constructing the English Gentleman in Eighteenth–Century France', *History of Education*, vol. 21, no. 3, 1992, pp. 241–57.
———, 'The Grand Tour: Language, National Identity and Masculinity', *Changing English*, vol. 8, no. 2, 2001, pp. 129–41.
———, '"Manners" Make the Man: Politeness, Chivalry, and the Construction of Masculinity, 1750–1830', *Journal of British Studies*, vol. 44, no. 2, 2005, pp. 312–29.
Cohler, Deborah, *Citizen, Invert, Queer: Lesbianism and War in Early Twentieth-Century Britain*, University of Minnesota Press, Minneapolis MN, 2010.
Cole, Sean, *The Story of Men's Underwear*, Parkstone, London, 2010.
Colley, Linda, 'Britishness and Otherness: An Argument', *Journal of British Studies*, vol. 31, no. 4, 1992, pp. 309–29.
———, *Britons: Forging the Nation, 1707–1837*, Yale University Press, New Haven CT, 2005.
Connolly, Cyril, *The Condemned Playground*, Routledge, London, 1945.

Cooke, John, *The Macaroni Jester, and Pantheon of Wit: Containing All that Has Lately Transpired in the Regions of Politeness, Whim, and Novelty*, John Cooke, London, *c.* 1773.

Coward, D.A., 'Attitudes to Homosexuality in Eighteenth-Century France', *Journal of European Studies* 10, 1980, pp. 235–59.

Coward, Noël, *The Noël Coward Diaries*, ed. Graham Payn and Sheridan Morley, Weidenfeld & Nicolson, London, 1982.

Crompton, Louis, *Byron and Greek Love: Homophobia in 19th-Century England*, Faber & Faber, London, 1985.

Dabydeen, David, *Hogarth's Blacks: Images of Blacks in Eighteenth Century English Art*, Dangaroo Press, Kingston-upon-Thames, 1985.

Dart, Gregory, *Metropolitan Art and Literature 1810–1840: Cockney Adventures*, Cambridge University Press, Cambridge, 2012.

David, Hugh, *On Queer Street: A Social History of British Homosexuality, 1895–1995*, HarperCollins, London, 1997.

David, Saul, *Prince of Pleasure: The Prince of Wales and the Making of the Regency*, Little, Brown, London, 1998.

De Jongh, Nicholas, *Not in Front of the Audience: Homosexuality on Stage*, Routledge, London, 1992.

Delpierre, Madeleine, *Dress in France in the Eighteenth Century*, trans. Caroline Beamish, Yale University Press, New Haven CT, 1997.

Denisoff, Dennis, '"Men of My Own Sex": Genius, Sexuality, and George Du Maurier's Artists', in Richard Dellamora (ed.), *Victorian Sexual Dissidence*, University of Chicago Press, Chicago IL, 1999, pp. 147–69.

——, 'Posing a Threat: Queensberry, Wilde and the Portrayal of Decadence', in Liz Constable, Dennis Denisoff and Matthew Potolsky (eds), *Perennial Decay: On the Aesthetics and Politics of Decadence*, University of Pennsylvania Press, Philadelphia PA, 1999, pp. 83–100.

——, *Aestheticism and Sexual Parody, 1840–1940*, Cambridge University Press, Cambridge, 2001.

Doan, Laura, *Fashioning Sapphism: The Origins of a Modern Lesbian Culture*, Columbia University Press, New York, 2001.

——, *Disturbing Practices: History, Sexuality, and Women's Experience of Modern War*, University of Chicago Press, Chicago IL, 2013.

Donald, Diana, *Followers of Fashion: Graphic Satires from the Georgian Period, Prints from the British Museum*, Hayward Gallery Publishing, London, 2002.

Donoghue, Emma, 'Imagined More than Women: Lesbians as Hermaphrodites, 1671–1766', *Women's History Review*, vol. 2, no. 2, 1993, pp. 199–216.

Douglas, Alfred, *Oscar Wilde and Myself*, Duffield, New York, 1914.

Dowling, Linda C., 'The Aesthetes and the Eighteenth Century', *Victorian Studies*, vol. 20, no. 4, 1977, pp. 357–77.

——, 'The Decadent and the New Woman in the 1890s', *Nineteenth-Century Fiction*, vol. 33, no. 4, 1979, pp. 434–53.

Drucker, Peter, 'Byron and Ottoman Love: Orientalism, Europeanisation and Same-Sex Sexualities in the Early Nineteenth-Century Levant', *Journal of European Studies*, vol. 42, no. 2, 2012, pp. 140–57.

Du Maurier, George, 'Intellectual Epicures', *Punch* 70, 5 February 1876, p. 33.

————, 'Nincompoopiana', *Punch* 77, 20 December 1879, p. 282.

————, 'A Love Agony. Design by Maudle', *Punch* 78, 5 June 1880, p. 254.

————, 'Maudle on the Choice of a Profession', *Punch* 80, 12 February 1881, p. 62.

Dutton, D.J., 'Power Brokers or Just "Glamour Boys"? The Eden Group, September 1939–May 1940', *English Historical Review*, vol. 118, no. 476, 2003, pp. 412–24.

Earle, Rebecca, '"Two Pairs of Pink Satin Shoes!!" Race, Clothing and Identity in the Americas (17th–19th Centuries)', *History Workshop Journal*, vol. 52, no. 1, 2001, pp. 175–95.

Eberle-Sinatra, Michael, 'A Revaluation of Leigh Hunt's *Lord Byron and Some of His Contemporaries*', *Byron Journal* 29, 2001, pp. 17–26.

Edwards, Jason, *Alfred Gilbert's Aestheticism: Gilbert amongst Whistler, Wilde, Leighton, Pater and Burne-Jones*, Ashgate, Aldershot, 2006.

Egan, Pierce, *Boxiana; or, Sketches of Antient [sic] and Modern Pugilism*, Smeeton, London, 1812.

————, *Life in London; or, the Day and Night Scenes of Jerry Hawthorne, Esq., and His Elegant Friend Corinthian Tom, Accompanied by Bob Logic, the Oxonian, in Their Rambles and Sprees Through the Metropolis*, Sherwood, Neely and Jones, London, 1821.

Egerton, Judy, *Wright of Derby*, Tate, London, 1990.

Elfenbein, Andrew, 'Byronism and the Work of Homosexual Performance in Early Victorian England', *Modern Language Quarterly*, vol. 54, no. 4, 1993, pp. 535–66.

————, *Romantic Genius: The Prehistory of a Homosexual Role*, Columbia University Press, New York, 1999.

————, 'Byron: Gender and Sexuality', in Drummond Bone (ed.), *The Cambridge Companion to Byron*, Cambridge University Press, Cambridge, 2004, pp. 56–73.

Etlin, Richard A., *In Defence of Humanism: Value in the Arts and Letters*, Cambridge University Press, Cambridge, 1996.

Farfan, Penny, 'Noël Coward and Sexual Modernism: *Private Lives* as Queer Comedy', *Modern Drama*, vol. 48, no. 4, 2005, pp. 677–88.

Ferdinand Twigem [pseud.], *The Macaroni: A Satire*, G. Allen, London, 1773.

Festa, Lynn M., 'Personal Effects: Wigs and Possessive Individualism in the Long Eighteenth Century', *Eighteenth-Century Life*, vol. 29, no. 2, 2005, pp. 47–90.

Fillin-Yeh, Susan, 'Introduction: New Strategies for a Theory of Dandies', in Fillin-Yeh (ed.), *Dandies: Fashion and Finesse in Art and Culture*, New York University Press, New York, 2001, pp. 1–34.

Fisher, Judith Law, '"In the Present Famine of Anything Substantial": Fraser's "Portraits" and the Construction of Literary Celebrity; or, "Personality, Personality is the Appetite of the Age"', *Victorian Periodicals Review*, vol. 39, no. 2, 2006, pp. 97–135.

Fordham, Douglas, and Adrienne Albright, 'The Eighteenth-Century Print: Tracing the Contours of a Field', *Literature Compass*, vol. 9, no. 8, 2012, pp. 509–20.

Friedman-Romell, Beth H., 'Breaking the Code: Toward a Reception Theory of Theatrical Cross-Dressing in Eighteenth-Century London', *Theatre Journal*, vol. 47, no. 4, 1995, pp. 459–79.

Garber, Marjorie, *Vested Interests: Cross-Dressing and Cultural Anxiety*, Routledge, New York, 1992.

Garelick, Rhonda K., *Rising Star: Dandyism, Gender, and Performance in the Fin de Siècle*, Princeton University Press, Princeton NJ, 1998.

Garrick, David, *The Fribbleriad*, Coote, London, 1761.

Gatcombe, George., 'The New Woman', *Fun*, 2 October 1894, p. 140.

Gatrell, Vic, *City of Laughter: Sex and Satire in Eighteenth-Century London*, Atlantic, London, 2006.

George, Laura, 'Byron, Brummell, and the Fashionable Figure', *Byron Journal*, vol. 24, no. 1, 1996, pp. 33–41.

———, 'The Emergence of the Dandy', *Literature Compass*, vol. 1, no. 1, 2004, pp. 1–13.

George, Mary Dorothy, *Catalogue of Political and Personal Satires Preserved in the Department of Prints and Drawings in the British Museum*, Volume 5: *1771–1783*, British Museum, London, 1935.

———, *Catalogue of Political and Personal Satires Preserved in the Department of Prints and Drawings in the British Museum*, Volume 9: *1811–19*, British Museum, London, 1949.

———, *English Political Caricature to 1792: A Study of Opinion and Propaganda*, Oxford University Press, Oxford, 1959.

Gilbert, Arthur N., 'Sexual Deviance and Disaster during the Napoleonic Wars', *Albion*, vol. 9, no. 1, 1977, pp. 98–113.

Gill, Miranda, 'The Myth of the Female Dandy', *French Studies*, vol. 61, no. 2, 2007, pp. 167–81.

Gillingham, Lauren, 'The Novel of Fashion Redressed: Bulwer-Lytton's *Pelham* in a 19th-Century Context', *Victorian Review*, vol. 32, no. 1, 2006, pp. 63–85.

Glick, Elisa, *Materializing Queer Desire: Oscar Wilde to Andy Warhol*, State University of New York Press, Albany NY, 2010.

Godfrey, Robert, *James Gillray: The Art of Caricature*, Tate, London, 2001.

Goldhill, Simon. *A Very Queer Family Indeed: Sex, Religion, and the Bensons in Victorian Britain*, University of Chicago Press, Chicago IL, 2016.

Goldsmith, Netta, 'London's Homosexuals in the Eighteenth-Century: Rhetoric Versus Practice', in Chris Mounsey and Caroline Gonda (eds), *Queer People: Negotiations and Expressions of Homosexuality, 1700–1800*, Bucknell University Press, Lewisburg PA, 2007, pp. 183–94.

Gottlieb, Julie V., *'Guilty Women', Foreign Policy, and Appeasement in Inter-War Britain*, Palgrave Macmillan, Basingstoke, 2015.

Greene, Jody, 'Public Secrets: Sodomy and the Pillory in the Eighteenth Century and Beyond', *Eighteenth Century*, vol. 44, no. 2–3, 2003, pp. 203–32.

Greig, Hannah, *The Beau Monde: Fashionable Society in Georgian London*, Oxford University Press, Oxford, 2013.

Grootenboer, Hanneke, *Treasuring the Gaze: Intimate Vision in Late Eighteenth-Century Eye Miniatures*, University of Chicago Press, Chicago IL, 2012.

Grossman, Jonathan H., 'The Mythic Svengali: Anti-Aestheticism in *Trilby*', *Studies in the Novel*, vol. 28, no. 4, 1996, pp. 525–42.

Gundle, Stephen, *Glamour: A History*, Oxford University Press, Oxford, 2008.

Haggerty, George, '*O Lachrymarum Fons*: Tears, Poetry and Desire in Gray', *Eighteenth-Century Studies* 30, 1996, pp. 81–95.

————, 'Queering Horace Walpole', *Studies in English Literature*, vol. 46, no. 3, 2006, pp. 543–62.

————, *Horace Walpole's Letters: Masculinity and Friendship in the Eighteenth Century*, Bucknell University Press, Lanham MD, 2011.

————, 'Smollett's World of Masculine Desire in *The Adventures of Roderick Random*', *Eighteenth Century*, vol. 53, no. 3, 2012, pp. 317–30.

Halberstam, Jack [Judith], *Female Masculinity*, Duke University Press, Durham NC, 1998.

Hall, John M., *Max Beerbohm Caricatures*, Yale University Press, New Haven CT, 1997.

————, *Max Beerbohm: A Kind of a Life*, Yale University Press, New Haven CT, 2002.

Hall, Radclyffe, *The Well of Loneliness*, Jonathan Cape, London, 1928.

Hallett, Mark, *The Spectacle of Difference: Graphic Satire in the Age of Hogarth*, Yale University Press, New Haven CT, 1999.

Hart-Davis, Rupert (ed.), *A Catalogue of the Caricatures of Max Beerbohm*, Macmillan, London, 1972, p. 158.

Harvey, John, *Men in Black*, Reaktion, London, 1995.

Harvey, Karen, 'The Century of Sex? Gender, Bodies, and Sexuality in the Long Eighteenth Century', *Historical Journal*, vol. 45, no. 4, 2002, pp. 899–916.

————, 'The History of Masculinity, circa 1650–1800', *Journal of British Studies*, vol. 44, no. 2, 2005, pp. 296–311.

Haselden, W.K., 'Coming and Going of the "Dandy"', *Daily Mirror*, 9 February 1906, p. 7.

Hatt, Michael, 'Space, Surface, Self: Homosexuality and the Aesthetic Interior', *Visual Culture in Britain*, vol. 8, no. 1, 2007, pp. 105–28.

Heap, Chad, *Slumming: Sexual and Racial Encounters in American Nightlife, 1885–1940*, University of Chicago Press, Chicago IL, 2009.

Hellman, Mimi, 'Interior Motives: Seduction by Decoration in Eighteenth-Century France', in Harold Koda and Andrew Bolton (eds), *Dangerous Liaisons: Fashion and Furniture in the Eighteenth Century*, Yale University Press, New Haven CT, 2006, pp. 14–23.

Hewitt, Emma Churchman, 'The "New Woman" in Her Relation to the "New Man"', *Westminster Review*, vol. 147, no. 3, 1897, pp. 335–7.

Heyl, Christoph, 'The Metamorphosis of the Mask in Seventeenth- and Eighteenth-Century London', in Efrat Tseëlon (ed.), *Masquerade and Identities: Essays on Gender, Sexuality and Marginality*, Routledge, London, 2003, pp. 114–34.

Hibbert, Christopher, *George IV: Regent and King, 1811–1830*, Allen Lane, London, 1973.

Hichens, Robert, *The Green Carnation*, William Heinemann, London, 1894.

Hitchcock, Tim, *English Sexualities, 1700–1800*, Palgrave Macmillan, Basingstoke, 1997.

Holland, Merlin, 'Biography and the Art of Lying', in Peter Raby (ed.), *The Cambridge Companion to Oscar Wilde*, Cambridge University Press, Cambridge, 1997, pp. 1–17.

————, *The Wilde Album*, Fourth Estate, London, 1997.

Hone, William, *The Man in the Moon: or, the 'Devil to Pay'. With Thirteen Cuts* [by George Cruikshank], William Hone, London, 1820.

Horrocks, Jamie, 'Asses and Aesthetes: Ritualism and Aestheticism in Victorian Periodical Illustration', *Victorian Periodicals Review*, vol. 46, no. 1, 2013, pp. 1–36.

Houlbrook, Matt, '"The Man with the Powder Puff" in Interwar London', *Historical Journal*, vol. 50, no. 1, 2007, pp. 145–71.

———, 'Queer Things: Men and Make-up between the Wars', in Hannah Greig, Jane Hamlett and Leonie Hannan (eds), *Gender and Material Culture in Britain since 1600*, Palgrave Macmillan, Basingstoke, 2016, pp. 120–37.

Hunt, Leigh, *Lord Byron and Some of His Contemporaries*, Henry Colburn, London, 1828.

Hussey, Mark, 'Clive Bell, "a Fathead and Voluptuary": Conscientious Objection and British Masculinity', in Brenda Helt and Madelyn Detloff (eds), *Queer Bloomsbury*, Edinburgh University Press, Edinburgh, 2016, pp. 240–57.

Hutchins, Frances E., 'The Pleasures of Discovery: Representations of Queer Space by Brassaï and Colette', in Renate Günther and Wendy Michallat (eds), *Lesbian Inscriptions in Francophone Society and Culture*, University of Durham, Durham, 2007, pp. 189–203.

Hutson, Lorna, 'Liking Men: Ben Jonson's Closet Opened', *ELH*, vol. 71, no. 4, 2004, pp. 1065–96.

Ishiguro, Kazuo, *The Remains of the Day*, Faber & Faber, London, 1989.

Janes, Dominic, *Victorian Reformation: The Fight over Idolatry in the Church of England, 1840–1860*, Oxford University Press, Oxford, 2009.

———, '*The Catholic Florist*: Flowers and Deviance in the Mid-Nineteenth-Century Church of England', *Visual Culture in Britain*, vol. 12, no. 1, 2011, pp. 77–96.

———, 'Frederick Rolfe's Christmas Cards: Popular Culture and the Construction of Queerness in Late Victorian Britain', *Early Popular Visual Culture*, vol. 10, no. 2, 2012, pp. 105–24.

———, 'Unnatural Appetites: Sodomitical Panic in Hogarth's *The Gate of Calais, or O the Roast Beef of Old England (1748)*', *Oxford Art Journal*, 35, no. 1, 2012, pp. 19–31.

———, *Oscar Wilde Prefigured: Queer Fashioning and British Caricature, 1750–1900*, University of Chicago Press, Chicago IL, 2016.

———, *Freak to Chic: 'Gay' Men in and out of Fashion after Oscar Wilde*, Bloomsbury, London, 2021.

Jenkins, Eugenia Zuroski, *A Taste for China: English Subjectivity and the Prehistory of Orientalism*, Oxford University Press, Oxford, 2013.

Jennings, Rebecca, 'From "Woman-Loving Woman" to "Queer": Historiographical Perspectives on Twentieth-Century British Lesbian History', *History Compass*, vol. 5, no. 6, 2007, pp. 1901–20.

Jerrold, William Blanchard, *The Life of George Cruikshank: In Two Epochs*, 2 vols, Chatto & Windus, London, 1882.

Jesse, William, *The Life of George Brummell, Esq., Commonly Called Beau Brummell*, Clarke & Beeton, London, 1854.

Jones, Jennifer M., 'Repackaging Rousseau: Femininity and Fashion in Old Regime France', *French Historical Studies*, vol. 18, no. 4, 1994, pp. 939–67.

Jones, Robert W., 'Notes on *The Camp*: Women, Effeminacy and the Military in Late Eighteenth-Century Literature', *Textual Practice*, vol. 11, no. 3, 1997, pp. 463–76.

Juvenis [pseud.], letter to the printer, *Middlesex Journal, or Universal Evening Post*, 7–10 November 1772.

Kaplan, Fred, *Thomas Carlyle: A Biography*, Cambridge University Press, Cambridge, 1983.

Kaplan, Joel H., and Sheila Stowell, *Theatre and Fashion: Oscar Wilde to the Suffragettes*, Cambridge University Press, Cambridge, 1994.

Kates, Gary, 'The Transgendered World of the Chevalier/Chevalière d'Eon', *Journal of Modern History*, vol. 67, no. 3, 1995, pp. 558–94.

Keenan, William J.F., 'Introduction: *Sartor Resartus* Restored: Dress Studies in Carlylean Perspective', in Keenan (ed.), *Dressed to Impress: Looking the Part*, Berg, Oxford, 2001, pp. 1–49.

Kelly, Ian, *Beau Brummell: The Ultimate Dandy*, Hodder & Stoughton, London, 2005.

Kennison, Rebecca, 'Clothes Make the (Wo)man: Marlene Dietrich and "Double Drag"', *Journal of Lesbian Studies*, vol. 6, no. 2, 2002, pp. 147–56.

Kenrick, William, *Love in the Suds: A Town Eclogue, Being the Lamentation of Roscius for the Loss of His NYKY*, Wheble, London, 1772.

Kimmel, Michael S., 'Masculinity as Homophobia: Fear, Shame and Silence in the Construction of Gender Identity', in Mary M. Gergen and Sara N. Davis (eds), *Toward a New Psychology of Gender*, Routledge, Florence KY, 1997, pp. 223–42.

King, Thomas A., *The Gendering of Men, 1600–1750*, Volume 1: *The English Phallus*, University of Wisconsin Press, Madison WI, 2004.

———, *The Gendering of Men, 1600–1750*, Volume 2: *Queer Articulations*, University of Wisconsin Press, Madison WI, 2008.

Knoppers, Laura Lunger, 'The Politics of Portraiture: Oliver Cromwell and the Plain Style', *Renaissance Quarterly*, vol. 51, no. 4, 1998, pp. 1283–1319.

Kuchta, David, *The Three-Piece Suit and Modern Masculinity: England, 1550–1850*, University of California Press, Berkeley CA, 2002.

———, '"Graceful Virile and Useful": The Origins of the Three-Piece Suit', in Andrew Reilly and Sarah Cosbey (eds), *Men's Fashion Reader*, Fairchild, New York, 2008, pp. 498–510.

Kuhn, William, *Disraeli: The Politics of Pleasure*, Free Press, London, 2006.

Kunzle, David, *Fashion and Fetishism: Corsets, Tight Lacing and Other Forms of Body-Sculpture*, Sutton, Stroud, 2004.

Kurnick, David, 'Thackeray's Theater of Interiority', *Victorian Studies*, vol. 48, no. 2, 2006, pp. 257–67.

Kwass, Michael, 'Big Hair: A Wig History of Consumption in Eighteenth-Century France', *American Historical Review*, vol. 111, no. 3, 2006, pp. 631–59.

Laqueur, Thomas, *Making Sex: Body and Gender from the Greeks to Freud*, Harvard University Press, Cambridge MA, 1990.

Lavater, Johann Caspar, *Essays on Physiognomy*, trans. H. Hunter, 3 vols, John Murray, London, 1789–98.

Layard, George Soames, *George Cruikshank's Portraits of Himself*, W.T. Spencer, London, 1897.

Leach, Peter, 'John Chute (1701–1776)', *Oxford Dictionary of National Biography*, Oxford University Press, Oxford, 2020; https://doi.org/10.1093/ref:odnb/37285.

Ludlow, Henry Stephen, 'Athletics v. Aesthetics', *Illustrated London News*, 17 March 1883, p. 377.

Lyons, Clare A., 'Mapping an Atlantic Sexual Culture: Homoeroticism in Eighteenth-Century Philadelphia', *William and Mary Quarterly*, vol. 60, no. 1, 2003, pp. 119–154.

MacDonald, Tara, 'Doctors, Dandies and the New Man: Ella Hepworth Dixon and Late-Victorian Masculinities', *Women's Writing: The Elizabethan to Victorian Period*, vol. 19, no. 1, 2012, pp. 41–57.

Mackenzie, Henry, *The Man of Feeling*, T. Cadell, London, 1771.

Mackie, Erin, *Rakes, Highwaymen, and Pirates: The Making of the Modern Gentleman in the Eighteenth Century*, Johns Hopkins University Press, Baltimore MD, 2009.

Mandler, Peter, *Aristocratic Government in the Age of Reform: Whigs and Liberals, 1830–1852*, Oxford University Press, Oxford, 1990.

Mangan, J.A., and J. Walvin (eds), *Manliness and Morality: Middle-Class Masculinity in Britain and America, 1800–1940*, Manchester University Press, Manchester, 1987.

Mann, Philip, *The Dandy at Dusk: Taste and Melancholy in the Twentieth Century*, Head of Zeus, London, 2017.

Mannings, David, *Sir Joshua Reynolds: A Complete Catalogue of His Paintings*, 2 vols, Yale University Press, New Haven CT, 2000.

Marcovitch, Heather, *The Art of the Pose: Oscar Wilde's Performance Theory*, Peter Lang, Bern, 2010.

Mariegold [pseud.], 'Mariegold in Society', *Sketch*, 12 January 1927, pp. 56–7.

——— , 'Mariegold Broadcasts', *Sketch*, 26 April 1933, p. 145.

McClive, Cathy, 'Masculinity on Trial: Penises, Hermaphrodites and the Uncertain Male Body in Early Modern France', *History Workshop Journal*, vol. 68, no. 1, 2009, pp. 45–68.

McCormack, Matthew, *Embodying the Militia in Georgian England*, Oxford University Press, Oxford, 2015.

McCormick, Ian, 'Sex, Sodomy, and Death Sentences in the Long Eighteenth Century', in Jolene Zigarovich (ed.), *Sex and Death in Eighteenth-Century Literature*, Routledge, New York, 2013, pp. 269–302.

McKenna, Neil, *Fanny and Stella: The Young Men Who Shocked Victorian England*, Faber & Faber, London, 2013.

McKeon, Michael, 'Historicizing Patriarchy: The Emergence of Gender Difference in England, 1660–1760', *Eighteenth Century Studies*, vol. 28, no. 3, 1995, pp. 295–322.

McNeil, Peter, '"That Doubtful Gender": Macaroni Dress and Male Sexualities', *Fashion Theory: The Journal of Dress, Body and Culture*, vol. 3, no. 4, 1999, pp. 411–47.

——— , 'Dissipation and Extravagance: Ageing Fops', UTS E-Press, Sydney, 2007, http://epress.lib.uts.edu.au/research/handle/10453/3030.

——— , 'Conspicuous Waist: Queer Dress in the "Long Eighteenth Century"', in Valerie Steele (ed.), *A Queer History of Fashion: From the Closet to the Catwalk*, Fashion Institute of Technology, New York, 2013, pp. 77–116.

——— , *Pretty Gentlemen: Macaroni Men and the Eighteenth-Century Fashion World*, Yale University Press, New Haven CT, 2018.

McPhee, Constance C., and Nadine M. Orenstein, *Infinite Jest: Caricature and Satire from Leonardo to Levine*, Metropolitan Museum of Art, New York, 2011.

Meyer, Moe, 'The Signifying Invert: Camp and the Performance of Nineteenth–Century Sexology', *Text and Performance Quarterly*, vol. 15, no. 4, 1995, pp. 265–81.

Miller, Monica L., *Slaves to Fashion: Black Dandyism and the Styling of Black Diasporic Identity*, Duke University Press, Durham NC, 2009.

Mills, Arthur Wallis, 'An Inducement', *Punch* 130, 1906, p. 261.

Mitchell, Leslie G., *Charles James Fox*, Oxford University Press, Oxford, 1992.

Moers, Ellen, *The Dandy: Brummell to Beerbohm*, Secker & Warburg, London, 1960.

Molineux, Catherine, 'Hogarth's Fashionable Slaves: Moral Corruption in Eighteenth-Century London', *ELH*, vol. 72, no. 2, 2005, pp. 495–520.

Moore, Thomas [pseud. Thomas Brown], *Replies to the Letters of the Fudge Family in Paris*, Pinnock and Maunder, London, 1818.

Morgan, Thaïs E., 'Victorian Effeminacies', in Richard Dellamora (ed.), *Victorian Sexual Dissidence*, University of Chicago Press, Chicago IL, 1999, pp. 109–26.

Morris, Roy, *Declaring His Genius: Oscar Wilde in North America*, Belknap Press, Cambridge MA, 2013.

Morton, J.B., 'Conscription for Young Pacifists', *Everyman: The World News Weekly* 247 (NS no. 4), 13 October 1933, p. 11.

Mosse, George L., *The Image of Man: The Creation of Modern Masculinity*, Oxford University Press, Oxford, 1996.

Mowl, Timothy, *Horace Walpole: The Great Outsider*, John Murray, London, 1996; repr. Faber & Faber, London, 2010.

Munns, Jessica, and Penny Richards (eds), *The Clothes that Wear Us: Essays on Dressing and Transgressing in Eighteenth-Century Culture*, University of Delaware Press, Newark DE, 1999.

Nadelhaft, Janice, '*Punch* and the Syncretics: An Early Victorian Prologue to the Aesthetic Movement', *Studies in English Literature, 1500–1900*, vol. 15, no. 4, 1975, pp. 627–40.

Neff, David S., 'Bitches, Mollies, and Tommies: Byron, Masculinity, and the History of Sexualities', *Journal of the History of Sexuality*, vol. 11, no. 3, 2002, pp. 395–438.

Newton, Esther, 'The Mythic Mannish Lesbian: Radclyffe Hall and the New Woman', *Signs*, vol. 9, no. 2, 1984, pp. 557–75.

Nichols, Beverley, 'The Devil and Disarmament', *Everyman: The World News Weekly* 246 (NS no. 3), 20 October 1933, p. 16.

Nicholson, Eirwen E.C., 'Consumers and Spectators: The Public of the Political Print in Eighteenth–Century England', *History*, vol. 81, no. 261, 1996, pp. 5–21.

Norton, Rictor (ed.), 'Mrs Piozzi's Reminiscences, 1770s-1790s', *Homosexuality in Eighteenth-Century England: A Sourcebook*, 20 April 2003, http://rictornorton.co.uk/eighteen/piozzi.htm.

——— (ed.), 'The Macaroni Club: Newspaper Items', *Homosexuality in Eighteenth-Century England: A Sourcebook*, 2005, https://rictornorton.co.uk/eighteen/macaroni.htm.

——— (ed.), 'The First Public Debate about Homosexuality in England: The Case of Captain Jones, 1772', *Homosexuality in Eighteenth-Century England: A Sourcebook*, 2007, http://rictornorton.co.uk/eighteen/jones1.htm.

——— (ed.), 'The He-Strumpets, 1707–10', *Homosexuality in Eighteenth-Century England: A Sourcebook*, 1 December 1999, updated 15 June 2008, www.rictornorton.co.uk/eighteen/dunton.htm.

Noyes, Dorothy, 'La Maja Vestida: Dress as Resistance to Enlightenment in Late-18th-Century Madrid', *Journal of American Folklore*, vol. 111, no. 40, 1998, pp. 197–217.

Nussbaum, Felicity A., *The Limits of the Human: Fictions of Anomaly, Race and Gender in the Long Eighteenth Century*, Cambridge University Press, Cambridge, 2003.

Nygren, Edward J., *Isaac Cruikshank and the Politics of Parody: Watercolors in the Huntingdon Collection*, Huntingdon Library Press, San Marino CA, 1994.

O'Connell, Lisa, 'The Libertine, the Rake and the Dandy: Personae, Styles, and Affects', in E.L. McCallum and Mikko Tuhkanen (eds), *The Cambridge History of Gay and Lesbian Literature*, Cambridge University Press, Cambridge, 2014, pp. 218–38.

O'Connor, Sean, *Straight Acting: Popular Gay Drama from Wilde to Rattigan*, Cassell, London, 1998.

Ogborn, Miles, 'Locating the Macaroni: Luxury, Sexuality and Vision in Vauxhall Gardens', *Textual Practice*, vol. 11, no. 3, 1997, pp. 445–61.

O'Gorman, Francis, and Katherine Turner (eds), *The Victorians and the Eighteenth Century: Reassessing the Tradition*, Ashgate, Aldershot, 2004.

O'Kell, Robert, *Disraeli: The Romance of Politics*, University of Toronto Press, Toronto ON, 2013.

O'Niall, Kate, 'Bachelor's Bounce', *Harper's Bazaar*, May 1932, p. 9.

Oram, Alison, *Her Husband Was a Woman! Women's Gender-Crossing in Modern British Popular Culture*, Routledge, London, 2007.

Orvis, David L., '"Old Sodom" and "Dear Dad": Vanbrugh's Celebration of the Sodomitical Subject in *The Relapse*', *Journal of Homosexuality*, vol. 57, no. 1, 2009, pp. 140–62.

Palmeri, Frank, 'Cruikshank, Thackeray, and the Victorian Eclipse of Satire', *SEL Studies in English Literature 1500–1900*, vol. 44, no. 4, 2004, pp. 753–77.

Park, Julie, *The Self and It: Novel Objects in Eighteenth-Century England*, Stanford University Press, Stanford CA, 2010.

Parker, George, *A View of Society and Manners in High and Low Life*, 2 vols, Printed for the author, London, 1781.

Patten, Robert L., *George Cruikshank's Life, Times, and Art*, Volume 1: *1792–1835*, Lutterworth, London, 1992.

———, 'Cruikshank, (Isaac) Robert (1789–1856)', *Oxford Dictionary of National Biography*, Oxford University Press, Oxford, 2004; www.oxforddnb.com/view/article/6845.

———, 'Signifying Shape in Pan-European Caricature', in Todd Porterfield (ed.), *The Efflorescence of Caricature, 1759–1838*, Ashgate, Farnham, 2011, pp. 137–58.

Paulson, Ronald, 'Smollett and Hogarth: The Identity of Pallet', *Studies in English Literature, 1500–1900*, vol. 4, no. 3, 1964, pp. 351–9.

Pearson, Neil, *Obelisk: A History of Jack Kahane and the Obelisk Press*, Liverpool University Press, Liverpool, 2007.

Perry, Gillian, and Michael Rossington (eds), *Femininity and Masculinity in Eighteenth-Century Art and Culture*, Manchester University Press, Manchester, 1994.

Pope, Alexander, *An Epistle from Mr. Pope, to Dr. Arbuthnot*, Printed by J. Wright for Lawton Gilliver, London, 1734.

———, *The Works of Alexander Pope, Esq*, 6 vols, Printed for Lawton Gilliver, London, 1735.

Porter, David, 'Monstrous Beauty: Eighteenth-Century Fashion and the Aesthetics of the Chinese Taste', *Eighteenth-Century Studies*, vol. 35, no. 3, 2002, pp. 395–411.

Postle, Martin (ed.), *Johan Zoffany RA: Society Observed*, Yale University Press, New Haven CT, 2011.

Potvin, John, 'The Aesthetics of Community: Queer Interiors and the Desire for Intimacy', in Jason Edwards and Imogen Hart (eds), *Rethinking the Interior, c. 1867–1896: Aestheticism and Arts and Crafts*, Ashgate, Farnham, 2010, pp. 169–84.

———, *Bachelors of a Different Sort: Queer Aesthetics, Material Culture and the Modern Interior in Britain*, Manchester University Press, Manchester, 2014.

Powell, Margaret K., and Joseph R. Roach, 'Big Hair', *Eighteenth-Century Studies*, vol. 38, no. 1, 2004, pp. 79–99.

Pugh, Martin, *We Danced All Night: A Social History of Britain Between the Wars*, Bodley Head, London, 2008.

Punch [pseud.], 'A Card', *Morning Chronicle and London Advertiser*, 7 August 1772.

Rauser, Amelia, 'Hair, Authenticity, and the Self-Made Macaroni', *Eighteenth-Century Studies*, vol. 38, no. 1, 2004, pp. 101–17.

———, *Caricature Unmasked: Irony, Authenticity and Individualism in Eighteenth-Century English Prints*, University of Delaware Press, Newark DE, 2008.

Regan, Shaun, '"Pranks, Unfit for Naming": Pope, Curll, and the "Satirical Grotesque"', *Eighteenth Century*, vol. 46, no. 1, 2005, pp. 37–57.

Rendell, Jane, 'Displaying Sexuality: Gendered Identities and the Early Nineteenth-Century Street', in Nicholas R. Fyfe (eds), *Images of the Street: Planning, Identity, and Control in Public Space*, Routledge, London, 1998, pp. 75–91.

———, 'Almack's Assembly Rooms – a Site of Sexual Pleasure', *Journal of Architectural Education*, vol. 55, no. 3, 2002, pp. 136–49.

———, *The Pursuit of Pleasure: Gender, Space and Architecture in Regency London*, Athlone, London, 2002.

Ribeiro, Aileen, *The Art of Dress: Fashion in England and France, 1750–1820*, Yale University Press, New Haven CT, 1995.

———, 'Portraying the Fashion, Romancing the Past: Dress and the Cosways', in Stephen Lloyd, Roy Porter and Aileen Ribeiro (eds), *Richard and Maria Cosway: Regency Artists of Taste and Fashion*, Scottish National Portrait Gallery, Edinburgh, 1995, pp. 101–5.

———, *Dress in Eighteenth-Century Europe, 1715–1789*, rev. edn, Yale University Press, New Haven CT, 2002.

———, *Fashion and Fiction: Dress in Art and Literature in Stuart England*, Yale University Press, New Haven CT, 2005.

———, *Clothing Art: The Visual Culture of Fashion, 1600–1915*, Yale University Press, New Haven CT, 2017.

Ritchie, Leslie, 'Garrick's Male-Coquette and Theatrical Masculinities', in Shelley King and Yaël Schlick (eds), *Refiguring the Coquette: Essays on Culture and Coquetry*, Bucknell University Press, Lewisburg PA, 2008, pp. 164–98.

Robinson, David M., *Closeted Writing and Lesbian and Gay Literature: Classical, Early Modern, Eighteenth Century*, Ashgate, Aldershot, 2006.

Roche, Daniel, *The Culture of Clothing: Dress and Fashion in the Ancien Regime*, trans. Jean Birrell, Cambridge University Press, Cambridge, 1996.

Rogers, Ben, *Beef and Liberty: Roast Beef, John Bull and the English Nation*, Vintage, London, 2004.

Rogister, J.M.J., 'D'Éon de Beaumont, Charles Geneviève Louis Auguste André Timothée, Chevalier D'Éon in the French Nobility (1728–1810)', *Oxford Dictionary of National Biography*, Oxford University Press, Oxford, 2004, www.oxforddnb.com/view/article/7523.

Rosenthal, Laura J., 'The Sublime, the Beautiful, "The Siddons"', in Jessica Munns and Penny Richards (eds), *The Clothes that Wear Us: Essays on Dressing and Transgressing in Eighteenth-Century Culture*, Associated University Presses, Cranbury NJ, 1999, pp. 56–80.

Ross, Charles, 'The Only Jones', *Judy*, 27 April 1881, p. 195.

Rothschild, Dorothy, 'Interior Desecration', *Vogue*, 1 May 1917, pp. 28, 62.

Rousseau, George, *Perilous Enlightenment: Pre- and Post-Modern Discourses – Sexual, Historical*, Manchester University Press, Manchester, 1991.

Rousseau, Jean-Jacques, *Dialogues*, Jackson, Lichfield, 1780.

Rowland, Michael, 'Shame and Futile Masculinity: Feeling Backwards in Henry Mackenzie's *Man of Feeling*', *Eighteenth-Century Fiction*, vol. 31, no. 3, 2019, pp. 529–48.

Russell, Leonard (ed.), *Press Gang: Crazy World Chronicle*, Hutchinson, London, 1937.

Santesso, Aaron, 'William Hogarth and the Tradition of the Sexual Scissors', *SEL: Studies in English Literature*, vol. 39, no. 3, 1999, pp. 499–521.

Schaffer, Talia, 'Fashioning Aestheticism by Aestheticizing Fashion: Wilde, Beerbohm, and the Male Aesthetes' Sartorial Codes', *Victorian Literature and Culture*, vol. 28, no. 1, 2000, pp. 39–54.

Schulz, David, 'Redressing Oscar: Performance and the Trials of Oscar Wilde', *TDR*, vol. 40, no. 2, 1996, pp. 37–59.

Schwandt, Waleska, 'Oscar Wilde and the Stereotype of the Aesthete: An Investigation into the Prerequisites of Wilde's Aesthetic Self-Fashioning', in Uwe Böker, Richard Corballis and Julie Hibbard (eds), *The Importance of Reinventing Oscar: Versions of Wilde During the Last 100 Years*, Rodopi, Amsterdam, 2002, pp. 91–102.

Schweik, Robert, 'Congruous Incongruities: The Wilde–Beardsley "Collaboration"', *English Literature in Transition, 1880–1920*, vol. 37, no. 1, 1994, pp. 9–26.

Scully, Richard, 'William Henry Boucher (1837–1906): Illustrator and *Judy* Cartoonist', *Victorian Periodicals Review*, vol. 46, no. 4, 2013, pp. 441–74.

Sedgwick, Eve Kosofsky, *Between Men: English Literature and Male Homosocial Desire*, Columbia University Press, New York, 1993.

———, *Epistemology of the Closet*, University of California Press, Berkeley CA, 2008.

Senelick, Laurence, *The Changing Room: Sex, Drag and Theatre*, Routledge, Abingdon, 2000.

Shannon, Brent, 'Refashioning Men: Fashion, Masculinity, and the Cultivation of the Male Consumer in Britain, 1860–1914', *Victorian Studies*, vol. 46, no. 4, 2004, pp. 597–630.

———, *The Cut of His Coat: Men, Dress, and Consumer Culture in Britain, 1860–1914*, Ohio University Press, Athens OH, 2006,

Shapiro, Susan C., '"Yon Plumed Dandebrat": Male Effeminacy in English Satire and Criticism', *Review of English Studies*, vol. 39, no. 155, 1988, pp. 400–412.

Shirland, Jonathan, '"A Singularity of Appearance Counts Doubly in a Democracy of Clothes": Whistler, Fancy Dress and the Camping of Artists' Dress in the Late Nineteenth Century', *Visual Culture in Britain*, vol. 8, no. 1, 2007, pp. 15–35.

Sinfield, Alan, 'Private Lives/Public Theater: Noël Coward and the Politics of Homosexual Representation', *Representations* 36, Autumn 1991, pp. 43–63.

Smeeton, George (ed.), *Doings in London; or, Day and Night Scenes of the Frauds, Frolics, Manners, and Depravities of the Metropolis*, 7th edn, O. Hodgson, London, *c.* 1840 (1828).

Smith, Hannah, and Stephen Taylor, 'Hephaestion and Alexander: Lord Hervey, Frederick, Prince of Wales, and the Royal Favourite in England in the 1730s', *English Historical Review*, vol. 124, no. 507, 2009, pp. 283–312.

Smollett, Tobias, *The Adventures of Roderick Random*, 2 vols, Osborn, London, 1748.
——— , *The Adventures of Peregrine Pickle*, 4 vols, Wilson, London, 1751.

Sontag, Susan, 'Notes on "Camp"', *Partisan Review*, vol. 31, no. 4, 1964, pp. 515–30.

Staves, Susan, 'A Few Kind Words for the Fop', *Studies in English Literature, 1500–1900*, vol. 22, no. 3, 1982, pp. 413–28.

Steele, Valerie, *Fetish: Fashion, Sex and Power*, Oxford University Press, Oxford, 1996.
——— , *The Corset: A Cultural History*, Yale University Press, New Haven CT, 2001.

Stephenson, Andrew, '"But the Coat Is the Picture": Issues of Masculine Fashioning, Politics and Sexual Identity in Portraiture in England, *c.* 1890–1905', in Justine de Young (ed.), *Fashion in European Art: Dress and Identity, Politics and the Body, 1775–1925*, I.B. Tauris, London, 2017, pp. 178–206.

Stern, Katherine, 'What is Femme? The Phenomenology of the Powder Room', *Women: A Cultural Review*, vol. 8, no. 2, 1997, pp. 183–96.

Stoppard, Tom, *The Invention of Love*, 2nd edn, Faber & Faber, London, 1997.

Straub, Kristina, *Sexual Suspects: Eighteenth-Century Players and Sexual Ideology*, Princeton University Press, Princeton N.J., 1992.
——— , 'Actors and Homophobia', in J. Douglas Cranfield and Deborah C. Payne (eds), *Cultural Readings of Restoration and Eighteenth-Century English Theater*, University of Georgia Press, Athens GA, 1995, pp. 258–80.

Styles. John, *The Dress of the People: Everyday Fashion in Eighteenth-Century England*, Yale University Press, New Haven CT, 2007.

Syme, Alison, *A Touch of Blossom: John Singer Sargent and the Queer Flora of Fin-de-Siècle Art*, Pennsylvania State University Press, University Park PA, 2010.

Tamagne, Florence, *A History of Homosexuality in Europe: Berlin, London, Paris, 1919–1939*, Algora, New York, 2006.

Taylor, Martin (ed.), *Lads: Love Poetry of the Trenches*, Constable, London, 1989.

Taylor, Miles, 'John Bull and the Iconography of Public Opinion in England *c.* 1712–1929', *Past and Present* 134, 1992, pp. 93–128.

Thackeray, William Makepeace, *An Essay on the Genius of George Cruikshank, with Numerous Illustrations of His Works (from the 'Westminster Review', no. LXVI)*, Henry Hooper, London, 1840.
——— , *The Four Georges*, Harper, New York, 1860.

Thienpont, Eva, 'Visibly Wild(e): A Re-evaluation of Oscar Wilde's Homosexual Image', *Irish Studies Review*, vol. 13, no. 3, 2005, pp. 291–301.

Thomas, Keith, 'Afterword', in Karen Harvey (ed.), *The Kiss in History*, Manchester University Press, Manchester, 2005, pp. 187–203.

Thrale, Hester Lynch, *Thraliana: The Diary of Mrs. Hester Lynch Thrale (Later Mrs. Piozzi), 1776–1809*, ed. Katharine C. Balderston, 2 vols, 2nd edn, Clarendon Press, Oxford, 1951.

Tilghman, Carolyn, 'Staging Suffrage: Women, Politics, and the Edwardian Theater', *Comparative Drama*, vol. 45, no. 4, 2011, pp. 339–60.

Tosh, John, *A Man's Place: Masculinity and the Middle-Class Home in Victorian England*, Yale University Press, New Haven CT, 1999.

Trumbach, Randolph, 'Sodomitical Assaults, Gender Role, and Sexual Development in Eighteenth-Century London', *Journal of Homosexuality*, vol. 16, no. 1–2, 1988, pp. 407–29.

——— , 'Sodomy Transformed: Aristocratic Libertinage, Public Reputation and the Gender Revolution of the 18th century', *Journal of Homosexuality*, vol. 19, no. 2, 1990, pp. 105–24.

——— , *Sex and the Gender Revolution*, Volume 1: *Heterosexuality and the Third Gender in Enlightenment London*, University of Chicago Press, Chicago IL, 1998.

——— , 'The Transformation of Sodomy from the Renaissance to the Modern World and Its General Sexual Consequences', *Signs*, vol. 37, no. 4, 2012, pp. 832–47.

Upchurch, Charles, 'Forgetting the Unthinkable: Cross-Dressers and British Society in the Case of the Queen vs. Boulton and Others', *Gender and History*, vol. 12, no. 1, 2000, pp. 127–57.

Vernon, James, '"For Some Queer Reason": The Trials and Tribulations of Colonel Barker's Masquerade in Interwar Britain', *Signs*, vol. 26, no. 1, 2000, pp. 37–62.

Wahrman, Dror, '"Percy's Prologue": From Gender Play to Gender Panic in Eighteenth-Century England', *Past and Present* 159, May 1998, pp. 113–60.

——— , *The Making of the Modern Self: Identity and Culture in Eighteenth-Century England*, Yale University Press: New Haven CT, 2004.

Walden, George, *Who Is a Dandy? On Dandyism and Beau Brummell*, Gibson, London, 2002.

Walpole, Horace, *The Yale Edition of Horace Walpole's Correspondence*, ed. W.S. Lewis, 48 vols, Yale University Press, New Haven CT, 1937–83.

Ware, J. Redding, *Passing English of the Victorian Era: A Dictionary of Heterodox English, Slang and Phrase*, George Routledge, London, 1909.

Weeks, Jeffrey, 'Inverts, Perverts, and Mary-Annes: Male Prostitution and the Regulation of Homosexuality in England in the Nineteenth and Early Twentieth Centuries', in Martin Duberman, Martha Vicinus and George Chauncey (eds), *Hidden from History: Reclaiming the Gay and Lesbian Past*, Penguin, Harmondsworth, 1991, pp. 195–211.

West, Shearer, 'The Darly Macaroni Prints and the Politics of "Private Man"', *Eighteenth-Century Life*, vol. 25, no. 2, 2001, pp. 170–82.

Wilde, Oscar, *The Picture of Dorian Gray*, ed. Joseph Bristow, Oxford University Press, Oxford, 2006.

Williams, Carolyn, 'Parody and Poetic Tradition: Gilbert and Sullivan's *Patience*', *Victorian Poetry*, vol. 46, no. 4, 2008, pp. 375–404.

Wilson, Cheryl A., 'Almack's and the Silver-Fork Novel', *Women's Writing: The Elizabethan to Victorian Period*, vol. 16, no. 2, 2009, pp. 237–52.

Wilson, Elizabeth, *Adorned in Dreams: Fashion and Modernity*, I.B. Tauris, London, 2003.

Wilton, Andrew, and Ilaria Bignamini (eds), *Grand Tour: The Lure of Italy in the Eighteenth Century*, Tate, London, 1996.

Woods, Gregory, 'British Homosexuality, 1920–1939', in Tony Sharpe (ed.), *W.H. Auden in Context*, Cambridge University Press, Cambridge, 2013, pp. 89–98.

Yazan, Senem, 'The Black Princess of Elegance: The Emergence of the Female Dandy', *Critical Studies in Fashion and Beauty*, vol. 3, no. 1–2, 2012, pp. 101–15.

Zatlin, Linda Gertner, 'Wilde, Beardsley, and the Making of *Salome*', *Journal of Victorian Culture*, vol. 5, no. 2, 2000, pp. 341–57.

Zoberman, Pierre, 'Queer(ing) Pleasure: Having a Gay Old Time in the Culture of Early-Modern France', in Greg Forter and Paul Allen Miller (eds), *The Desire of the Analysts*, State University of New York Press, Albany NY, 2008, pp. 225–52.

Zonneveld, Jacques [Sjaak], *Sir Brooke Boothby: Rousseau's Roving Baronet Friend*, De Jacques Nieuwe Haagsche, Voorburg, 2004.

Picture credits

Acknowledgements

Research was carried out over several years but is particularly indebted to Keele University for its award of a School of Humanities Fellowship and a period of research leave in 2019. This enabled me to take up the position of Humfrey Wanley Fellow in the Centre for the Study of the Book at the Bodleian Library, University of Oxford. I also benefited greatly from the award of a Travel Grant to the Lewis Walpole Library, Yale University.

I thank Bloomsbury for their permission to allow the publication of Chapter 2. This is composed of a revised version of material that first appeared as 'Gender and Sexuality', in Peter McNeil (ed.), *A Cultural History of Fashion*, Volume 4: *Fashion in the Age of Enlightenment (1650–1800)*, Bloomsbury, London, 2017, pp. 105–22.

To Samuel Fanous, Publisher at the Bodleian Library, goes the credit for having suggested to me that I write this book. Thanks also go to Dr Andrew Rudd for drawing my attention to Ian Fenwick's cartoon of a pacifist in *Everyman: The World News Weekly* (1933) and to Duncan Horne for his invaluable comments on the final draft of the book's text.

Index